THE LAW OF BUSINESS ASSOCIATIONS IN ZAMBIA: AN INTRODUCTION

THE LAW OF BUSINESS ASSOCIATIONS IN ZAMBIA: AN INTRODUCTION

by

Mumba Malila SC
LLB (Zambia) LLM (Cambridge) LLD (Pretoria)
Judge of the Supreme Court of Zambia

and

Chanda Chungu
LLB LLM (Cape Town)

First Edition 2019

© Juta and Company (Pty) Ltd
First Floor, Sunclare Building, 21 Dreyer Street, Claremont 7708

ISBN: 978 1 48513 360 5

Typeset in 12/14 Times New Roman
Typesetting by Helanna Typesetting

ABOUT THE AUTHORS

Justice Dr Mumba Malila currently serves as a Judge of the Supreme Court of Zambia. Prior to his appointment directly into the Supreme Court in 2014, Dr Malila served in various positions in the Zambian legal profession, including those of a private legal practitioner, university law teacher, assessor and lecturer at the Zambia Institute of Advanced Legal Education (ZIALE), corporation counsel and government advisor. He held many public service appointments, including Honorary Secretary of LAZ, and membership of the Judicial Service Commission, the Law Development Commission, and the Citizens' Economic Empowerment Commission. Justice Dr Malila took silk as State Counsel in 2009 and has twice served as Attorney General of Zambia and leader of the Bar. He has also served as Chairperson of the Zambian Human Rights Commission, Vice Chairperson of the African Commission on Human and Peoples' Rights, Chairperson of the ZIALE Council, Chairperson of the Legal Practitioners Disciplinary Committee, and Chairperson of the Anti Money Laundering Unit in the Drug Enforcement Commission.

Justice Dr Malila holds an LLB from the University of Zambia, an LLM from the University of Cambridge and an LLD from the University of Pretoria. He obtained a Certificate in Human Rights from the Rene Casin Institute of Human Rights in Strasbourg, France and is a member of the Chartered Institute of Arbitrators. He recently completed further LLM studies at the University of Cumbria. He has authored three books, co-authored one book, contributed several book chapters and authored numerous articles in peer reviewed journals.

Chanda Chungu is a Legal Practitioner at Mulenga Mundashi Kasonde Legal Practitioners in Zambia. He obtained both his Bachelor of Laws (LLB) and Master of Laws (LLM) in Commercial and Labour Law from the University of Cape Town. His research interests are in labour law, industrial relations, administrative and constitutional law. He was previously a teaching assistant and junior lecturer at the University of Cape Town as well as a researcher for the International Labour Organisation and the World Bank Africa Mining Project. He also served for two years on the University of Cape Town Council and Senate and was selected for the Mandela Washington Leadership Fellowship. He is currently pursuing his Doctor of Philosophy (PhD) degree at the University of Cape Town.

ABOUT THE COMMISSIONING AND SERIES EDITOR

Evance Kalula is Chair of the ILO Committee on Freedom of Association (CFA) and Emeritus Professor of Law at the University of Cape Town. He served as Director of the International Academic Programmes Office and the Confucius Institute from 2012 until 2017. He held a personal chair as professor of employment law and social security. He holds several degrees in law, including a PhD. He was educated at the University of Zambia School of Law; Kings College, London; Balliol College, Oxford (where he was a Rhodes scholar) and the University of Warwick School of Law. He specialises in international and comparative labour law, international trade, regional integration and social security. He previously served as Chair of the South African Employment Conditions Commission (ECC), member of the International Labour Organization (ILO) Commission of Inquiry on Freedom of Association in Zimbabwe, and Chair of the University of Lusaka (UNILUS) Council. He is currently a member of the Ministerial Advisory Panel of the South African Economic Development Department (EDD), fellow of the African Academy of Sciences (AAS), advisor to the Council of the Academy of Sciences of South Africa (ASSAf) and member of the Board of Institute for African Alternatives (IFAA). He is also the immediate Past President of the International Labour and Employment Relations Association (ILERA).

EDITOR'S PREFACE

The Law of Business Associations in Zambia: An Introduction is the latest addition to Juta's growing number of titles on Zambian law. Although billed as an introduction, this book is in fact more than a primer; it is an authoritative, comprehensive and up-to-date presentation of the law as set out in legislation and case law.

The book sets out the history and current state of business associations law in Zambia, providing a clear overview of all relevant legislation, case law and implied policy. In six comprehensive and well-conceived chapters, the book covers types of business associations, sole traders and sole proprietorships, partnerships, co-operative societies, registered companies and parastatal organisations. It thus deals with the regulation of enterprise in both the private sector and public sector in a balanced, clear and accessible way, giving both lawyers and non-lawyers the tools of the trade. A useful feature that enhances the accessibility and understanding of the issues dealt with is the inclusion of key points at the end of each chapter, providing a summary of the issues discussed. This is a feature that some readers, particularly those using the book as a companion and reference book, such as students, will find very useful.

The authors are well placed to provide this expansive and clear exposition. The first author, Judge Mumba Malila, has for many years been and continues to be a leading law teacher, policy maker, and scholar. He is now a member of the Supreme Court bench. He is undoubtedly an acknowledged authority on business law and company law. He has been 'present at the creation' of the reform of the law as Attorney General, a position he has held twice with distinction. He has disseminated the law as a scholar, and has implemented it as a judge. The second author, Chanda Chungu, is a remarkable emerging young scholar who is quickly putting his stamp on this field and other related areas of the law.

The Law of Business Associations in Zambia: An Introduction provides all the essential elements that one needs to know about this area of the law. The book will therefore be useful to a broad range of readers who are either interested in or need to understand business law, including students, legal practitioners, other professionals who use the law in their work, policy makers, investors and the general public.

I would like to sincerely thank the authors for their diligence in making time to produce this book speedily, along with another forthcoming title on

Company Law. As always, our publisher Linda van de Vijver has been outstanding in her encouragement and support.

Evance Kalula
Commissioning and Series Editor
Cape Town
March 2019

CONTENTS

Chapter 4: CO-OPERATIVE SOCIETIES

TABLE OF CASES

TABLE OF STATUTES

Chapter 1

TYPES OF BUSINESS ASSOCIATIONS IN ZAMBIA

1.1 INTRODUCTION

A person seeking to set up a business in Zambia will have to consider the various forms of business enterprises that are available in order to ascertain which one of them offers the best medium through which he could conduct his business, considering the convenience, cost and appropriateness of each of these forms of business enterprise. Choosing an organisational structure for one's business is important because the structure will define one's legal responsibilities and how the profit and losses of the business may be treated.

Business associations as commercial entities in Zambia are broadly classified into four categories, namely: sole proprietorships, partnerships, registered companies (which may be limited (private or public) or unlimited companies) and co-operative societies. Another category of business association which may really be treated as a subset of registered companies are statutory corporations and parastatals.

Within these broad categories, many forms of business arrangements may be assumed such as joint ventures and unit trusts or collective investment schemes. Except for statutory corporations and parastatals, all these forms of business enterprises are available to private persons and present an intending investor with a medium through which to do business with varying differences in the method of registration and operation. Of course, different considerations ranging from the availability of capital to the desire for simplicity in set up, operation and winding up of operations will influence the choice of one or the other of these forms of business association.

This introductory chapter gives a bird's eye view of the various forms of business associations before considering each of these in detail in subsequent chapters.

1.2 SOLE TRADER OR SOLE PROPRIETORSHIP

A sole proprietorship is a lone or solitary business undertaking. It is an easy form of business entity often, but not always, associated with small-scale business enterprises. A sole trader or sole proprietor runs his business as an individual, incurs all operational costs for the business and keeps all the business' profits after he has paid tax on them. He is personally responsible for any losses the business makes; for settling bills for items procured for the business such as stock, equipment and services; and for maintaining and keeping records of the business' sales and expenditure.

Being a sole trader or proprietor means the individual is responsible for the business in every sense of the word. This does not necessarily mean that he must work alone. It is not possible for any business proprietor to act on his own behalf all the time. Acting through other persons is a practice that has been employed by mankind from time immemorial. In the area of business and commerce especially, it is impossible for businessmen not to employ the services of other people, whether with special expertise, or without any expertise, to help ensure that assignments relevant to the success of the business undertaken are accomplished.

The Latin maxim *qui facit per alium facit perse* sums up the common-law position that he who can act for himself may act through an agent. The sole trader or proprietor can thus delegate functions to agents, employ staff or can be otherwise assisted in his business. Chapter 2 examines the sole trader form of business enterprise in detail.

1.3 BUSINESS PARTNERSHIP

A partnership exists where two or more persons (natural or artificial) associate for a shared business objective. It normally involves contribution in the running of the business enterprise and ensuring its success. It also entails the sharing of the profits generated from the business. Each partner pays tax on his share of the profits.

A partnership relationship brings about fiduciary duties and potential liability on the individual partners. The partners share not only the profits of the business but responsibilities too.

The Registration of Business Names Act 16 of 2011 provides for the registration of business enterprises that are not corporations. These include sole proprietorships and partnerships. Entities registered under this Act can conduct business legally under a trading or business name, but their owners are personally liable for the acts and omissions of the business. Since these firms do not benefit from corporate personality and limited liability, as they would if they were incorporated companies, they are not attractive to outside investors. However, they may be of interest as an initial mechanism for start-ups of new business associations.

Chapter 3 examines in detail the main attributes of partnerships as a form of business association.

1.4 CO-OPERATIVE SOCIETY

A co-operative society (or co-operative) is any enterprise or organisation owned jointly by its members and managed for their mutual socio-economic benefit and whose activities are not prohibited by law. It often affords for its members a combination of business and service benefits. Membership of co-operatives is often restricted to groups of persons having a common interest or occupation or living in a well-defined neighbourhood or community.

The Co-operative Societies Act 20 of 1998 provides for the formation and registration of co-operative societies as corporate bodies with perpetual succession and limited liability. As forms of business associations, these entities do have legal personality, subject to the provisions of the Act and the by-laws of the particular society. They generally operate on the same lines as registered companies.

Several business enterprises such as microfinance institutions, thrift societies, and producer or marketing organisations may be registered as co-operative societies under the Act. Many co-operative societies that are formed for the promotion of savings and provision of financing to their members are registered as credit unions.

Chapter 4 is devoted to co-operative societies and discusses this business association in more detail.

1.5 REGISTERED COMPANY

The Companies Act 10 of 2017[1] is the principal Act for incorporating business entities called registered companies. There are various kinds of companies that may be registered under the Act, each bearing different attributes.

Section 12 provides that only the types of companies listed under s 6 of the Act may be incorporated. These are: *(a)* public companies; *(b)* private companies—being either (i) limited by shares or (ii) limited by guarantee or (iii) unlimited companies.

Registered companies are primarily governed by the provisions of the Companies Act and the rules and regulations laid down in the articles of

---

[1] This Act received Presidential assent to become law and replace the Companies Act 1994 on 20 November 2017. The law became operational on 7 June 2018 following the passage of Statutory Instrument No 47 of 2018.

association of the company together with any shareholders' agreement. The nature of a company and the business it is set up to undertake normally determines what other legal requirements specified in other pieces of legislation will have to be complied with. Companies undertaking businesses as diverse as commodities trading, banking, mining, manufacturing and farming will use the legal framework set out by the Companies Act for purposes of their set up before moving on to comply with other legal requirements under separate, specific Acts of Parliament or other regulations governing particular aspects of their business. For example, a company that wishes to undertake banking business or financial services will inevitably have to ensure compliance with the Banking and Financial Services Act 7 of 2017 and the regulations made under that Act. A company intending to undertake insurance will be required to comply with the provisions of the Insurance Act Chap 382 of the Laws of Zambia.

A company set up to manufacture pharmaceutical products or to undertake mining activities will, likewise, have a whole host of laws and regulations to meet. Similarly, a public company will have several rules and regulations to abide by as set out in the Securities Act 41 of 2016. It is also always important to bear in mind that there are various sector regulators which may also prescribe safety and licencing requirements that must be met before a business enterprise can commence or continue to undertake business.[2]

The documents required to incorporate a company under the Companies Act include the application for incorporation form, the articles of association, a consent form signed by at least two directors and a company secretary to act in those roles, and a Statutory Declaration of Compliance, which may require some professional input to formulate or complete. This may initially appear complicated for small enterprises that cannot afford professional fees. Such associations may prefer registration under the Registration of Business Names Act as an initial step, though this need not necessarily be so.

Chapter 5 considers each of the types of companies and their registration requirements in detail.

---

[2] For example, the Bank of Zambia, the Competition and Consumer Protection Commission, the Securities and Exchange Commission, the Energy Regulation Board, the National Council for Construction, the National Water and Sanitation Council, the Pharmaceuticals Regulation Authority, the Zambia Bureau of Standards, the Zambia Information and Technology Authority, the Weights and Measures Agency and the Environmental Council of Zambia.

1.6 STATE-OWNED ENTERPRISES AND PARASTATAL AND STATUTORY CORPORATIONS

The term parastatal or state-owned enterprise describes a public undertaking (ie, state-owned or state-controlled) which is quasi-autonomous and outside the regular civil service structure. Parastatals comprise two categories of enterprises: those of a purely commercial nature set up under the Companies Act, and Statutory Boards, Commissions and Agencies established under specific Acts of Parliament. These generally conduct business in one form or another.

This form of business enterprise is technically not available to individuals as an optional vehicle for carrying on business because, by definition, they are state-owned or quasi-government enterprises that conduct business in competition with or together with private parties. In some cases, both state (public) and private shareholding in parastatal companies is possible. It is here where private parties may also be involved. In some cases, however, both state (public) and private shareholding in parastatal companies may exist.

The establishment, ownership and manner of operation do offer parastatal bodies their distinguishing attributes in their role as business enterprises. Parastatal companies could be an important vehicle for private business enterprises where, for example, a public-private partnership is contemplated.

Chapter 6 is dedicated to discussing this type of business association.

1.7 FACTORS THAT INFLUENCE THE CHOICE OF BUSINESS ASSOCIATION TO ESTABLISH

There are various factors that may influence one's choice as to the type of business association one will set up. These factors are normally assessed and balanced against each other to determine the form of business association that may conveniently and cheaply be formed and run.

First, persons intending to form a business association should consider the proposed size of the business. If the business intended to be undertaken is small-scale, a sole proprietorship or partnership would be more appropriate than a registered company. The nature of the business to be undertaken is also important. Some activities may not lawfully be carried out within business formations under particular laws even if they may have an underlying business objective or purpose. For example, in terms of s 12(9) of the Companies Act, a person or entity seeking to carry out religious or faith-based activities is not permitted to incorporate a company. The same restrictions apply to those carrying out legal and accounting services. Where the nature of the business to be undertaken is motivated more by the need to provide an essential social or community service, a statutory organisation or a parastatal company would be a more appropriate vehicle to employ.

In some instances, government policy will inform the type of business association to establish in particular sectors. Co-operatives in the agricultural sector are an example of government-policy-inspired business associations in a sector of the economy. The government deliberately encouraged the formation of agricultural co-operatives to enable small-scale farmers to pool their resources and to easily access credit and farmer inputs. If a statute creates an entity, that business will operate as a statutory corporation. Furthermore, the intended level and nature of control of the business entity may play a significant role in the choice of the kind of business enterprise to set up to be used. Where government seeks to have control in a manner that would not fit within the provisions of the Companies Act, it may initiate legislation to form statutory corporation.

In some instances, one person or a few of them may seek to have total or almost complete control of the business entity and may equally wish to minimise regulation and public scrutiny of their business. Here, a sole proprietorship or a partnership may be ideal.

The level of finance required to run the business association is an equally relevant consideration. Some forms of business associations such as partnerships and sole proprietorships require less start-up capital than others. They also normally raise operating finance from personal resources and may find it more difficult than companies to raise capital from external sources.

1.8 COMPLIANCE WITH LAWS IN THE BUSINESS ENVIRONMENT

Whatever structure one chooses to use as a business vehicle, it is important for one to familiarise oneself with the legal environment under which such business is expected to operate. It is equally important to appreciate the legal issues that are likely to be encountered and which could greatly affect the success of the business. Such laws could be in the realm of either public or private regulation. Public-law requirements involve compliance with statutory obligations such as satisfying mandatory licencing registration, compliance with health and safety regulations and meeting statutory payment obligations.

The private realm may essentially involve two key areas, namely contract and tort law. Contract law is the foundation of all commercial transactions. Virtually all that a business does revolves around contract. Thus, whenever it sells goods or services or procures these from others, contracts of one form or another are concluded.

The law of tort on the other hand involves private, civil actions for wrongful deeds. It may also involve civil wrong to the public or sections of it which would entitle those injured to personal remedies. This branch of the law may in some instances impose a duty on an individual or company to refrain from certain activity, such as not discharging dangerous waste emissions into the environment, ensuring that products are safe for use by consumers, and making sure that people who enter a business's premises are not subjected to harm. Typically, the sort of tort action a business might face could include negligence claims for work injuries.

Registration of a name under which a business enterprise shall operate is one of the earliest considerations that anyone intending to set up a business should have. A considerable part of Chapter 2 is devoted to this aspect.

Taxation is a crucial area of the law that calls for proper appreciation on the part of business managers. The law and rules of taxation are bound to affect a business and define its success or failure. Managing taxation often depends on the organisational structure of the business. While the employee tax contributions must always be remitted to tax authorities by the business, the question whether the business is expected to pay corporate tax, value added tax or any other form of tax will pretty much depend on its legal form. It is therefore important that a business familiarises itself from the onset about these issues.

Intellectual property presents another area of law which requires careful understanding by some businesses, particularly those engaged in producing new products or commercial goods. Copyright, patents, industrial designs and trademarks are all types of intellectual property protection that ought to be appreciated. When a business knows its intellectual rights, it is better able to stop people stealing or copying the names of its products or brands, its inventions and the design or look of its products. Similarly, such business will also ensure that it does not infringe other peoples' intellectual property rights.

Licencing a business is an issue that every new business should consider seriously before it commences operations. Simply defined, a licence is permission granted by the authorities for a business to carry out a type of activity. Many types of business are regulated, either at municipal or at the state level, especially if they are engaged in activities that carry the risk of exposing members of the public to some form of physical harm or injury to health. Obvious examples include the supply of alcohol, drugs, food or fuel, and the disposal of toxic waste.

There are sector regulators in virtually all areas of business that are responsible for issuing sector specific licences.[3]

While applications for licences should normally be straightforward and do not normally demand a high level of legal expertise, it may be necessary to seek expert advice as failure to comply with licencing requirements could lead to a business operating illegally with potential criminal prosecution.

A well-functioning business will invariably encounter employment-related issues in its operations. This is inevitable considering that a business will often time employ staff to conduct some of its activities. Employment issues will be encountered at various levels, including at the stage of engaging and disengaging staff, negotiating and determining their terms and conditions of employment, registering them for and paying for their social security schemes such as National Pension Scheme Authority, taking account of their work environment safety and health, and contributing to the Workers Compensation Fund. They also include dealing with strike action and work-related disputes. It is crucial in this regard for a business to seek advice on all these issues.

Insolvency is an issue that a new business enterprise will hardly find necessary to consider, at least at set-up stage, yet it is crucial to begin to think of it from inception. When the business enterprise is unable to meet its financial obligations (ie discharge its financial obligations as they fall due) there are legal rules that come into play to deal with such an eventuality.

When a person, trading as a sole proprietor, or in partnership or as a shareholder in a company, is unable to pay debts as and when they fall due, legal procedure exists that may be invoked to get the court to take over the administration of his estate, which is then distributed among creditors. It is thus important to be alive to these issues even at the time of setting up a business undertaking.

---

[3] See part 1.5 note 2.

KEY POINTS

- Zambia generally recognises five types of business associations.
- Various factors influence the choice of the type of business association to use. These include the proposed size of the business, the level of control wanted by the owners of the business and the legal framework governing the nature of the business.
- A sole proprietorship is a lone or solitary business undertaking and is usually associated with small-scale business enterprises.
- A partnership entails two or more persons coming together to form a business for the purpose of making a profit.
- A co-operative society (or co-operative) is any enterprise or organisation owned jointly by its members and managed for their mutual socio-economic benefit and whose activities are not prohibited by law.
- Parastatals comprise two categories of enterprises: those of a purely commercial nature set up under the Companies Act, and Statutory Boards, Commissions and Agencies established under specific Acts of Parliament.

Chapter 2

SOLE TRADER OR SOLE PROPRIETORSHIPS

2.1 INTRODUCTION

A sole proprietorship, also known as a sole trader or simply as a proprietorship, is a type of business entity which is owned and run by one individual with no legal distinction between the owner and the business. It is a 'sole' proprietorship in the sense that the owner has no business partner(s). It is a solo entrepreneurship business project.

Such an enterprise, though run commercially, is conducted purely on a personal basis, and is usually owned by an individual who runs it either alone or, as tends to be the case in Zambia, with the assistance of family members or friends. A sole trader or proprietor can and often does engage employees. All profits and all losses accrue to the owner of the business. In other words, all assets of the business are owned by the proprietor and all its debts are the proprietor's debts and must be paid from personal resources. This means that the owner has unlimited liability. The concept of limitation of liability is considered later in this part.

A sole proprietorship is also sometimes loosely referred to as a 'one man' company though this nomenclature may cause considerable confusion, particularly when one has in mind companies registered under the Companies Act. As a sole trader is dissimilar from a registered company in both form and substance, and in the manner of operation, it is advisable to avoid any reference to a sole proprietorship as a company.

Sole proprietorships run a wide range of businesses, usually small-scale. In Zambia these include retail grocer's shops, transport businesses, (especially passenger transport—taxis and mini buses), bottle stores, clinics, tailoring shops, barber shops and small-scale farms. They may also extend to professional service-providing outfits such as consultancy providers.

Sole proprietorships are easy to form and normally operate very informally. They are a major attraction for start-up, small-scale business enterprises.

2.2 THE OPTION TO USE OR NOT TO USE A BUSINESS OR TRADE NAME

A sole proprietor may choose to use her own name in undertaking a business or may opt to use a business or trade name other than her legal or true name. The latter option allows the proprietor to open a business account in the name of the business with banking institutions. This could also shield the identity of the person or persons behind the business for immediate purposes, and thus creates a thinly veiled factual (not legal) separation between the owner of the business and the business enterprise itself.

The broader question is: what lies in a trading or business name? What is the difference, if any, between a business name and a trading name? The answers to these questions lie in the realisation that the name of any business is the identity of the business itself. It helps customers find and connect with a particular business. It is remarkable how vital a business or trading name can be to the success of the business.

The name of any business creates an impression in the customers of the business and, therefore, could make a powerful impact immediately. It can easily become an entrepreneurial landmark and a determining factor in the success of the enterprise. As the name is the first thing a customer interacts with, it is desirable that it conveys the right message. The business or trade name says a lot about the business and the person or persons behind it, and could, thus, make a powerful and lasting impression on customers and potential customers. The name could, in this sense, play a huge role in the growth of the business and the public or customers' perception of it.

Conversely, the name of a business may inappropriately represent the business or the brand, and the enterprise would suffer because of it. It is therefore crucial that some time is invested in reflecting on the name that one intending to set up a business would use for her business. It is advisable to settle for a business name that is easy to pronounce, easy to spell and just as easy to remember. It would, for example, be unhelpful to give such difficult a name in a local dialect to one's lodge as *'Mavutoyoipisisa Lodge'* or *'Kulelabana Nkuyuma-yuma* Guest House' when the target market is foreign tourists who are unfamiliar with local dialects.

As regards the terms 'trade name' and 'business name' all that needs to be said is that the two terms refer to essentially the same thing and may thus be used interchangeably. The term 'trade name' is an old term while 'business name' is a more modern and probably more correct term and is the term of choice in contemporary legislation.

When a sole proprietor opts to use a business or trade name, it will be relevant to consider whether the requirements of registration set out below apply. While sole proprietorships must comply with various laws, particularly tax legislation and licensing regulations, they may also need to satisfy the provisions of other laws such as environmental regulations, depending on the kind of business they are engaged in. It is not mandatory, however, that preceding their commencement of business they comply with the provisions of the law as set out in the Registration of Business Names Act 16 of 2011[1] unless they chose to use a trade name.

The Registration of Business Names Act directs that every individual carrying on business under a business name which does not consist of her true surname without any addition other than the true forename or the initials thereof must be registered in the manner directed by the Act. In specific terms, s 4 of the Act provides:

(1) Subject to the provisions of this Act, the following shall apply for registration under the provisions of this Act:

(a) Every individual or firm with a place of business in Zambia and carrying on business under a business name which does not consist of the true surname of the individual or surnames of all the partners who are individuals and the corporate names of all the partners who are corporations without any addition other than the true forename or forenames of the individual partners or initials of the forenames; and

(b) Every individual or firm with a place of business in Zambia, who, or a member of which, has either before or after the commencement of this Act changed the individual's or firm's name, except in the case of a woman in consequence of marriage.

Provided that—

(i) where two or more individual partners have the same surname, the addition of an 's' at the end of that surname shall not of itself render registration necessary;

(ii) where the business is carried on by a trustee in bankruptcy or a receiver or manager appointed by a court, registration shall not be necessary; and

(iii) a purchase or acquisition of property by two or more persons as joint tenants or tenants in common is not of itself to be deemed as carrying on a business, whether or not the owners share any profits arising from the sale thereof.

The following examples further illustrate instances when one should register one's business name:

- Chebo Chibangula, engaged in a consultancy business, would be obliged to register a business name if he includes other words with his true names such as *Chebo Chibangula Consultants*, or *Chebo Chibangula & Sons*.

---

[1] This Act repealed and replaced the Registration of Business Names Act 29 of 1931, Chapter 389 of the Laws of Zambia.

- Mubita Banda runs an ice cream business as a sole trader. His true first and surname is Mubita Banda. He wants his business to be known as *Mubita Banda Creams*. He is obliged to register it.
- Habwalo Chimfwembe and Kambita Samundengu run a brick-laying business together, operating as a partnership. Their partnership's legal name is Habwalo and Samundengu and they now want their business to be known as *Habwalo and Samundengu Bricklayers*. They must register it.

In all these examples, the true names of the entrepreneur is combined with a description of the business they are into to form a totally new name, hence the need to register it under the provisions of the Act set out above. Examples of when registration would not be required are as follows:

- Chomba Bwenkaubune owns a law firm and operates as a sole trader. Her true names are Chomba Bwenkaubune. Because she is happy to run her business as a sole trader under her legal name, she does not have to register her business name.
- Harry Shiompa, Ndoni Mwachisompola and Likezo Nasilele have a building business together, operating as a partnership. Their partnership's legal name is *Harry Ndoni and Likezo*. They are happy to operate under their legal name, using all of the partners' names. They do not need to register a business name although they may do so.

Although s 4(1) refers to applying for registration, s 5(1) does in fact make it plain that the application is for a certificate. It seems that an applicant under s 4 would in essence be applying to be registered and to be issued with a certificate of registration.

It is perhaps worth noting that under the repealed Registration of Business Names Act,[2] there was reference to a person's true Christian name. The present Act has omitted reference to 'Christian' and merely refers to the person's true name. In a setting such as we have in Zambia, where circular, multi-religion and paganism beliefs co-exist with Christian beliefs, the reference specifically to 'Christian name' had, for very understandable reasons, to be dropped. The present Act now refers to a person's forename rather than Christian name. This is notwithstanding the fact that, by declaration contained in the Constitution, Zambia is designated as a Christian nation.

As regards the extent of application of the Act, a reading of s 4 makes it plain that it covers and thus applies to individuals, firms and partnerships.

---

[2] Registration of Business Names Act 29 of 1931, Chapter 389 of the Laws of Zambia.

2.3 RESERVATION OF A NAME FOR REGISTRATION

A person wishing to register a name may apply to the Registrar to reserve such name for a period not exceeding three months. The Registrar of Business Names or the 'Registrar' is the person appointed as Registrar under the Patents and Companies Registration Agency Act 15 of 2010.[3]

The facility for reservation of a name is provided for in s 6 of the Act and mirrors a similar provision in the Companies Act. The benefits of reserving a business name for an enterprise when one plans to go into the business only in the future lies in the fact that such name may not, in the meantime, be taken and be used by any other person. This course of action is understandable when one considers that having a good private name for a business enterprise could be a key factor in the business' success.

A name of a business may be sharp and memorable to the public and may describe what the firm or business enterprise does. Given the likelihood that a name may have remarkable appeal at any one point, it may be necessary to block a particular name for use at a later stage. In Zambia, for example, at the dawn of the new millennium in 2000, it was fashionable for people establishing new businesses to have the word 'millennium' as part of the business name. The same could be said about the country's silver jubilee of independence when the word 'jubilee' gained sudden attraction for businesses.

The wisdom in reserving a name is, however, obviated or undermined by the maximum period available for reservation. It is as likely as it is improbable that a business name available now will be available or unavailable after three months.

In practice, a person desiring to register a business name will ordinarily proceed with the application for registration as soon as the name is cleared. The benefits of having a name reserved before the registration would have been immense had there been provision for reserving names for an indefinite period. As the law allows renewal of a name reservation after three months have elapsed, one could argue though that a person reserving a name for three months could perpetually renew a reservation for subsequent indefinite three-month periods. Effectively this would circumvent the mischief intended to be averted by confining the period of reservation to three months.

---

[3] He or she is commonly referred to as the Registrar of Companies.

2.4 REGISTERING A SOLE PROPRIETORSHIP AS A BUSINESS NAME

Where, as indicated above, it is necessary to register a sole proprietorship as a business name, certain practical steps must be undertaken. These are simple and fairly straightforward and do not generally require specialised professional input.

The procedure for registration of a business name is set out in s 5 of the Act. The firm or person required by the Act to be registered will deliver to the Registrar of Business Names a completed application form together with the prescribed fee. The application form for registration of a business name certificate is obtainable from the office of the Registrar. In terms of the Registration of Business Names Regulations, 1998, made pursuant to s 18 of the repealed Act,[4] corporations, firms and individuals seeking registration will be expected to complete different forms.[5] Generally, however, the particulars required to be given in the form include:

(a) the business name;

(b) the general nature of the business;

(c) the principal place of the business;

(d) where the registration to be effected is that of a firm, the forename and surname; any former forename or surname; the nationality, and if that nationality is not the nationality of origin, the nationality of origin; the usual residence; and the other business occupation (if any) of each of the individuals who are partners, and the corporate name and registered or principal office of every corporation which is a partner;

(e) where the registration to be effected is that of an individual, the forename and surname; any former forename or surname; the nationality, and if that nationality is not the nationality of origin, the nationality of origin; the usual residence; and the other business occupation (if any) of such individual;

(f) where the registration to be effected is that of a corporation, its corporate name and registered or principal office;

(g) if the business is commenced after the commencement of this Act, the date of commencement of the business;

---

[4] The Regulations were made following s 26 of the repealed Act. These Regulations remain applicable by virtue of s 15 of the Interpretation and General Provisions Act Chapter 4 of the Laws of Zambia which provides that 'where any Act, Applied Act or Ordinance or part thereof is repealed, any statutory instrument issued under or made by virtue thereof shall remain in force so far as it is not inconsistent with the repealing written law, until it has been repealed by a statutory instrument issued or made under the provisions of such repealing written law, and shall be deemed for all purposes to have been made thereunder'.

[5] Registration of Business Names Forms 1, 2 and 3.

(h)   where the registration to be effected is that of a firm, the age of each partner thereof; and

(i)   where the registration to be effected is that of an individual, the age of such individual.

The Registration of Business Names Regulations of 1998 must, of course, be applied *mutatis mutandis* under the new Act.

Section 5 of the repealed Act contained an interesting proviso that where any such partner or individual is of or over the age of 21 years, it shall be sufficient for her to state her age as 'full age'. This may have been a tacit recognition or acknowledgement of the fact that persons below the age of majority were entitled to register business names. This provision was omitted in the new Act.

2.5   THE CERTIFICATE OF REGISTRATION

Once an application for a certificate is duly made in accordance with s 5, the Registrar is obliged to issue a certificate to the applicant within 14 days of receipt of the application if the application accords with the provisions of the Act and the activity of business to be carried out does not contravene any law. This requirement is set out in s 7 of the Act. A certificate so granted is infinite in validity. It remains in force unless surrendered by the holder, suspended or cancelled in accordance with the provisions of the Act.

The prescription of a time frame for issuing a certificate of registration appears to be a deliberate measure designed to encourage efficiency in the registration of business names. Considering that there is really nothing more than merely checking availability of the name and the correctness of the documents submitted, it can be argued that the period of 14 days is in fact too long.

2.6   REJECTION OF APPLICATION BY THE REGISTRAR

Although the whole process of registration appears fairly straightforward and, in many respects, seems more of a formality than anything else, it could in fact turn out to be bothersome to an applicant. The Registrar does have the power to decline an application for registration. Section 9 of the Act provides situations when the Registrar may decline registration of a business name. These are:

(a) Where a business name is identical with that of another existing business name or is similar to, or is the same as, the name of another business name and is likely to mislead the public.

Speaking of the acceptability or otherwise of a business name proposed to be registered, it should be acknowledged that, generally, every person is by law entitled to call herself by whatever name she desires or by different names for different purposes as long as she does not use this liberty as a means of perpetrating fraud or interfering with the rights and entitlements of others. This extends as much to business transactions as it does to other aspects of life. In *Maughan v Sharpe*[6] Erle CJ observed that 'individuals may carry on business under any names and style they may choose to adopt'.[7] No person is to be prevented from carrying on any lawful business in her own name by the mere fact of her name and business resembling that of another person,[8] yet the mere fact that the name is her own does not of itself entitle her to do with it in such a way as to deceive or mislead the public.[9]

The right to the exclusive use of a name in connection with a trade or business is not unfamiliar in our law. This right is in many ways analogous to, but certainly not identical with, the right to a trademark proper. The possessor of a trademark in the strict sense is entitled to prevent competitors from trading on her reputation and passing her goods as their own by means of copies or colourable imitations of the visible sign or device which she has appropriated to her business. The right of the possessor of a trade name stands on like footing. Giffard, LJ explained the rationale for this position succinctly in *Lee v Harley*[10] thus:

> The principle upon which the cases on this subject proceed is not that there is property in the word, but that it is a fraud on a person who has established a trade, and carries it on under a given name, that some other person should assume the same name, or the same name with a slight alteration, in such a way as to induce persons dealing with him in the belief that they are dealing with the person who has given a reputation to the name.

Normally, a trader or business entrepreneur will only be entitled to restrain another from using her name if both are engaged in a similar or common commercial undertaking.

The Registrar's power under this provision to decline to register a business name is exercisable first where she is satisfied that the offending business name is identical, similar to, or the same as an existing business name. Here it would appear that the time of registration is of the essence. The name that is registered earlier in time will, of course, receive protection under the provision in preference to a name presented for registration later

---

[6] [1864] 17 C.B.N.S at 402.

[7] See also remarks of Jessel MR in *Merchant Banking Co of Fondon v Merchants' Joint Stock Bank* [1878] 9 Ch.D 560; *Levy v Walker* [1879] 10 Ch. Div 436.

[8] *Burgess v Burgess* [1894] 3 De G.M. & G. 896; *Turton v Turton* [1889] 42 Ch D. 128; *Saunders v Sun Life Assurance of Canada* [1884] 1 Ch 537.

[9] *Holloway v Holloway* [1850] 13 Beav 209; *Massam v Thorley' Cattle Food Co* [1880] 14 Ch Div 748; *Taussaud v Taussaud* [1890] 44 Ch D 678.

[10] LR (5 Ch App) 155.

in time. The Registrar also considers whether the existence of or continued use of the offending business name is likely to mislead the public. It is possible to have similar names that do not in fact mislead the public.

2.6.1 Where the business name is repugnant or otherwise undesirable

Under s 9 of the Act no firm or individual shall be registered by a business name which, in the opinion of the Registrar, is repugnant or undesirable. If any firm or individual, through inadvertence or otherwise, is registered by a business name which, in the opinion of the Registrar, is repugnant or undesirable, the Registrar shall remove such business name from the register. The Act does not define repugnance and undesirability. It is therefore to be determined on a case-by-case basis. Because of the discretion that this provision reposes in the Registrar, the Act also allows any person aggrieved by a decision of the Registrar under that section to appeal to the Minister responsible for commerce and industry.

2.6.2 Where the business name includes the word 'Zambia', 'government', 'state' or any other word, abbreviation or initial which (i) imports or suggests that the applicant enjoys the patronage of the Head of State, the government or administration of any foreign state or of any department or institution of the government or a foreign state; or (ii) is calculated to mislead the public to believe that the business is under Zambian ownership or control

Such name is considered as plainly misleading and the Registrar could refuse to register it or, as the case may be, could remove it from the register. It is not immediately obvious why the provision on the use of the word 'Zambia' in a trade name was allowed in the law. Quite apart from identifying the roots, domicility or territory of operation, a business name that contains the word Zambia could be a patriotic device designed to showcase Zambian entrepreneurship. In itself and by itself alone, the name Zambia in a business name should not therefore be understood as designed to mislead any right-thinking member of the public about state ownership of the business enterprise. One only assumes that this provision may be one of the many hangovers of the state dominance of the trading sector in the Second Republic.

In like manner, under s 9(1)(c)(i) the Registrar shall not register any business name which includes any word which suggests or is calculated to suggest the business or firm enjoys the patronage of the President. If any business name is, through inadvertence or otherwise, registered in conflict with the provisions of that subsection, the Minister may require the firm or individual carrying on business under that name to change the name and, upon such change being made, the Registrar shall enter the new name on the register in place of the former name and shall issue a new certificate of registration.

2.6.3 Where a business name is calculated to deceive or to mislead the public or to cause annoyance or offence to any person or class of persons or is suggestive of blasphemy or indecency

It is unlikely that the wording of this subsection of s 9 properly conveys the intention of the legislature as regards the mischief that was intended to be averted. One gets the impression that the intention here was to make the obligation strict, so that whether by a particular business name one 'calculated to deceive' or not, as long as the name actually deceives, it should be removed.

2.6.4 Where the name suggests or implies a connection with a political party or a leader of a political party

It is not clear what mischief was intended to be cured or avoided by this provision. Political parties can engage in lawful business in order to raise operational and campaign funds. In the absence of a law which prevents political parties from undertaking business venture, it seems ill-advised to have a provision which clearly seeks to distance political parties from business ventures. One can think of a whole host of reasons why it would be unwise for the businesses of a political party to be identified through the name of the party. Yet one could equally conceive many reasons why it should. Whether a political party wishes its business outfits to be readily identified with it should be purely a matter of strategy and, more importantly, choice.

Perhaps what could be viewed as an incongruous omission from the Act is a clear statement that a name is undesirable if it includes the name of a registered trademark unless a document signed by the owner of the trademark and indicating consent to its use is provided. This could obviate some interpretation questions that are bound to arise where business names with names similar to existing registered trademarks are registered or are sought to be registered.

The Registrar is under a duty, whenever she removes any business name from the register, to send to the firm or individual carrying on business under such name, by registered post, a notice that such name has been removed from the register. In any event, where an aggrieved person appeals to the Minister, the decision of the Minister on the matter shall be final. This is as far as the legal theory goes. The decision of the Minister is, of course, open to judicial challenge through judicial review.

The Registrar is also empowered by the Act (s 9(2)) to reject an application for a certificate where it can be demonstrated that the activity or business to be carried out contravenes any law in force, or where the certificate previously held by the applicant has been revoked by the Registrar, or in situations where the applicant submits false information in relation to the requirements for the application.

Where the Registrar rejects an application for registration, she is under a duty to inform the applicant accordingly and give the reason or reasons for such rejection. Under s 22 of the Act any person aggrieved with the decision of the Registrar taken in exercise of the powers under the Act has the right to appeal to the Minister within 30 days of the Registrar's decision. There is a further right of appeal against the Minister's decision to the High Court within 30 days of the Minister's decision.

2.7 CHANGES IN REGISTERED PARTICULARS

In terms of s 15 of the Act, whenever a change is made or occurs in some of the particulars registered in respect of any firm or person, such firm or person shall, within 14 days after such change occurs, furnish to the Registrar a statement in writing in the prescribed form[11] specifying the nature and date of the change. This is consistent with the general purpose of registration in the first place. The Register of Business Names is kept at the offices of the Agency and is, in terms of s 19(2), open to inspection by the public at such times and on such conditions, including the payment of a fee for inspection, as the Agency may determine. Being open to the public, the need to keep the records of a registered business name up-to-date becomes imperative. This is complemented by the obligation imposed on the Agency by s 21 of the Act to publish the names of all the individuals and firms registered under the Act in a daily newspaper of general circulation in Zambia.

The Act lists five items whose change would require notification to the Registrar. These are: *(a)* the business name itself; *(b)* the ownership of the business; *(c)* the physical address of the principal or other place of business; *(d)* the nature of the business; and *(e)* the name of the partners. Allowance for extension of the period for filing of the statement specifying the changes may be made. Criminal sanctions may attend any firm or person required by

---

[11] Registration of Business Names Form 6.

the Act to notify the Registrar of any change in particulars who, without reasonable excuse, makes default in doing so in the manner and within the time specified by this Act.[12] Similarly, there are criminal penalties for furnishing incorrect information.[13] Additionally, the Act imposes a disability on the person who defaults as far as enforcement of certain contracts go. To appreciate the extent of the disability imposed by s 15, which is a re-enactment of s (1) of the repealed Act, it is instructive to consider that section in detail. It enacts as follows:

In addition to the penalty imposed under subsection (4), the rights of the individual or firm under or arising out of any contract made or entered into by or on behalf of such defaulter in relation to the business in respect to the carrying on of which particulars were required to be furnished at any time while he is in default shall not be enforceable by action or other legal proceeding whether in the business name or otherwise: Provided that—

(a) the individual or firm may apply to the court for relief against the prohibition referred to in this subsection, and the court may, upon being satisfied that the default was accidental, or due to inadvertence, or some other sufficient cause or that on other grounds it is just and equitable to grant relief, grant such relief either generally, or as respects any particular contract, on condition of the costs of the application being paid by the individual or firm, unless the court otherwise orders, and on such other conditions, if any, as the court may impose, but such relief shall not be granted except on such service and such publication of notice of the application as the court may order, nor shall relief be given in respect of any contract if any party to the contract proves to the satisfaction of the court that, if this Act had been complied with, he would not have entered into the contract;

(b) nothing shall prejudice the rights of any other parties as against the individual or firm in respect of such contract as aforesaid; or

(c) where any action or legal proceeding shall be commenced by any other party against the individual or firm to enforce the rights of such party in respect of such contract, nothing shall preclude the individual or firm from enforcing in that action or proceeding, by way of counter-claim, set-off or otherwise, such rights as he may have against that party in respect of such contract.

While this interesting provision appears never to have been considered by any court in Zambia, an equivalent provision was a subject of consideration by an English court in *Watson v Park Royal (Caterers) Ltd* where, commenting on a similar provision in the English Act, Edmund Davies J stated:

It is clear that relief under s 8 can be granted in proper circumstances even after judgment and that, if granted, it operates retrospectively right back to the institution of proceedings: *Re Shaer*. But while the court undoubtedly has the widest powers to grant

---

[12] Under s 15(4) an individual who, or a firm which, contravenes sub-s (1) commits an offence and is liable on conviction to a fine not exceeding five hundred penalty units for every day during which the default continues.

[13] According to s 23 of the Act, any person required under the Act to furnish any information or other particulars who, without reasonable excuse, fails to provide it shall, on conviction, be liable to a fine not exceeding two thousand penalty units for each day during which the default continues.

relief (*Weller v Denton*) and is required to construe the disabling section broadly, it is at the same time necessary to inquire in each case whether it would be proper in all the circumstances to grant the relief sought. I turn accordingly to the facts of the present case.[14]

His Lordship then referred to the facts and the correspondence, commenting in relation to the correspondence down to and including the letter dated 15 December 1958, from the plaintiff's solicitor (see p 349 of the judgment), that it was directly material in considering whether it would be 'just and equitable' to grant the plaintiff relief under s 8(1)(*a*) of the Act of 1916.

Further, the fact that from the outset of the proceedings the defendants had maintained that the plaintiff was not registered in accordance with the Act of 1916 was material to the plaintiff's plea of inadvertence or ignorance made in support of her application for relief under s 8. Another matter material to her plea of inadvertence was the fact that although the defendants, in their letter of 7 July 1960, had pointed out that the plaintiff's name did not appear in the Register of Business Names, the plaintiff had still not applied for relief. The plaintiff could clearly have applied for relief earlier in the proceedings as was done by the defaulting plaintiff in *Weller v Denton* but she had not done so and her application was made only now when His Lordship pointed out the peril in which she stood under the Act. His Lordship continued:

> It has already been demonstrated by the correspondence and other documents that from the outset, and long before these proceeding were begun, the defendants were taking the point that there had been no registration and were giving due notice of their intention to rely on that plea were any proceedings instituted, which they in due course did. The plaintiff must therefore be held to have been amply warned and fully aware at all material times of the statutory requirement. Her duty was then to register and thereafter to apply for relief under s 8 either generally or in respect of these particular deliveries, as was done in *Re Smith*.
>
> However 'broadly' s 8 be construed (as Sargant LJ directed in *Re Shaer* ([1926] All ER Rep at p 424; [1927] 1 Ch at p 359)) before granting relief from the disability thereby imposed the Act still requires the court to be 'satisfied' of the matters therein set out, that is 'that the default was accidental, or due to inadvertence, or some other sufficient cause, or that on other grounds it is just and equitable to grant relief.
>
> The only 'other sufficient cause' suggested appears to be, in effect, 'I did not apply for relief simply because I thought that relief would be mine for the asking'. That is not the law and that is not 'sufficient cause' for failing to register. Judges do, of course, from time to time refuse relief, as, indeed, Roche J and Salter J each, in turn, originally did in *Hawkins v Duché*, and to hold that it is automatically granted on request would simply be to put a pencil through the provisions of an Act of Parliament which obviously had security and stability in business dealings as its object. Nor, in view of the events and correspondence preceding the writ and subsequent thereto to which reference has already been made, am I in any degree satisfied that it would now be 'just and equitable

---

[14] [1961] 2 All ER 346.

to grant relief'. This is not a case where the defendants have had the plaintiff's goods and are withholding payment. They have parted with every penny of the £918 odd sued for, and the only question that remains is whether they or the plaintiff are to have the costs of the action. For these reasons I decline to exercise my discretion in favour of the plaintiff and the relief sought is refused.

2.8   TRANSFER OF CERTIFICATE OF REGISTRATION

Section 14 of the Act allows for the transfer of a certificate from the holder to a third party. Such transfer requires the approval of the Registrar upon application by the holder. Naturally, once the transfer is sanctioned by the Registrar, the changes in the registered particulars would ironically trigger the need to notify the Registrar of changes in the registered particulars as provided for in s 15 of the Act.

2.9   SUSPENSION AND CANCELLATION OF CERTIFICATE OF REGISTRATION

The Registrar has power under s 16 to suspend or cancel a certificate in four circumstances, namely:
(1)   where the holder obtained it by false information or statements;
(2)   in the case of a partnership, where it is dissolved;
(3)   where the holder fails to submit annual returns for two consecutive years; and
(4)   where the holder contravenes the Act or any other written law.

The Act provides for the due process to be followed before a certificate is suspended or cancelled. Under s 16(2) the Registrar is obliged in the first place to give written notice to the holder of the certificate of the intention to suspend or cancel the certificate. In doing so, the Registrar must give reasons for the intended suspension or cancellation. The holder then has at least 30 days to show cause why the certificate should not be suspended or cancelled.

Where notice is given to the holder of the certificate and remedial measures are taken within the period of 30 days to the satisfaction of the Registrar, the Registrar is obliged not to suspend or cancel such certificate. Where a certificate is cancelled, the holder is under an obligation to return the certificate to the Registrar, who shall cancel the name and particulars relating to the certificate from the register.

2.10   REREGISTRATION AND REISSUE OF CERTIFICATE

Where a certificate has been cancelled or suspended the holder concerned may apply for re-registration in the prescribed manner and form. A lost certificate may be replaced by a duplicate certificate issued by the Registrar on application by the holder in accordance with s 18 of the Act.

2.11   OBLIGATION TO DISPLAY CERTIFICATE OF REGISTRATION AND BUSINESS NAME STATIONERY

A certificate issued in respect of any business name ought, in accordance with s 11 of the Act, to be displayed in a conspicuous place at the place of business. It is a criminal offence to fail to do so and is punishable on conviction.[15] Although the wording of s 11 does not state so, it would appear that displaying a fair copy of the original certificate would suffice for purposes of the Act, particularly when one considers that the same business may operate from more than one business premises.

The Act also obliges all holders of a certificate issued under the Act to set out the business name in legible characters in all official correspondence, contracts, invoices, negotiable instruments and orders for goods or services issued or made on behalf of the holder of the certificate.[16] It is noteworthy that s 18 of the Co-operative Societies Act 20 of 1998 contains a similar requirement.

2.12   NOTICE OF CESSATION AND SURRENDER OF CERTIFICATE

Where a registered business name ceases to carry on business under the registered name, the person or firm behind the name should within three months after the business ceases to carry on business notify the Registrar in writing. This requirement is imposed by s 20 of the Act on the person who was the sole proprietor or partner in the firm at the time when it ceased to carry on business, or if she is dead, on her personal representative, within three months after the business has ceased to be carried on. The notice is given by sending it by post or delivery to the Registrar in the prescribed form.[17] If any person whose duty it is to give such notice fails to do so within the time prescribed, she shall be liable, on conviction, to criminal penalties.[18]

Once the Registrar receives notice of cessation, she may remove the firm or individual from the register. The Registrar may also on her own volition, where she has reasonable cause to believe that any firm or individual

---

[15] Such person is liable upon conviction to a fine not exceeding 100 000 penalty units.
[16] Section 10 of the Act.
[17] Registration of Business Names Form 7.
[18] A fine not exceeding 1 500 units.

registered under the Act is not carrying on business, send to the firm or individual by registered post a notice that, unless an answer is received to such notice within one month from the date thereof, the firm or individual may be removed from the register. If the Registrar either receives an answer from the firm or individual to the effect that the firm or individual is not carrying on business or does not within one month after sending the notice receive an answer, she may remove the firm or individual from the register.

2.13 ANNUAL RETURNS UNDER THE REGISTRATION OF BUSINESS NAMES ACT

The Registration of Business Names Regulations, 1998[19] introduced the requirement for all businesses registered under the Registration of Business Names Act to file annual returns with the Registrar. Regulation 10 provides:

> (1) A firm, corporation, foreign company or individual registered in accordance with this Act shall, not later than three months after the end of its financial year, complete and submit an annual return in Form 8 set out in the First Schedule.

The Act now goes further to criminalise failure to file annual returns. Section 10(2) provides as follows:

> A person who contravenes subsection (1) commits an offence and is liable, upon conviction, to a fine not exceeding two hundred thousand penalty units.

Section 26 empowers the Minister on the recommendation of the Agency, by statutory instrument, to make regulations concerning any of the following matters for the better carrying out of the provisions of the Act:

(a) the procedure and forms to be used, and the fees payable for registration and other matters under the Act;
(b) the information to be supplied in an application for registration;
(c) the format of the returns to be submitted; and
(d) anything required to be prescribed under the Act.

It is important for anyone registered under the Registration of Business Names Act to remember that registering a business name does not confer on the person registered the same rights as those acquired when one registers a trademark.

A person registered as a business name does not own the name or have exclusive rights to use the name by reason only of the registration under the Act. Where one wishes to protect a registered business name from being used by a competitor, one will need to have the name also registered as a trademark. It is only then that one can control the use of the name or any part of the name. Conversely, registering a business name will not stop

---

[19] Statutory Instrument No 100 of 1998.

someone who has registered the same name as a trademark from using it. It is thus advisable to conduct a trademark search before deciding on a business name.

2.14 THE ROLE OF THE REGISTRAR OF BUSINESS NAMES

From what has been discussed above it is clear that the Registrar wields enormous powers in regard to business names. The divide between the powers and the duties of the Registrar is blurred, and it is possible to classify some power as a responsibility. She is charged with the general day-to-day application and enforcement of the Act. In particular her duties are to receive applications for registration of business names, assess the suitability of the names proposed, register business names and issue certificates as appropriate, and maintain an index of business names. The Registrar also has the responsibility of removing inappropriate names from the register of business names.

The Registrar, in undertaking any of the duties cast upon her by the Act, is performing an administrative public function. Her discretion must be exercised judiciously and may be open to challenge through judicial review. It is perhaps important to point out that the wide discretion given to the Registrar will not be lightly interfered with by the court. The classic test which will guide a court in reviewing a decision of the Registrar is that of Bristowe J in *African Trust v Johannesburg Municipality*:[20]

> It is obvious from the provisions of the Business Names Act that most of those provisions are never enforced in practice. Take the requirement to file change of registered particulars, for example. Many changes that occur to these registered names are never reported to the Registrar who has neither the human nor the financial resources to carry out inspections. The same can be said about business names that cease to operate. They depend on the goodwill of individuals to comply. Until the Registrar's inspectorate division and prosecution team are established the provisions of the law will remain largely a dead letter.

2.15 ADVANTAGES OF SOLE PROPRIETORSHIPS

There are several advantages that a sole proprietorship enjoys over other forms of business associations. These include the following six.

First, sole proprietorships are easy to start up. They require little paper work to fill in and little money on setting up. They are thus one of the easiest types of business to start.

Secondly, they are subject to fewer regulations relative to other types of businesses and this can serve much time and cost. It above all minimises

---
[20] [1960] TH 179 at 182.

exposure of this form of business to statutory penalties for failure to comply with laws and regulations. As already pointed out, the requirements for registration under the Registration of Business Names Act are not mandatory in all cases. A sole trader will, however, be required to comply with specific licensing regulations which, in many cases, are not onerous. Thirdly, the sole trader or proprietor has full autonomy regarding business decisions and there is never the tension that is sometimes common among partners when it comes to decision making. There is absolute flexibility on what the business should invest in at any particular moment and how the profits will be used. Besides having a quick decision-making process, a sole proprietor does not have any opposition when making a decision as she has total control of her business.

Fourthly, sole proprietorships are easy to discontinue. Unlike other forms of business entities that have elaborate winding-up procedures, a sole proprietorship does not. A fifth advantage is that the owner takes all the profits of the business. Linked, the sole trader is in direct and full control of all the elements and aspects of the business association. This is one of the main reasons that most businesses of this type are an attractive option.

Lastly, from a tax point of view, these enterprises also enjoy certain advantages. A sole proprietorship is not a corporation; it does not pay corporate taxes, but rather the person who organised the business pays self-employment taxes on the profits that the business makes, making tax filing much simpler. Similarly a sole proprietorship also does not have to be concerned with double taxation, as a corporate entity would.

2.16 DISADVANTAGES OF SOLE PROPRIETORSHIPS

As against all the advantages one can think of for opting for a sole proprietorship as opposed to other forms of business enterprises, there are some obvious disadvantages. First, the most significant disadvantage of this form of business association is that they have no separate legal personality from the owner and consequently in the event of failure to pay debts, a creditor may have recourse to the personal property of the owner of the business. The owner of the business has unlimited liability as she is responsible for the business's debts because she has control over the business. The personal property of the proprietor can be attached to settle the debt arising purely out of a business transaction.

Because they have no separate legal existence, sole proprietorships cannot enter into contracts in their own right, nor can they sue or be sued *eo nomine*, ie, in their own name.

Secondly, because of lacking corporate personality, a business organised as a sole trader is likely to encounter difficulties raising capital and the owner has to make up for all the business' funds. Another disadvantage of a sole proprietorship is that it can only be operated at a certain scale and no more. As the business becomes more successful, the risks accompanying the business tend to grow. To minimise those risks, a sole proprietor has the option of forming a limited liability company. Thirdly, a sole trader lacks perpetual succession. This means that when the proprietor dies or is declared bankrupt, the business association ceases to exist.

Lastly, compared to other business associations, because sole traders are generally smaller businesses, they usually find it more difficult to raise external finance and capital. Most banks and financial institutions are less inclined to lend to sole traders because it is a larger risk to lend to sole traders who may have less assets to offer as collateral.

KEY POINTS

- A sole proprietorship is a type of business entity which is owned and run by one individual and where there is no legal distinction between the owner and the business.
- A sole proprietor may choose to use her own name in undertaking a business or opt to use a business or trade name other than her legal or true name.
- Advantages of sole traders include the fact that they are easy to start and discontinue, have full autonomy and have fewer regulations.
- Disadvantages of sole traders are that they lack corporate capacity, separate legal personality and perpetual succession.

Chapter 3

PARTNERSHIPS

3.1 GENERAL NATURE OF A PARTNERSHIP

At a very elementary level a partnership exists where two or more persons (natural or artificial) associate for a business objective. It is obvious from a very basic understanding that a partnership involves at least two persons coming together for purposes of making a profit. Needless to say, there can be no such thing as a one-man partnership. The purpose of the association of the two or more persons is to make a profit.

A partnership typically entails direct participation in the success and profits of the business and involvement (to one extent or another) in the running of the firm. It brings fiduciary duties and potential liability, depending on the type of partnership structure, but it may also bring about favourable tax treatment. The English Partnership Act 1890[1] defines a business partnership in s 1, as 'the relationship which subsists between persons carrying on business in common with a view to profit'.

A non-profit association of persons would, therefore, not be regarded as a partnership within the meaning of the law. In ordinary parlance, however, it is usual to describe all forms of association as partnerships. It is not uncommon for a matrimonial relationship to be referred to as a partnership. This also applies to unmarried couples who may be engaged in a common activity—say an outing for a wedding or a holiday. Two people on a hunting expedition or a country side drive will quite often be described as partners. Though they may be loosely called partners, however, there is no partnership within the meaning of the Partnership Act.

It is important for a proper appreciation of the real nature of a partnership to consider various definitions given of the concept of partnership. Useful guidance is also to be found in the following passage from *Halsbury's Laws of England*:[2]

> Partnerships involve a contract between the partners to engage in a business with a view to profit. As a rule each partner contributes property, skill or labour but this is not essential. A person who contributes property without labour, and has the rights of a partner, is usually termed a sleeping partner or dormant partner. A sleeping partner may,

---

[1] [54 & 54 VICT] [CH 39].
[2] Lord Hailsham of Marylebone (ed) *Halsbury's Laws of England* 4 ed (1989) 5 at para 2.

however, contribute nothing. The question whether or not there is a partnership is one of mixed law and fact.

At paragraph 4 on the same page it defines a business as follows:

The existence of a business is essential to a partnership, and for this purpose business includes every trade, occupation or profession the idea involved is that of a joint operation for the sake of gain.

Hardy Ivamy in his work *Principles of the Law of Partnership*[3] defines partnership as

the relation which subsists between persons carrying on a business in common with a view of profit. This definition is neat and epigrammatic, and, no doubt, puts the matter in a nutshell; but it is easier to concoct an epigram than to interpret it, and, as a witty and learned Lord of Appeal has remarked, it is one thing to put a case in a nutshell and another to keep it there.

At page 3 of the same book, he continues as follows:

Let us examine the definition a little more closely. There are three essential facts without which no partnership can exist. There must be: (i) a business; (ii) carried on in common; (iii) with a view of profit.

The essentials of a partnership agreement were set out by Stratford AJA in *Rhodesia Railways and Ors v Commissioner of Taxes*[4] as follows:

I think we are safe if we adopt the essentials which have been laid down in Pothier on Partnership . . . . These essentials are fourfold. First, that each of the partners brings something into the partnership, or binds himself to bring something into it, whether it be money, or his labour or skill. The second essential is that the business should be carried on for the joint benefit of both parties. The third is that the object should be to make profit. Finally, the contract between the parties should be a legitimate contract.

Subsequently, in *Bester v Van Niekerk*[5] the fourth essential, ie that the contract between the parties should be a legitimate contract, was dropped, on the ground that illegality as a ground of invalidation was part of the general law of contract and was not an essential peculiar to partnership agreements.

A partnership relationship arises by agreement. Such agreement may be express or implied. Most partnerships arise by express mutual agreement between the parties to it. Such express agreement may be in writing or it may be oral. Where it is reduced to writing, the partners may draw up a partnership contract, which is also referred to as a partnership deed or partnership articles, setting out the details of their association. It is possible

---

[3] A Underhill & ER Hardy Ivamy *Principles of the Law of Partnership* 10 ed (1975) 1.
[4] [1925] AD 438 at 465.
[5] 1960 (2) SA 779 (AD).

for people engaged in a business relationship in which they make profit and share it to be in a partnership without realising it or indeed calling it as such.

Provided their business relationship can fit within the definition of a partnership as set out in the Partnership Act, they will be treated as such by the law even if they did not intend this to be the case. In the case of *Musaku Mukumbwa and Rody Musatwe v Northern Breweries Limited and Kalinde Trading Limited*[6] the Zambian Supreme Court reiterated this point when it made the following observations:

> The evidence on the appeal, in our view, clearly establishes that the appellant and the 1st respondent entered into a business partnership whereby they obtained beers from the 2nd respondent for resale. They may not, themselves, have called it a joint business venture but in our view, it actually was . . . . A further examination of the appellant's testimony establishes that his business partnership with the 1st respondent was based on an agreement that the duo would share profits realized from the beer sales.

As will be shown later, the Supreme Court's view on a joint venture partnership is consistent with the views expressed in *United Dominions Corporation Ltd v Brian Pty Ltd and Others*.[7]

In the Nigerian case of *Ojemen v Okoafuda*[8] the plaintiff and the defendant agreed orally to establish a cinema and to run it for their mutual benefit. Each of them made a financial contribution to the venture and they used the money to purchase necessary equipment. There was no formal agreement, nor was the total amount of capital expected from each party settled. What the parties did was simply to sign a document setting out the amount already contributed. An action was brought by one of the parties for a declaration that on the facts, a partnership existed between the two, and that the defendant was liable to account for money received on behalf of the partnership and for the recovery of property bought with partnership funds. It was held that on the facts, a partnership existed between the parties. According to Uwaifor J:

> The formation and terms of a partnership may be evidenced by partnership articles under seal, by an agreement signed by the partners, by an unsigned document drafted by one partner and acted on by the others, and even by an informal document initialed by the parties intended only to form instructions for a formal document. Furthermore, a partnership may be established by parole evidence and this may be so even when articles of partnership are in existence.[9]

---

[6] SCZ Judgment No 47 of 2014.

[7] [1985] 157 CLR 1.

[8] [1977] NCRL 192. See also *Sterios Thomopoulos v John Mandilas* [1946] 10 WACA 269 where the court held that even an agreement to agree may give rise to a partnership.

[9] [1977] NCRL 192 at 197–98.

Equally in the Kenyan case of *Mworia & Another vs Kiambati*, the court of appeal reiterated that a partnership can take any form. The court had this to say:

> In some cases, partners establish their business by entering into a deed. In many cases, the agreement is oral. In a verbal contract of partnership, a person has to prove the existence of it by proving material items. These can be proved by their conduct, the mode they have dealt with each other and with other people.[10]

While there is no legal requirement to have a formal partnership agreement or deed to regulate the partnership relationship, individuals contemplating forming a partnership will be well advised to have a formal, written partnership agreement. Such formal document gives them a framework for outlining each partner's obligations, the dispute settlement mechanism, and other difficult-to-resolve issues that naturally occur in nearly every business relationship. Ultimately, it will help ensure the long-term well-being of their business.

The written partnership agreement should be crafted with the assumption that anything that can go wrong with the partnership will in fact go wrong. Friction between partners over things such as use and sharing of money, power or ego frequently undo these business relationships. The partnership agreement should prepare one for all possible 'what-if' situations and set methods for resolving them. It pays to be extra cautious. The following are some of the key areas that intending partners will want to cover in their written partnership agreement:

Preliminaries
- Under what name does the partnership intend to trade?
- What business does the partnership intend to undertake?
- Is the partnership for a fixed duration?

Administration, responsibilities and remuneration
- How are the roles to be shared out between or amongst the partners?
- What level of performance is expected?
- Are partners expected to make a full-time commitment to the venture, or are business activities permitted?
- What will be the income of each partner, and how will profits or losses be distributed?

Contributions
- What will each partner be contributing to the partnership in terms of cash, assets, loans, investments and/or labour?

---

[10] [1988] KLR 665.

- If a partner loans the company money, what will be the terms of repayment?
- Will the partners be expected to make additional contributions to the partnership, and if so, how will that be handled?

Withdrawal of partners/admission of new partners
- What guidelines should be followed if one partner wants to leave the partnership?
- Will partners be allowed to sell their interests in the business to outsiders?
- On what grounds can a partner be expelled from the partnership (misconduct, non-performance of duties)?
- How will new partners be admitted to the partnership?

Buy-out procedures
- What guidelines should be followed if one partner wants to retire or leave the partnership?
- What happens if a partner is incapacitated or dies?
- Will the partnership take out 'key man' life insurance to ensure the surviving partner is able to buy the deceased partner's shares from his heirs?
- Will partners who leave have to sign a non-compete agreement?

Dispute resolution
- What methods will be used to settle disputes that cannot be otherwise resolved?
- What procedures should be used if there is a tie vote between partners on crucial partnership decisions?
- Will mediation or binding arbitration be used?
- If disputes cannot be resolved, is there a mechanism in place for dissolving the partnership?

Financial arrangements
- What banking arrangements will be made for the partnership?
- Which partners will have cheque-signing privileges?
- Who will be authorised to draw on the partnership's accounts?
- How will the books be kept?

Method for dissolving the partnership
- When can the partnership be dissolved?

•   What happens to the partnership if the partners decide they cannot work together?

Valuation

•   What methods will be used to determine the value of the business in the event of a sale, dissolution, death, disability or withdrawal of a partner?

A firm or a partnership is a mere collection of individuals and is not in law regarded as a separate legal entity. It has no corporate status like a registered company. In *Green v Beesley*[11] Tindal CJ stated that 'I have always understood the definition of partnership to be a mutual participation', yet the participants do not create a legal entity when they create a partnership.

Each of the individuals making up the partnership has a responsibility for the transactions, the debts and liabilities of the firm. The private property of each individual partner is liable to be attached in settlement of the debts of the firm or partnership. Innocent and prudent partners may end up answering for the business recklessness or poor judgment of one partner who transacts on behalf of the partnership.

Like other unincorporated associations such as political parties and clubs, a partnership generally lacks capacity to sue and to be sued in its own name. This point was well articulated in *Harry Mwaanga Nkumbula and Simon Mwansa Kapwewe v United National Independence Party*,[12] a case which involved not a partnership, but a different form of unincorporated association called a political party, the United National Independence Party (UNIP). This party was named as the respondent in court proceedings. The Attorney-General, appearing on behalf of UNIP, made a preliminary objection on the ground that UNIP, an unincorporated body, was not a legal entity and could not, therefore, be sued in its name. He equated it to a members' club, and adopting the definition of a 'club', submitted that UNIP is a society of persons associated together for the purpose of the promotion of politics and as such it has no legal existence apart from the members it is composed of. Counsel for the applicants submitted that the law on the point was unclear but that, under s 36 of the Societies Act, UNIP could be named as a party. In the alternative, he submitted that the court had discretion to amend the proceedings and make the Attorney-General appear on behalf of UNIP.

---

[11] [1835] 2 Bing NC 108 at 112.
[12] [1978] ZR 388.

It was held that an unincorporated body is not a legal entity and is therefore not capable of suing or being sued in its name. It could only sue and be sued in a representative capacity. Hence, UNIP could only be sued in such a capacity. A materially similar conclusion was arrived at by the Supreme Court of Zambia in *National Milling Company Limited v A Vashee (Suing as Chairman of Zambia National Farmers Union)*[13] where it held that an unincorporated association is not a legal person and therefore cannot sue or be sued. However, the court further held that a contract purportedly made by or with an incorporated association is not necessarily a nullity.

These two cases, though not dealing with partnerships specifically, illustrate the general approach that will be taken in dealing with actions involving unincorporated entities. The rules and procedure for commencement of actions by and against partnership are discussed later.

3.2 LAW APPLICABLE TO PARTNERSHIPS IN ZAMBIA

3.2.1 The English Partnership Act of 1890

Zambian law recognises unincorporated firms or associations called partnerships. The law governing partnerships in Zambia is basically English law as contained in the English Partnership Act of 1890, which is applicable to Zambia by virtue of the English Law (Extent of Application) Act.[14] The statutory law contained in the Partnership Act of 1890 has been

---

[13] SCZ Judgment 23 of 2000.

[14] Chapter 11 of the Laws of Zambia. It is important to state that at independence in 1964, Zambia, a former British colony, retained most of the imported English law, both common law and statutory law with minor adjustments to suit local circumstances. This was effected through various pieces of legislation, notably the Zambia Independence Act (section 2(1)) of 1964 and the Zambia Independence Order (ss 4(1) and 6), both of which in effect provided that all existing laws in force in the territory on 24 October 1964 or which were passed before that date but were to come into force thereafter, continued in force unless expressly revoked by Parliament. Two other pieces of legislation are worth mentioning. These are the English Law (Extent of Application) Act (chapter 11 of the Laws of Zambia) and the British Acts Extension Act (chapter 10 of the Laws of Zambia). The former Act provides that subject to the provisions of the Constitution of Zambia and to any other written law, the common law, the doctrines of equity and the statutes which were in force in England on 17 August 1911 (being the commencement date of the Northern Rhodesia Order in Council,1911) as well as any statute of a later date than 17 August 1911 in force in England, now applied to the Republic, or which would be applied by any Act or otherwise, and the Supreme Court Practice Rules in force in 1999 shall apply in Zambia. The British Acts Extension Act, on the other hand, provides for the extension or application of certain British Acts to Zambia and for amendments to certain British Acts in their application to Zambia. A schedule to that Act lists a number of British Acts passed after 17 August 1911. These are: the Conveyancing Act 1911, the Forgery Act 1913, the Industrial and Provident Societies (Amendment) Act 1913, the Larceny Act 1916, the Bills of Exchange (Time of Noting) Act 1917, the Married Women (Maintenance) Act 1920, the Gaming Act 1939, and the Law Reform (Enforcement of Contracts) Act 1954.

supplemented and interpreted by judicial decisions and general common-law principles. The English Partnership Act of 1890 is a codifying statute like the English Bills of Exchange Act.[15] Its applicability to partnerships is, however, not total to all partnerships. Where partners opt to draw up a partnership deed, the partnership articles will ordinarily contain detailed provision as to management issues, accounts, profit and loss matters, termination, etc. In the case of a conflict between a provision in the articles and the Act, the provision of the articles will generally prevail. The Act assumes the default applicability role. Where there are no partnership articles or where the articles are silent on any aspect, the Act will apply fully. Some provisions of the Act, however, apply to all partnerships whether the partners desire it or not. It is therefore absolutely necessary that one is familiar with the provisions of general application and those whose application may be excluded by the parties through agreement.

In England, by the Limited Partnership Act of 1907,[16] partners may set up a limited partnership in which one or more members of the partnership limit their liability to an agreed amount. That Act, however, requires that there should be at least one partner known as a general partner whose liability is unlimited. Limited partners contribute an amount of money as capital, or some in-kind contribution in the form of property valued at a stated amount. They are not liable for the debts and obligations of the firm beyond the amount contributed. During the lifetime of the partnership, limited partners may not draw out or receive back any part of their contributions to the partnership, nor do they take part in the management of the firm's business, and therefore do not have power to bind the partnership. If they do any of these things, they become liable for all the debts and obligations of the firm up to the amount drawn out or received back or incurred while taking part in the management, as the case may be. General partners on the other hand have unlimited liability. They are liable for all debts and obligations of the firm. A person cannot be both a general and a limited partner at the same time.

Under the Limited Partnership Act 1907, a limited partnership must be registered. This is done by delivering a statement in a prescribed form, signed by all the partners, to the Registrar of Companies. As a statute passed before the 17 of August 1911, the Limited Partnership Act of England of 1907 technically applies to Zambia so that it is theoretically possible under the law in Zambia to form a limited partnership in terms of

---

[15] (1882) Chapter 61 45 and 46 Vict.
[16] Chapter 24 7 Edw 7.

that English Act. It is doubtful, however, that facilities for registration of such partnerships are available. In practice, no such partnerships exist in Zambia, for where limitation of liability is desired, it is usual for the association to be formed into a limited company under the Companies Act.[17]

A rather significant development in partnership law in the United Kingdom was the passage of the Limited Liability Partnerships Act 2000.[18] This Act provides for the creation of a limited liability partnership (LLP) as a distinct body with legal personality separate from its members. The LLP is governed under a mixture of company law and partnership law rules and principles. The liability of members of an LLP on winding up is limited to the amount of capital they contributed to the LLP.

Incorporation of LLPs is by subscription to an incorporation document, which must be delivered to the Companies Registrar. Once all the formalities have been complied with, the Registrar retains the incorporation document and issues a certificate of incorporation. The relationship between members is governed by agreement between the members. Where no such agreement exists, the Act provides that regulations may be made specifying the default form of such an agreement. As with normal partnerships, the members of an LLP are deemed to be agents of the LLP, and the LLP is liable for the actions of a member when that member commits wrongs or omissions. Unlike ordinary partnerships, however, the members of an LLP are not jointly and severally liable for the actions of a co-partner because the LLP itself has legal personality separate from its members. The Limited Liability Partnership Act of 2000 does not, of course, apply to Zambia. Therefore, LLPs cannot be set up under current Zambian law.

3.2.2 The Registration of Business Names Act

A partnership that intends to conduct its business under a trade name consisting of a name other that the true Christian names and surnames of the partners will require to be registered under the Registration of Business Names Act 16 of 2011. This aspect has been covered in detail in the part dealing with sole proprietorships.

It ought to be remembered that registration under that Act is not mandatory and does not entail exemption from other forms of registration

---

[17] 10 of 2017.
[18] Chapter 12.

necessary to carry on particular businesses such as licensing requirements or compulsory registration such as that required for tax purposes.

3.2.3 Other legislation

As partnerships are set up for a diverse range of business activities, they are obliged to comply with all other laws, both of a general nature such as that relating to taxation, environmental protection and public health, and of particular application such as those relating to sector regulation and licensing.

3.2.4 Common law and equity

It has already been indicated that general principles of law, especially the principles of common law and equity, will apply to partnerships where these have not been modified or excluded by the Partnership Act or the articles of partnership. Considering that partnerships are effectively a form of contract, this position should hardly be surprising.

3.3 ILLEGAL ASSOCIATIONS

A partnership is illegal if it is formed for a purpose which is contrary to public policy or which cannot be carried on without breaking the law. An association or partnership which is rendered illegal has no legal recognition and its members will be precluded from enforcing any claims arising out of the transaction of the association, but are individually liable for debts to a creditor dealing with such an association without notice of illegality. In *Shaw v Benson*[19] one of the objects of the Thornhill Arms Society was to form a fund from which money might be lent to shareholders, on interest. The society was made up of more than 20 members and was not incorporated. It lent money to the defendants, who offered promissory notes as security for the loan. An action was brought on the notes. The court held that the action could not be maintained. Brett MR remarked:

> [T]he Thornhill Arms Society is prohibited by the Companies Act . . . and is illegal. Is the contract illegal? The mere contract to lend is not illegal, and the question is whether the contract of the borrowers is not merely a contract to repay money advanced: it seems to me that their contract is not a mere contract of repayment, for the liability was undertaken, and the money was to be repaid according to the rules of the society; therefore, the rules of the society form part of the contract of repayment, and as the society is illegal, the contract for repayment also must be illegal. The borrowing and the lending were parts of one transaction, which had for its object the carrying out of the illegal purpose of the society.

---

[19] [1883] 11 QBD 563.

Similarly, in *Wilkinson v Levison*[20] an unincorporated and unregistered loan society consisting of over 20 members was held not to be entitled to recover a loan advanced to a member in accordance with the rules of the society because the society was illegal. However, in *Greenberg v Cooper-stein*[21] the court held that an action for a refund of moneys paid to an illegal association could succeed. In that case, members of an illegal association sued its treasurer and secretary on behalf of all the members for an account of the subscriptions received by the defendants and payment of the account found due. The action succeeded. The court observed that in all cases where an illegal association was seeking to recover money lent by it, it was necessarily held that as a result of the association being illegal, the contract with it could not be enforced. Tomlin J then remarked:

> [I]t is a different case where those who have subscribed money for an illegal purpose come requiring the agents in whose hands it is and who were to apply it for that purpose and have not done so, to return it to them. I am happy to think that the law is not so feeble that it cannot protect the subscribers by ordering an account.[22]

In *R v Twala*[23] a South African court employed the same reasoning as in *Greenberg*. In that case, an employee of an illegal loan fund association was convicted of theft after he had appropriated moneys to his own use. The Appellate Division confirmed his conviction. His defence was that as an illegal body, the association had no right to own or possess property. This was rejected, with Fagan JA stating:

> English decisions ... have held an association formed in contravention of the corresponding provision in the English company law to be incapable of suing or of being sued, and have refused to give legal effect to the agreement purporting to set out the constitution of the association or to contracts purporting to have been entered into by or concluded with the association. I am assuming that our courts will apply section 4 of our Act in the same way .... But that does not mean that assets purporting to be owned, possessed or controlled by such an association are *res nullius*. The assets must have been derived from people who had a legal title to them, and who if no legal bond was created by the conditions under which they purported to hand over those assets, must have retained the fight to reclaim them in so far as they had not yet been expended in terms of those conditions.[24]

In the case of *Fort Hall Bakery Supply Co v Wangoe*[25] the Supreme Court of Kenya dealt with an action that was brought by the plaintiff for the recovery of a certain sum of money from the defendant. During the trial

---

[20] [1925] 42 LTR 97.
[21] [1926] Ch 627.
[22] [1926] Ch 627 at 665–66.
[23] 1952 (2) SA 599 (A).
[24] 1952 (2) SA 599 (A) at 608.
[25] [1959] EA Rep 474.

the evidence adduced indicated that the plaintiffs were an association of more than 20 persons (in fact, that they were 45 in number) trading in partnership for gain. Further evidence showed that the association was not registered under the Registration of Business Names Ordinance. Defence counsel submitted that the action was not properly before the court as the association was illegal under s 388 of the Registration of Business Names Ordinance. The court held that the plaintiffs could not be recognised as having any legal existence, were incapable of maintaining the action and, that the action could therefore not be allowed to proceed. Likewise, in the Nigerian case of *Akinlose v A.I.I. Co Ltd*[26] a partnership of more than 100 persons was held to be illegal for exceeding the statutory limit of 20 persons.

However, regard must always be had to the purpose of the section before declaring any association as illegal. In *Smith v Anderson*[27] the case concerned an arrangement similar to the modern unit trust under which members of the public were invited to buy units, represented by certificates, in a fund of securities vested in trustees. The issue that fell to be determined was whether the holders of those units constituted an illegal association under the Companies Act then in force. The Court of Appeal held that the arrangement did not violate the Companies Act. James LJ stated:

> [T]he Act was intended, as it appears to me, to prevent the mischief arising from large trading undertakings being carried on by large fluctuating bodies, so that persons dealing with them did not know with whom they were contracting, and so might be put to great difficulty and expense, which was a public mischief to be repressed. . . . The Act says no company, association, or partnership consisting of more than twenty persons shall be formed after the commencement of this Act. For what? For the purpose of carrying on any business . . . I cannot arrive at the conclusion that the certificate holders form an association within the meaning of this Act of Parliament . . . .

Francis Palmer[28] was of the view that an illegal partnership association was a mere phantom with no legal existence. This does not mean, however, that all contracts made with the persons forming the illegal association have no legal validity.

In the South African case of *South African Flour Millers' Mutual Association v Rutowitz Flour Mills Limited*[29] it was held that once the membership of an association exceeded the statutory limit, the association ceased to be recognised by the law and did not revive in the event of members being subsequently reduced below the statutory limit.

---

[26] [1961] WNLR 213.
[27] [1880] 15 Ch 247.
[28] F Palmer *Company Law* 22 ed (1976) 1037.
[29] [1938] CPD 199.

A partnership will be illegal on the same grounds as a general contract, namely, when its objects are forbidden by the law, or are immoral or contrary to public policy, or where they have become illegal by some supervening illegality.

3.4 ANALYSING THE STATUTORY DEFINITION OF A PARTNERSHIP

Section 1 of the Partnership Act defines a partnership as the relation 'which subsists between persons carrying on a business in common with a view of profit'. The precise meaning of this section has been a subject of judicial interpretation in many cases. The individual components of that definition must be examined carefully if a proper conclusion is to be reached as to whether or not an association is a partnership within the meaning of that section of the Act. It is necessary for a proper appreciation to break down and consider the facets of that definition.

As regards the meaning of the term 'business' in s 1, it must be noted that s 45 of the Act states that business includes 'every trade, occupation or profession'. This is hardly a useful definition but could be called in aid for purposes of guidance only. Elsewhere the term has been defined to include

> a professional practice and includes any other undertaking which is carried on for gain or reward or which is an undertaking in the course of which goods or services are supplied otherwise than free of charge.[30]

The term 'carrying on business' was given judicial interpretation by the High Court of Northern Rhodesia in the case of *Daniel James van der Westhuizen v The Commissioner of Taxes*.[31] The appellant in that case was a South African national. He had ceased to reside in Northern Rhodesia, as Zambia was then called, in 1961, although he returned to the country from time to time to stay with his children. He also retained certain business interests in Northern Rhodesia and pursued them during his brief return visits to the country. He appealed against his being assessed for super tax during the assessment years ending on 31 March 1962 and 31 March 1963 respectively on grounds that during those years he was neither ordinarily resident nor carrying on business in Northern Rhodesia. In deciding the dispute, the court made extensive reference to the judgment of Beadle CJ in *Estate G v Commissioner of Taxes*[32] on the correct approach to the question of whether a particular activity or set of activities amounted to 'carrying on

---

[30] In *Words and Phrases Legally Defined* 3 ed (1988).
[31] [1963–64] ZR 183 (Reprint).
[32] [1964] 26 SATC 168.

business'. The court, in particular, considered the following passage from the judgment:

> It is quite impossible to define precisely the 'commercial' meaning so as to have a yardstick with which to measure any particular activities. The sensible approach, I think, is to look at the activities concerned as a whole, and then ask the question: are these the sort of activities which, in commercial life, would be regarded as 'carrying on business?' The principle feature of the activities which might be examined in order to determine this are their nature, their scope and magnitude, their object (whether to make profit or not), the continuity of the activities concerned, if the acquisition of property is involved, the intention with which the property was acquired. This list of features does not purport to be exhaustive, nor is it possible to generalize and state which features should carry most weight in determining the problem. Each case must depend on its own particular circumstances.

Guided by this dictum, Charles J explained the meaning of the term 'carrying on business' under s 86(2)*(a)* of the Income Tax Act of 1954 in regard to the facts before him. As the receipt of rent from the three leasehold properties was the result of separate and unconnected transactions entered into for purposes of using the properties pending their sale and not for purposes of carrying on the business of leasing real estate, he opined:

> I cannot see how the fact could convert a single transaction into carrying on business of letting . . . . As to the appellant's continued interest and active participation in the business of A company, both as director and as the predominant shareholder, and his being a substantial shareholder in the B company during the relevant assessment years, that clearly was not 'carrying on business.'

In *Smith v Anderson*,[33] Jessel MR stated that 'when a person habitually does a thing which is capable of producing a profit, for the purpose of producing a profit, he is carrying on a business'. In *Re Griffin, Ex parte Board of Trade*[34] Esher MR pushed the point further when he opined:

> [W]hether one or two transactions make a business depends upon the circumstances of each case. I take the test to be this: if an isolated transaction, which if repeated would be a transaction in business, is proved to have been undertaken with the intent that it should be the first of several transactions, that is, with the intent to carrying on a business, then it is a first transaction in an existing business. The business exists from the time of the commencement of that transaction with the intent that it should be one of a series.

It seems that a business should mean a series of acts which if successful will lead to a gain being made. One isolated transaction, or a series of transactions which, no matter how successful, will not produce a gain, may not be appropriately called a business. However, it appears that it is

---

[33] [1880] 15 Ch D 247 at 258.
[34] [1890] 60 LJQB 235 at 237.

possible for persons to form a partnership for purposes of undertaking a single business transaction. The need or necessity of establishing an intention to continue in business beyond one transaction has been overlooked in some cases, impliedly acknowledging the validity of a partnership in a single venture. There is authority for the proposition that an association of persons to carry out one deal only may constitute a business. In the case of *United Dominions Corporation Ltd v Brian Pty Ltd and Others*[35] an agreement entered into on 23 July 1974, although describing the parties as engaging in a 'joint venture' was in essence found to be a partnership agreement dealing with a 'partnership for one transaction'. On this point Dawson J noted:

> The requirement that a business should be carried on provides no clear means of distinguishing a joint venture from a partnership. There may be a partnership for a single adventure or undertaking, for the Act provides that, subject to any agreement between the partners, a partnership, if entered into for a single adventure or undertaking, is dissolved by the termination of that adventure or undertaking. See, for example, Partnership Act 1892 (NSW), s 32*(b)*. A single adventure under our law may or may not, depending upon its scope, amount to the carrying on of a business: *Smith v Anderson* (1880) 15 Ch D 247 at 277–278; *Re Griffin; Ex parte Board of Trade* (1890) 60 LJQB 235 at 237; *Ballantyne v Raphael* (1889) 15 VLR 538. Whilst the phrase 'carrying on a business' contains an element of continuity or repetition in contrast with an isolated transaction which is not to be repeated, the decision of this court in *Canny Gabriel Castle Jackson Advertising Pty Ltd v Volume Sales (Finance) Pty Ltd* (1974) 131 CLR 321 suggests that the emphasis which will be placed upon continuity may not be heavy.[36]

This finding, supporting the existence of single venture partnerships, can cause some confusion regarding non-partnership joint ventures and syndicates. Some reference to this dilemma was made in *United Dominions Corporation Ltd v Brian Pty Ltd*. On this point the High Court stated:

> The term 'joint venture' is not a technical one with a settled common-law meaning. As a matter of ordinary language, it connotes an association of persons for the purposes of a particular trading, commercial, mining or other financial undertaking or endeavour with a view to mutual profit, with each participant usually (but not necessarily) contributing money, property or skill. Such a joint venture . . . will often be a partnership. The term is, however, apposite to refer to a joint undertaking or activity carried out through a medium other than a partnership such as a company, a trust, an agency or joint ownership. The borderline between what can properly be described as a 'joint venture' and what should more properly be seen as no more than a simple contractual relationship may on occasions be blurred. Thus, where one party contributes only money or other property, it may sometimes be difficult to determine whether a partnership is a joint venture in which both parties are entitled to a share of profits or a

---

[35] [1985] 157 CLR 1.
[36] [1985] 157 CLR 1 at 15.

simple contract of loan or lease under which the interest or rent payable to the party providing the money or property is determined by reference to the profits made by the other.[37]

In *Mann v D'Arcy and Others*[38] the plaintiff claimed that towards the end of May 1958, an agreement was made whereby he entered into a partnership with the three defendants for a single venture, namely, the purchase and resale of some 350 tons of potatoes. Megarry J said:

> It is important not to be bewitched by words. There are partnerships and partnerships. A general partnership for a period of years may be very different in substance from a partnership in a single venture; and one single venture may differ greatly from another. In *Towne v Eisner* ((1918), 245 US Rep 418 at p 425) Holmes J reminded us that 'a word is not a crystal, transparent and unchanged, it is the skin of a living thought and may vary greatly in colour and content according to the circumstances and the time in which it is used.' One must, I think, penetrate beyond the word 'partnership' to the substance of the transaction and not generalise the words of either James LJ or Lindley's Law of Partnership beyond anything that they can fairly have intended.

One may be justified in suggesting that these decisions can be supported by thoughts that a codifying statute like the Partnership Act is intended, in part at least, to clarify unclear positions brought about by conflicting case law by a categorical statement of what the law is to be. It is therefore not normally proper to look to earlier cases alone for guidance as to interpretation of the Act. It will be noted that the pre-1890 cases were not interpreting the Partnership Act and therefore sufficient room for departure from those decisions exist.

There is no partnership when it is shown that the persons concerned were preparing to carry on business as a company as soon as they could. In *Keith Spicer Limited v Mansell*,[39] the defendant and Mr Bishop agreed to go into business together and to form a limited company to carry on business in the defendant's restaurant. Before the incorporation of the company, Bishop ordered goods from the plaintiffs which he intended for the use of the company. The defendant and Bishop opened a bank account in the name of the proposed company without the word 'Limited'. In an action against the defendant for the price of the goods, which was just under £150, the plaintiffs alleged that the defendant and Bishop were in partnership (having failed to prove that Bishop was the agent of the defendant), that Bishop had ordered the goods for the partnership and that the defendant was liable for the price. Edmund Davies LJ noted:

---

[37] [1985] 157 CLR 1 at 10.
[38] [1968] 2 All ER 172.
[39] [1970] 1 All ER 462 CA.

An apposite statement of the relevant law is to be found in Lindley on Partnership–
'Persons who are working together to form a company, although they may intend to
become members of the company after its formation, are not partners if this be the only
relation between them; they are, it is true, engaged in a common object, and that object
is ultimately to acquire profit; but their immediate object is the formation of a company,
and even if the company is not to be incorporated they are only in the position of
persons who intend to become partners after the company is formed.'
... Not every transaction between two people preparatory to the formation of a
company is sufficient to constitute them partners.

Widgery LJ concluded by saying:

Like my Lords, I find the evidence and the judge's finding quite insufficient to show that
there was here a carrying-on of business in common with a view of profit between Mr
Bishop and the defendant at the material time. All the transactions as far as I can see,
were transactions which might perfectly well have been preparatory to the formation of
the company, and accordingly, whatever the truth of the matter might have been if it had
been more fully investigated in the evidence, there is in my judgment no material here
on which we can say that the learned county court judge erred.

The substratum of the *Keith Spicer* judgment was that the defendant was
not liable as there was not a partnership between him and Mr Bishop as
they were not carrying on a business together in partnership but merely
preparing to carry on business as a company as soon as they could.

In *Henshaw v Roberts*[40] where a syndicate executed a written agreement
to form a partnership within a specified time and the partnership was not
formed within that time it was held that 'the existence of a partnership
depends on the carrying on of business and not on the agreement to form a
partnership'.[41] If the parties had begun to carry out business (though
prematurely), a partnership relationship would have been readily inferred
from their conduct.

The situation may be less easy to understand where parties have
performed acts and incurred expenses in preparation to carrying on the
business of a partnership. However, in *Khan and Another v Miah and
Others*[42] in May 1993 the first and second respondents wished to open a
restaurant but lacked sufficient capital. They therefore approached the
appellant, K, with a view to interesting him in the venture. It was agreed
that they would be partners in the business, that K would provide most of
the initial capital, that the first respondent would manage the business and
that the second respondent would be the chef. The third respondent was
later brought in to provide the business experience and financial standing
required by a prospective landlord. By 1 December 1993 the parties had

---

[40] [1967] I ALR Comm 5 at 11–12.
[41] *Henshaw v Roberts* [1967] I ALR Comm 5 at 11–2.
[42] [2001] 1 All ER 20 HL.

found suitable premises, obtained planning permission for its conversion to a restaurant, taken a lease on the premises and agreed to buy the freehold reversion, opened a partnership bank account in the names of K and the third respondent, arranged to borrow money from the bank towards the purchase of the freehold, entered into a contract with a firm of builders for the conversion and fitting out of the premises, and contracted for the purchase of equipment and table linen. Nearly all the moneys in the partnership account were provided by K. Subsequently, K's relationship with the respondents broke down, and any partnership between them determined on 25 January 1994. By that time, the parties had acquired the freehold, bought and taken delivery of furniture, entered into a credit agreement for the purchase of carpets and a contract for the laundry of table linen, and advertised the restaurant in the local press. However, the restaurant did not open for business until 14 February 1994. The respondents thereafter carried on the business on their own account, without any settling of accounts with K, hence the court proceedings. Lord Millett observed that

> whether parties who propose entering into a business venture in partnership together have actually done so is a question of fact into which your Lordships would not normally enter. But the majority of the Court of Appeal did not reverse the judge's findings of fact. They reversed his conclusion because they considered that there was a rule of law that the parties to a joint venture do not become partners until actual trading commences . . . They identified the business of the partnership as the carrying on of a restaurant business from the premises in Newbury, and (at 486) posed the question: 'were the four parties carrying on a restaurant business at [the premises] prior to 25 January 1994?' So expressed, the question could only be answered in one way. The restaurant was not open for business.
>
> . . . I think that the majority of the Court of Appeal were guilty of nominalism. They thought that it was necessary, not merely to identify the joint venture into which the parties had agreed to enter, but to give it a particular description, and then to decide whether the parties had commenced to carry on a business of that description. They described the business which the parties agreed to carry on together as the business of a restaurant, meaning the preparation and serving of meals to customers, and asked themselves whether the restaurant had commenced trading by the relevant date. But this was an impossibly narrow view of the enterprise on which the parties agreed to embark. They did not intend to become partners in an existing business. They did not agree merely to take over and run a restaurant. They agreed to find suitable premises, fit them out as a restaurant and run the restaurant once they had set it up. The acquisition, conversion and fitting out of the premises and the purchase of furniture and equipment were all part of the joint venture, were undertaken with a view of ultimate profit, and formed part of the business which the parties agreed to carry on in partnership together.
> . . . There is no rule of law that the parties to a joint venture do not become partners until actual trading commences. The rule is that persons who agree to carry on a business activity as a joint venture do not become partners until they actually embark on the activity in question. It is necessary to identify the venture in order to decide whether the parties have actually embarked upon it, but it is not necessary to attach any particular

name to it. Any commercial activity which is capable of being carried on by an individual is capable of being carried on in partnership. Many businesses require a great deal of expenditure to be incurred before trading commences. Films, for example, are commonly (for tax reasons) produced by limited partnerships. The making of a film is a business activity, at least if it is genuinely conducted with a view of profit. But the film rights have to be bought, the script commissioned, locations found, the director, actors and cameramen engaged, and the studio hired, long before the cameras start to roll. The work of finding, acquiring and fitting out a shop or restaurant begins long before the premises are open for business and the first customers walk through the door. Such work is undertaken with a view of profit, and may be undertaken as well by partners as by a sole trader.

The question in the present case is not whether the parties 'had so far advanced towards the establishment of a restaurant as properly to be described as having entered upon the trade of running a restaurant', for it does not matter how the enterprise should properly be described. The question is whether they had actually embarked upon the venture on which they had agreed. The mutual rights and obligations of the parties do not depend on whether their relationship broke up the day before or the day after they opened the restaurant, but on whether it broke up before or after they actually transacted any business of the joint venture. The question is not whether the restaurant had commenced trading, but whether the parties had done enough to be found to have commenced the joint enterprise in which they had agreed to engage. Once the judge found that the assets had been acquired, the liabilities incurred and the expenditure laid out in the course of the joint venture and with the authority of all parties, the conclusion inevitably followed.

The phrase 'with a view to profit' as used in s 1 of the Partnership Act literally means with the intention to create a profit. Persons associating together in a partnership must have the intention of making some gain from their partnership. In *Re Arthur Average Association for British Foreign, and Colonial Ships, Ex parte Hargrove and Co.*,[43] Jessel MR put the position thus:

[I]f you come to the meaning of the word 'gain', it means acquisition. It has no other meaning that I am aware of. Gain is something obtained or acquired. It is not limited to pecuniary gain. We should have to add the word 'pecuniary' so as to limit it. And still less is it limited to commercial profits. The word used, it must be observed, is not 'gains', but 'gain' in the singular. Commercial profits, no doubt, are gain, but I cannot find anything limiting gain to imply commercial profit. I take the words as referring to a company which is formed to acquire something, or in which the individual members are to acquire something, as distinguished from a company formed for spending something, and in which the individual members are simply to give something away or to spend something, and not to gain anything . . .

In *Armour v Liverpool Corporation*[44] Simonds J remarked:

Neither 'business' nor 'gain' is a word susceptible of precise or scientific definition. The test appears to me to be whether that which is being done is what ordinary persons would describe as the carrying on of a business for gain . . . .

---

[43] [1875] LR 10 Ch App 542.
[44] [1939] Ch 422 at 437.

In the case of *South African Flour Millers' Mutual Association v Rutowitz Flour Mills Limited*[45] the court held that a trade association whose purpose was to rationalise production and distribution in an industry was, in fact, carrying on business for 'gain'.

Gain literally means profit. This limb of the definition confines partnerships to associations formed for making a profit. This can be contrasted with clubs and societies formed for the promotion of religious, social, educational and recreational activities and which are not run in order to create profits for the individual members. Lord Linley in *Wise v Perpetual Trustee Co Ltd*[46] stated of clubs in contradiction with partnerships as follows:

> Clubs are associations of a peculiar nature. They are not partnerships; they are not associations for gain; and the feature which distinguishes them from other societies is that no member as such becomes liable to pay to the funds of the society or to anyone else any money beyond the subscription required by the rules of the club to be paid so long as he remains a member. It is upon this fundamental condition, not usually expressed but understood by everyone that clubs are formed; and this distinguishing feature has been often judicially recognised.

Members of societies, unlike partners, do not expect to gain monetarily by their membership. They may, however, gain in other ways by, for example, improving their knowledge or skills, enhancing their social contacts and status, or personal satisfaction from participation in the association's activities. Association members cannot obtain a distribution of pecuniary gains or profits made by the association, although associations may incidentally make profits in the furtherance of their objects.

It is important to note that the Partnership Act provides that for a business to be a partnership there must be *'a view of profit'*, ie an intention to achieve profit. It does not say that there must be an intention to *share profit*. In theory any persons conducting business with a view of profit are partners. In practice, the courts will not treat an association as a true partnership unless the desire is not merely to achieve profit but also to share that profit, that is to say they will interpret the words 'with a view of profit' as meaning 'with the intention of sharing profits'.

By 'carrying on business in common' as used in s 1 of the Act is simply meant that the partners undertake their business together through their respective tasks and responsibilities as may be defined in the partnership agreement. This they may do either by themselves or through their employees. This does not mean, however, that the share of profits of each of

---

the partners is necessarily equal, the sharing ratio being a matter for agreement between them.

To constitute a partnership the business must be carried out by or on behalf of all the partners; however, all the partners need not take an active role. In *Re Ruddock*,[47] Ruddock, who carried on business as a sole trader, became indebted to Mrs Bear, the grandmother of one of his employees. The employee was 19 years old. Ruddock entered into an agreement under seal with Mrs Bear whereby she was to purchase a one-quarter share of the business—the ultimate benefit would go to the grandson. Under the agreement, Mrs Bear had full control over the share, including the power of disposition (until the grandson attained 21 years, died before attaining such an age or if he displeased her in any way). The purchase price of the share was to be treated as having been paid by the discharge of the debt owing to Mrs Bear. Mrs Bear would receive a one-quarter share of the net profits. However, it was expressly agreed that she should not be liable as a partner for any losses and that Ruddock would indemnify her. Mrs Bear's name was not to be used and she was not to be held out as a partner. Mrs Bear had access to the books and Ruddock was to behave and manage the business 'as one partner should do to another'.

At a subsequent date, Ruddock consulted with Mrs Bear as to the disposal of another quarter share in the business and, at all times during the negotiations for the sale of this share, acted on the basis that her consent was essential. Mrs Bear replied that she had no objection to the sale. Later Ruddock became bankrupt and Mrs Bear put in proofs of debts for money paid to Ruddock. The other creditors sought to have these proofs expunged. The court agreed with the other creditors. Although Mrs Bear took no part in the day-to-day management of the business, she was a partner and could not prove against the estate of the insolvent debtor in competition with his other creditors. According to Molesworth J:

> The general principle of the authorities is, that a right to participate in profits constitutes a partner: and that, notwithstanding stipulation of being dormant or not liable to losses. But there are cases in which it has been held that the relative rights and liabilities of the persons dealing so far varied from those usual between partners, that the general rule should not apply. Many of those cases regard loans which continue to be such. This matter had nothing like a loan; it was a purchase for a price never to be repaid. As to what was said of the grandson, though it may have been the motive for the dealing, no rights to him formed part of the contract. He got nothing which was not subject to Mrs Bear's discretion. She retained all the rights of a dormant partner . . . .
>
> The cases show that the relation of partners is the result of their respective substantial rights, not of the words employed, and that the result of the partnership liability from

---

[47] [1879] 5 VLR (IP & M) 51.

participation of profits cannot be evaded by the form of conveyance. In subsequent matters Mrs Bear and Mr Ruddock treated each other as partners, as to his contemplating to sell another fourth and add another partner, which she was willing to do, but in which they corresponded on the mutual understanding that her consent was necessary . . .[48]

The term 'persons' as used in s 1 of the Act has the usual meaning attributable to it in law, ie it means both natural and unnatural persons. As will be pointed out in the part dealing with capacity to enter into partnership, it is possible for an individual to enter into a partnership with an artificial person, eg a limited company.

3.5 TYPES OF PARTNERS

There are different classes of partners who as between themselves hold different rights and responsibilities. The classification of partners within a partnership is a normal phenomenon. It usually identifies the contribution, role or rights of designated partners in the management of the partnership business. Whatever the name given to a particular partner in a firm, however, the ultimate rights and duties of the partner will be a matter of agreement by the partners so that the mere designation of a partner by a specific title may not be a conclusive indication of that partner's rights and duties in the firm. Some of the usual terms used to identify partners are as follows below.

3.5.1 Actual partner

This is the usual type of partner. He is the person who by agreement has entered into partnership and takes an active part in the conduct of the business of the firm. This type of partner, also referred to as an ostensible partner, is the agent of the other partners of the firm for purposes of the partnership business. What he does in the ordinary course of the partnership business, so far as third parties are concerned, bind him and his co-partners.

3.5.2 Normal partner

This is a person whose name is used as if he were a member of a partnership, but who is really not a member and is not entitled to share the profits of the firm. Such a person is not a necessary party to an action relating to the firm, except in cases of suits on negotiable instruments. He is, however, liable for all acts of the firm as if he were a real partner.

---

[48] [1879] 5 VLR (IP & M) 58.

3.5.3 Sleeping/dormant partner

This is a partner who does not take an active part in the management of the firm on a day-to-day basis. He is in reality a partner whose name may not even appear in any way as a partner, and, therefore, unknown to outsiders as a partner in the firm. In the Nigerian case of *Ojemen v Okoafuda*,[49] Uwaifo J put the matter thus:

> A person's contribution towards a partnership may be in property, skill or labour and there is what we call a sleeping or dormant partner . . . who contributes property but does not contribute labour.

Such partner will, however, be liable to third parties who transact with the firm even without knowing of his being a partner. As will be seen, s 5 of the Partnership Act makes every partner bound by the acts of a partner who does anything in the usual way. No distinction based on the active participation of a partner is made in that section. A dormant partner's liability may in fact be said to be premised on his position of an undisclosed principal. For as long as he remains a partner, he is liable for the debts and wrongs of the partnership although such liability is typically limited to the amount invested in the partnership. In the Indian case of *Sushila Devi v The State of Jharkhand and Another*,[50] DGR Patnaik J of the High Court, however, held that a sleeping partner is not liable for criminal acts attributable to the partnership. In that case, Messrs Ashk and Co was a partnership firm constituted by partners, namely the petitioner and her husband (who was at the time of the action deceased). A raid was conducted by the Police (Food) Crime Investigations Department, Jamshedpur. Upon detection of several irregularities and violations of the provisions of the Bihar Finance Act, a case was registered against the firm, including the petitioner for alleged infraction of the Penal Code and the Bihar Finance Act. Before the trial commenced, the petitioner filed an application praying to be discharged from the case on ground that she was a sleeping partner and was never involved in running or managing the affairs of the business of the firm in any manner. The court held that for it to impose criminal liability on any person, the element of *mens rea* and consciousness of the nature of the acts should also to be taken into account, and that if such elements are lacking, then the accused cannot be held liable for the offence.

Often, it is common that some of the partners of a firm may not even be aware of what is happening in the firm on a day-to-day basis. There may be partners, better known as sleeping partners who are not required to

---

[49] [1977] NCLR 193.
[50] Cr. M.P. No 979 of 2006.

participate in the business of the firm. These include women and minors who were admitted for the benefit of the partnership only and who may not know anything about the business of the firm.

It would be a travesty of justice to prosecute all partners and ask them to prove under the proviso to sub-s (1) that the offence was committed without their knowledge. It is significant to note that the obligation resting on the accused to prove under the proviso that the offence occurred without his knowledge, or that he exercised all due diligence to prevent such offence, arises only when the prosecution establishes that the requisite condition mentioned in sub-s (1) is established. The requisite condition is that the partner was responsible for carrying on the business and was, during the relevant time, in charge of the business. In the absence of such proof, no partner can be convicted.

3.5.4 Partner in profits only

By agreement between them, partners may stipulate that one or more of the partners will be entitled to a certain share of the profits without being liable for the losses. This kind of arrangement might be preferable for a number of reasons, such as where the partners' contributions to the partnership differ. One partner may invest only cash, while another may invest both cash and skill. It may well be that the partner who invests cash only might wish to absolve himself by insisting that he participates in profits only and not the losses caused by any possible mismanagement of the firm by the partner solely responsible for management. Although partners of this kind hardly have a role in the management of the business of the firm, they will, however, be liable to third parties for all acts of the firm.

3.5.5 Undisclosed partners

The right of an undisclosed partner to the benefit of any contract of the firm is, like that of an undisclosed principal, subject to equities and defences which the defendant may have against the partner who actually contracted.[51] Where a contract is made with one partner in his own name only, without mention of his firm, on account of the partnership business, the other partners may join with him in suing on it, or he may sue on it alone, upon the same principle that where an agent contracts for an undisclosed principal, either the former or the latter may sue upon it.

---

[51] *Beckham v Drake* [1849] 9 M & M 79; *S Kaprow & Co v Maclelland* [1948] 1 KB 618 at 627.

Where a contract is made by one partner in his own name on account of the partnership business, and the other partners are not disclosed, he may be sued alone upon it, or the other partners may be sued with him as co-defendant at the option of the person with whom the contract is made. But when he has sued and obtained judgment against the partner who made the contract, he cannot afterwards sue the non-disclosed partners.

Where the contract is made in a partnership name, and there are partners who did not appear in the transaction and were unknown to the other contracting party, the secret partners are in the position of undisclosed principals, and, although they may join in suing upon the contract, the other party cannot be compelled to sue them.

3.5.6 Partner by estoppel

Any person who, by words spoken or written or by his actions and conduct, represents himself, or knowingly allows himself to be represented as a partner in a firm, is liable as a partner to anyone who has on the face it contracted with the firm on that basis. Therefore, although such a person is not really a partner in the true sense, a third party may sue him as if he was a partner in respect of particular transactions.

3.5.7 Salaried partner

Some partnerships, as an incentive to an experienced or highly productive and/or efficient employee, may offer them the position of salaried partner. According to Megarry J in *Stekel v Ellice*:[52]

> The term 'salaried partner' is . . . to some extent . . . a contradiction in terms. However, it is a convenient expression which is widely used to denote a person who is held out to the world as being a partner, with his name appearing as partner on the notepaper of the firm and so on. At the same time, he receives a salary as remuneration, rather than a share of the profits, though he may, in addition to his salary, receive some bonus or other sum of money dependent upon the profits. Quoad the outside world it often will matter little whether a man is a full partner or a salaried partner; for a salaried partner is held out as being a partner, and the partners will be liable for his acts accordingly. But within the partnership it may be important to know whether a salaried partner is truly to be classified as a mere employee, or as a partner . . . What must be done . . . is to look at the substance of the relationship between the parties.[53]

Depending on any agreement to the contrary, a salaried partner remains an employee of the firm and is not an 'official partner' entitled to share in the profits of or even manage the firm but is seen as the penultimate step before being invited into the partnership. Whether or not the salaried

---

[52] [1973] 1 All ER 465.
[53] [1973] 1 All ER 465 at 198.

partner would be able to bind the company or exercise any other the other rights that other partners hold will depend on the partnership agreement.

3.6 USE OF THE TERM 'FIRM'

Section 4 provides that 'persons who have entered into partnership with one another are for the purposes of this Act called collectively a firm, and the name under which their business is carried on is called the firm name'. Partners may carry on business under any name and style which they choose. However, the firm's name should not be one that deceives the public.

A firm name may require to be registered under the Registration of Business Names Act 16 of 2011.[54] In law 'a firm' is only a convenient phrase for describing the two or more persons who constitute the partnership. In Zambia, the terms 'firm' and 'partnership' have been used to describe arrangements which do not in the least qualify as partnerships under the law of partnerships. For example, many one-man law practices are erroneously referred to as law firms. The names themselves are even more confusing because it is not infrequent that sole proprietors described themselves as partners. This, however, has largely been harmless in practice and its toleration by the relevant authority (Registrar of Business Names) is therefore understandable.

A firm is thus the association by which the partners are collectively carrying on business. However, since by its juridical nature a firm is not a legal entity, it has no existence apart from its individual members who carry on businesses both as principles and as agents of each other.

3.7 CAPACITY TO BE A PARTNER

Capacity to enter into a partnership agreement is generally coextensive with ordinary contractual capacity. Infants and persons of unsound mind require special consideration.

An infant can validly enter into a partnership contract. The obligations of such infant's business transactions would then be governed by the general law of contract, including the Infant's Relief Act of 1874.[55] As a general rule, a minor is not bound by any contract made during his minority. There are three exceptions:

---

[54] See Chapter 1.
[55] Which applies to Zambia.

(1) Contracts for necessaries—under which the infant will be bound. The term 'necessaries' is not restricted to things required to maintain bare existence like bread and clothes, but it includes articles determined in relation to the minor's station in life.

(2) Educational and employment contracts for the minor's benefit—contracts for a minor's education, service or apprenticeship, or for enabling them to earn a living (other than trading contracts) are binding unless they are detrimental to the interests of the minor.

(3) Voidable contracts—when a minor acquires an interest in a subject of a permanent nature (for example, lease, partnership, shares in a company) which imposes a continuous liability on him, the contract cannot be enforced against him during his minority. But after he attains full age, it will be binding on him unless he avoids it within a reasonable time.

In *Mercantile Union Guarantee Corp. Ltd v Ball*,[56] which decided that in the ordinary course of things a hire-purchase contract cannot be for the benefit of an infant, Finlay J made a pertinent observation as follows:

> [T]he law on this matter has been discussed in many cases. The position is thus stated in Coke upon Littleton, p 172: 'An infant may bind himself to pay for his necessary meat, drink, apparel, necessary physique, and such other necessaries, and likewise for his good teaching or instruction, whereby he may profit himself afterwards.
>
> It is true that there are certain contracts which, if they are for the infant's benefit, can be enforced against him; and it is said this trading contract was for the benefit of the infant because it was for the benefit of the infant that he should learn how to carry on a trade. But in my opinion there is no authority for saying that a trading contract, even if for the benefit of the infant, is an exception to the rule that an infant is not, except in certain cases, liable on contracts made by him.' Not only must the contract be within the class of contracts by which an infant may be bound, but also it must be one beneficial to the infant, and whether it is so is a question to be decided on the facts of each particular case.

Any contract of partnership entered into by an infant is not binding upon the infant during infancy. During such infancy the infant can repudiate the agreement and could do so for a short period of grace upon attainment of the age of majority. If after attainment of the age of majority the infant holds himself out or allows the firm to hold him out as still being a partner, he becomes liable for such of the partnership debts as were incurred after he reached majority. In other words, he will be estopped from taking any other position other than the one represented.

---

[56] [1937] 2 KB 498.

In *Goode v Harrison*[57] a minor who was a partner in a partnership took no steps to avoid the partnership upon attaining his majority; he was held liable for the debts of the partnership incurred after he came of age.[58] Such contracts are to be distinguished from contracts which are not binding on an infant unless the minor ratifies them upon attaining majority. Under the Infant's Relief Act of 1874 such ratification is void even if for new consideration. In *Hamilton v Vaughan Sherrin Electrical Engineering Co*[59] an infant partner on reaching majority expressly adopted the partnership agreement. It was held that the adoption rendered him liable both for partnership debts incurred before and after his attaining majority. However, a minor who repudiates the partnership may be able to recover on grounds of total failure of consideration.[60]

Persons of unsound mind are bound by partnership agreements under general rules of contract unless they can show that at the time of making the agreement (1) they were sufficiently ill not to understand what they were doing, and (2) that the other person/party to the agreement was aware of this fact. This is no doubt a very heavy burden of proof to discharge. Under s 35 of the Partnership Act, lunacy of any partners is a ground for application to court for dissolution of the firm.

Unnatural persons such as incorporated companies may enter into partnerships like natural persons. It is possible to have a partnership constituted between a natural person and an artificial person.

3.8   THE DISTINCTIVE FEATURES OF A PARTNERSHIP

In law a partnership is not regarded as an entity separate and distinct from its members. It is a collection of individuals who each have individual responsibility for the business activities of the partnership as a whole. The assets and liabilities of a partnership are the assets and liabilities of its members. In this regard, a partnership can be contrasted with a registered company on a number of grounds. While a company has a potentially perpetual existence, a partnership ordinarily ends with a change in the makeup or composition of the membership. Sir WM James LJ of the Court of Appeal in *Re Agriculturist Insurance Co (Baird's case)*[61] summed up the essential attributes of a partnership which distinguishes it from a company when he said:

---

[57] [1821] 5 B & Ald1 47.
[58] See also *Lovell and Christmas v Beauchamp* [1894] AC 607.
[59] [1894] 3 Ch 589.
[60] See *Steinberg v Scala (Leeds) Ltd* [1923] Ch 452; *Pearce v Brain* [1929] 2 KB 310.
[61] [1870] LR 5 Ch App 725.

Ordinary partnerships are essentially in kind, and not merely in the magnitude of the partnership or the number of the partners, different from joint stock companies. Ordinary partnerships are by law assumed and presumed to be based on the mutual trust and confidence of each partner in the skill, knowledge, and integrity of every other partner. As between the partners and the outside world (whatever may be their private arrangements between themselves), each partner is the unlimited agent of every other in every matter connected with the partnership business, or which he represents as partnership business, and not being in its nature beyond the scope of the partnership. A partner who may not have a farthing of capital left may take the moneys or assets of this partnership to the value of millions, may bind the partnership by contracts to any amount, may give the partnership acceptances for any amount, and may even—as has been shown in many painful instances in this Court—involve his innocent partners in unlimited amounts for fraud which he has craftily concealed from them.

3.9 LEGAL PROCEEDINGS BY AND AGAINST PARTNERS

A partnership not being a distinct persona means that all partners must be joined in a legal suit arising from transactions in the conduct of partnership business. This common-law position which actually disadvantaged litigants against partners was mitigated by the rules of court which now provide that an action can be brought against a firm. The particular rules relating to partners are contained in the Rules of the Supreme Court (RSC) (White Book) Order 81. By Order 81 rule 1,

[a]ny two or more persons claiming to be entitled, or alleged to be liable, as partners in respect of a cause of action and carrying on business within the jurisdiction may sue, or be sued, in the name of the firm (if any) of which they were partners at the time when the cause of action occurred.

Since the firm is not a legal entity, the use of the firm name is simply a means to identifying as partners the individuals who are suing or being sued. If court process is issued in the name of a firm as plaintiffs, any defendant is entitled to demand a written statement of the names and places of residence of all the persons who were partners in the firm when the cause of action occurred; likewise, a plaintiff who sues a partnership in its firm name is entitled to demand for the defendants the like details of all persons who were partners in the defendant firm when the cause of the action arose (Order 81 rule 2). Except where a partnership has, a plaintiff suing a partnership in the firm name may serve the writ on anyone or more of the partners, or at the principal place of business of the partnership within the jurisdiction on any person who at the time of service has the control or management of the partnership business there, or by sending a copy of the writ by post to the principal place of business of the partnership (Order 81 rule 3). Persons sued as partners in the name of the firm must acknowledge service in their own names, but the action may nevertheless continue in the firm name (Order 81 rule 3).

The point that a partnership is but a collection of persons and that it is not separate from those individuals means that a partner cannot ordinarily sue other partners in relation to a matter arising out of the partnership business. This point was made in *Shingadia Brothers v Karson Jadavjee Shingadia*.[62] There a partnership of three persons owned immovable property which they leased out to one of their number. The lessee fell into arrears in his rent obligation. The other partners brought an action against the defaulting lessee. The Federal Supreme Court (of Rhodesia and Nyasaland) held that the partnership as such could not sue because a party cannot be both plaintiff and defendant in the same action. Similarly, on the same principle that a firm name is merely an expression, the Kenyan High Court in *Nterekeiya Bus Service v Republic of Kenya*[63] declared the conviction of a firm name as a nullity.

3.10 PARTNERSHIPS AND REGISTERED COMPANIES CONTRASTED

It is important to understand the essential distinction between a partnership and other forms of business associations in Zambia. However, since by far the bulk of business entities in Zambia are registered companies, it is probably unnecessary to examine the differences with all the other forms of business associations as these will become apparent when those enterprises are examined. In any case, apart from sole proprietorships, which have already been considered in the Chapter 1, the rest of the business associations, that is to say, co-operative societies and parastatal companies, are very similar, if not the same, in form and substance as registered companies.

The table below summarises some of the principal differences between a partnership and a registered company.

Partnership	Registered Company
(1) Generally, no formalities required on formation. The agreement of the parties involved, express or implied, is sufficient.	(1) Formation is by application to the Registrar of Companies upon filing of certain prescribed documents under the Companies Act 17 of 2017.
(2) On formation, does not acquire any distinct legal personality, and is a mere association of persons.	(2) On registration acquires a separate legal personality distinct from its members or shareholders.

---

[62] [1958] R & N 1.
[63] [1966] 1 ALR Comm 452. See also *Sadler v Whiteman* [1910] KB 889.

Partnership	Registered Company
(3) The liability of its members is not limited (except in the case of a limited partnership).	(3) The liability of the individual members can and is often limited.
(4) A partnership dissolves when one of the partners dies, unless the partnership is for a fixed period of time or there is an agreement to the contrary.	(4) As an entity distinct from its members, a company has perpetual succession and continues to exist even after the death of one of its shareholders.
(5) The number of members is unrestricted unless it is a partnership for exempted professional undertakings.	(5) The number of members is between two and 50 in a private company (not including employees past and present) and seven and above in the case of a public company.
(6) The objects and powers of partnership together with its internal rules are spelt out in the Partnership Deed or Partnership Article (if any) or by the Partnership Act, 1890, and may be changed by the agreement of the partners.	(6) The objects and powers of a company as well as its internal regulation are fixed by its articles which can be altered in the manner prescribed by the articles and the Companies Act.
(7) Partners cannot transfer their interest in the partnership without the agreement of the other partners.	(7) Shares in a public company are freely transferable. Consent of the other shareholders is usually required in a private company.
(8) Each partner is an agent of the firm and may bind the firm by his acts.	(8) A shareholder of a company is not by virtue only of that membership an agent of the company, and cannot bind a company by his acts, unless the shareholder is also a director, or the articles provide otherwise. Directors of the company are the authorised agents of a company.

3.11 ADVANTAGES OF A PARTNERSHIP

From the foregoing distinctions between a partnership and a registered company, it is easy to discern that a partnership has certain advantages over a registered company. These are, however, outweighed by the advantages of a registered company over a partnership. The chief advantages of a partnership over a limited liability company can be summed up as follows:

(1) There are fewer formalities in setting up a partnership and in operating. This means that the costs of running a partnership are generally relatively low. This offers small entrepreneurs who may not have huge start-up capital a cheap option to set up their business undertaking.

(2) There are no formalities required of partnerships to file resolutions and accounts at public offices such as the office of the Registrar of Companies. Unlike companies, therefore, there is less publicity and even less public scrutiny of the affairs of a partnership. A partnership's

accounts are never open to public inspection. This allows persons who choose to operate discretely a perfect vehicle for their business, subject always to the tax man's guide for probity.

(3) The rules relating to raising and maintenance of share capital to which registered companies are subject do not apply to partnerships. These rules can be restrictive and onerous.

(4) A partnership can make any arrangement with its creditors that the partners think fit and appropriate without resorting to complex legal procedures that apply to companies.

Usually, partnerships in Zambia are relatively small-scale business enterprises. Most law firms, accountancy firms and medical services firms operate as partnerships. Due to the well-known disadvantages that go with unincorporated associations, such as borrowing restrictions, incorporation of business associations under the Companies Act[3] is usually preferred.

3.12 RULES FOR DETERMINING THE EXISTENCE OF A PARTNERSHIP

As already pointed out, a partnership may subsist between persons who may not even have agreed to enter into a partnership or between persons who do not even know that the relationship between them is indeed a partnership. We saw how in the case of *Musaku Mukumbwa and Another v Northern Breweries*[64] the Zambian Supreme Court readily for a partnership to be subsisting even where the parties had not used the term partnership.

Conversely, persons associating together may think they are in partnership when they are in fact not in any such relationship. It is often difficult to determine in the absence of a definite partnership agreement whether a partnership does or does not exist. The indicators to determine whether a particular relationship is in fact a partnership are set out in s 2 of the Partnership Act. However, it should be noted that these rules are not solely determinative of the existence of a partnership. A court will have regard to all the circumstances to arrive at the true substance of the agreement between the parties. In this regard, recourse will be had to both the express and implied intention of the parties in order to determine whether a partnership relationship exists. According to Roper J in *Wiltshire v Kuenzli*:

> [I]t having been ascertained that the parties intended to do all the things which would constitute them partners in law, no effect can be given to their declared intention not to become partners. Of course, if the facts are equivocal the expressed intention not to become partners is of the utmost importance as showing the proper inference to be

---

[64] SCZ Judgment 47 of 2014.

drawn from the facts, but if the facts are unequivocal the same expressed intention is meaningless and useless.[65]

On close scrutiny of the rules for determining the existence of a partnership as set out in s 2 of the Partnership Act, however, one notices that these are more of factors that point at when a partnership is not, rather than when it is, in existence. This is borne out of the use in s 2 of the words *does not.* The section provides:

> In determining whether a partnership does or does not exist, regard shall be had to the following rules:
> (1) Joint tenancy, tenancy in common, joint property, common property, or part ownership *does not* of itself create a partnership as to anything so held or owned whether the tenants or owners do or do not share any profits made by the use thereof.

This rule is quite instructive when one must determine a partnership in regard to some property use or ownership. To constitute a partnership the co-owners must agree to share the management of the property with a view of profit and must regard each other as agents for their joint venture. Explaining the import of s 2(1) of the Partnership Act, Romilly MR remarked in *Kay v Johnson*:

> [A] partnership means . . . that the joint property shall be enjoyed for some purpose which shall produce a return in the share of proceeds, or so as to add to its value, but nothing of the sort took place here. It was in fact nothing more than joint occupation, under a joint ownership of the property.[66]

Where two persons agree to buy an estate jointly and then incorporate a company to run the property on a commercial basis, the two are not partners in the sense envisioned in the Partnership Act. Their agreement relates only to the purchase of the property and not to the running of the future business which will be undertaken based on their joint-owned property.[67] In *Keith Spicer Ltd v Mansell*,[68] which was considered under the part dealing with the legal definition of a partnership, two individuals, X and Y, purchased premises upon which they hoped to establish a restaurant. They intended to form a company for this purpose. Prior to the formation of the company, X purchased furniture from a third party. The furniture was not paid for and the third party thereupon sued Y on the basis that he was in partnership with X. The court said there was no partnership as X and Y were not carrying on business in common but were preparing to do so as a company. Acts carried out in contemplation of a business being undertaken in the future did not

---

[65] [1945] 63 WN 47.
[66] [1856] 21 Bear 536.
[67] See *London Financial Association v Keck* [1884] 26 Ch D 1007.
[68] [1970] 1 All ER 462 CA.

point to a partnership. Further, the holding of property jointly did not change things.

In the Nigerian case of *Oginni v Oginni*[69] the appellant and the respondent were both members of a musical band. They entered into a contract which provided that that the musical equipment and vehicles used by the band were joint property. Their agreement also provided that the members of the band were equal in respect of the property and the share of the moneys which they generated. It also provided that if any one of them left the band, he would be entitled to receive one third of whatever assets they had as his own share. The respondent later told the appellant that the agreement was inoperative. Subsequently the appellant left the band and instituted an action praying for the dissolution of the partnership, an account and distribution of the assets. Two issues that fell to be decided were whether the agreement between the two was proof of the existence of a partnership between them and whether the co-ownership of the instruments used by the band and their sharing of profits was evidence of a partnership between the parties.

It was held that co-ownership of property does not of itself create a partnership between co-owners, whether or not they share profits made by use of it. The agreement between the parties was merely declaratory of their rights in the property and the band and, consequently, there was no obligation to render an account on such assets. Whether or not co-owners are also partners is a question of evidence. The manner in which property has been dealt with and divided as well as the way in which the proceeds and income there from have been treated in the books are all important factors to be taken into consideration. Persons who are only co-owners keep their books differently from those who are partners.

Subsection (2) of s 2 of the Partnership Act provides:

> The sharing of gross returns *does not* of itself create a partnership, whether the persons sharing such returns have or have not a joint or common right or interest in any property from which the returns are derived.

It is important to note that while the sharing of profits does raise the presumption of partnership, the sharing of gross returns does not. Yet, persons who share the gross returns of a business may be partners provided they satisfy all the other aspects of the definition of a partnership in s 1.

Where A, for example, owns a theatre and lets it to B, a producer, on terms that A will be responsible for the costs associated with the upkeep and maintenance of the theatre while B will be responsible for the costs of

---

[69] [1975] 2 ALR Comm 93.

production, and that they would share gross returns, they are not partners.[70] In *Cox v Coulson*,[71] the defendant was the manager of a theatre and agreed with a Mr Mill to provide the theatre and pay for the lighting together with the play bills. He was to receive 60 per cent of the gross takings, while Mr Mill was to provide and pay for a theatrical company and provide the scenery and receive the remaining 40 per cent. The plaintiff was injured by a shot fired by one of the actors during the performance of a play at the theatre. She sought, inter alia, to make the defendant liable on the ground that he was a partner of Mr Mill. It was held that the defendant was not a partner by s 2(2) since the sharing of gross returns did not of itself create a partnership.

Section 2(3) of the Partnership Act provides:

> The receipt by a person of a share of the profits of a business is *prima facie* evidence that he is a partner in the business, but the receipt of such a share or of a payment contingent on or varying with the profits of a business, *does not* of itself make him a partner in the business.

This is a very important subsection and it calls for careful understanding. Its import is that sharing of profit raises a presumption of partnership, and the burden is then cast on the person denying the existence of the partnership to disprove the presumption. The difficulty in interpreting this subsection lies in the use of the expression '*prima facie*' to qualify evidence. The fact of a profit-sharing scheme is seemingly admissible in evidence as to the existence of a partnership, but that fact by itself is not enough to draw the inference that there was a partnership. There is seemingly a contradiction here, for how can a fact be *prima facie* evidence of partnership and yet be insufficient of itself to prove the partnership? North J explained in the case of *Davis v Davis*[72] that

> adopting then the rule of law which was laid down before the Partnership Act, and which seems to be precisely what is intended by s.2(3) of the Act, the receipt by a person of a share of the profits of a business is *prima facie* evidence that he is a partner in it, and if the matter stops there, it is evidence upon which the courts must act. But if there are other circumstances to be considered, they ought to be considered fairly together not holding that a partnership is proved by the receipt of a share of the profits unless it is rebutted by something else; but taking all the circumstances together, not attaching undue weight to any of them but drawing an inference from the whole.

The Supreme Court of Somalia declared in *Osma Ismail v Jaji Mohamed Ajib Osman*:

---

[70] *Lyon v Knowles* [1863] 32 LJ QB 71.
[71] [1916] 2 KB 177.
[72] [1894] 1 Ch 393.

The receipt by a person of a share of the profits of a business is strong evidence that he is a partner, but whether or not the relationship exists depends on the real intention and agreement of the parties and not upon the mere fact of participation in the profits.[73]

The position espoused by these cases appears to declare the pre-existing law that the sharing of profits without any other facts being proved implies partnership, but if it is one of several facts, then all the facts must be considered together, and no particular weight should be given to the fact of profit sharing. The sharing of profits does raise a presumption of partnership whereas the sharing of gross returns does not, yet it is true to say persons who share gross returns may be partners provided they satisfy all other requirements of the s 1 definition. This means that the sharing of profits, without more, proves a partnership, but this may be rebutted by proving other facts which show that the parties did not intend to be partners. The burden is cast on the person denying the existence of a partnership to disprove such assumption.

Subsection 3 of s 2 of the Partnership Act states that the instances listed in paragraphs *(a)–(e)* do not themselves create a partnership, that is to say, a partnership may exist, but not necessarily. These instances are:

(a) The receipt by a person of a debt or other liquidated amount by instalments or otherwise out of profits of a business does not of itself make him a partner in the business or liable as such. In *Cox v Hickman*[74] a debtor who was in difficulty transferred his business to trustees with instructions to carry on the business and use the profits for paying his creditors. It was held that the creditors were not partners of the business. Wightman J[75] remarked:

> It is said that a person who shares in net profits is a partner; that may be so in some cases, but not in all; and it may be material to consider in what sense the words, 'sharing in the profits' are used. In the present case, I greatly doubt whether the creditor, who merely obtains payment of a debt incurred in the business by being paid the exact amount of his debt, and no more, out of the profits of the business, can be said to share the profits. If in the present case, the property of the Smiths had been assigned to the trustees to carry on the business, and divide the net profits, not amongst those creditors who signed the deed, but amongst all the creditors, until their debts were paid, would a creditor, by receiving from time to time a ratable proportion out of the net profits, become a partner? I should think not.

(b) A contract for the remuneration of a servant or agent by a share of the profits of the business does not of itself make the servant or agent a

---

[73] [1966] 1 ALR Comm 471.
[74] [1880] 8 HL Cas 268.
[75] [1880] 8 HL Cas 268 at 296; ER 443.

partner in the business or liable as such.[76] In *Walker v Hirsch*[77] Walker had been a clerk to the defendant's firm when he and the firm's proprietors entered into an agreement for Walker to be paid a fixed salary in addition to the right to participate in one eighth of profits and losses. Walker further agreed to deposit £1 500 in the business while the agreement continued, receiving 5 per cent per annum interest. The firm's name was not altered, nor was Walker mentioned in firm circulars or bills. Furthermore, Walker was not introduced to customers as a partner, did not sign bills of exchange, and signed letters and receipts 'Walker for [the firm]'. In 1884 the defendant gave him notice and excluded him from the office. Walker sought to wind up the business, sought an injunction restraining dealings with the business's assets, and sought the appointment of a receiver and manager. The trial judge refused the injunction and appointment of a receiver and ordered the defendant to pay the £1 500 into court. The trial judge, Lindley LJ, focused on Walker's lack of ability to control the defendant in the management of the business. Walker was regarded as a servant 'not in the position of a partner having an equal voice or control in the management of the concern'. Therefore, the injunction was refused.

(c) A person being a window or child of a deceased partner receiving by way of annuity a portion of the profits made in the business is not by reason of such receipt a partner in the business and liable as such. In *Commissioners of Inland Revenue v Lebus*[78] the Commissioners attempted to recover income tax on the amounts which were due under a will to a widow of a partner. The court found that a beneficiary under a will would only have to pay tax on the amounts which were paid to her during the years of assessment. The widow did not have to pay tax on a share of the profits earned by the business.

(d) The advance of money by way of loan to a person engaged in any business on a contract that the lender shall receive a share of the profits does not of itself make the lender a partner and liable as such provided that the contract is in writing and signed by or on behalf of all the parties thereto. This provision protects a creditor who has advanced money in return for a share of the profits. In *Steward v Buchanan*,[79] A financed B in business. When B became insolvent, A attempted to

---

[76] *Ross v Parkyns* [1875] LJ Ch 610.
[77] [1884] 27 Ch D 460.
[78] [1946] 1 All ER 476.
[79] [1904] 6 F (Court of Session Cases) 15.

evade liability as a partner by asserting that he was merely a lender of money receiving a share of the profits and so is protected by paragraph *(d)* of s 2(3). It was held that he was a partner and fully liable because *(a)* he could not produce the written contract of loan required by the proviso to the enactment, and *(b)* he had interfaced in the management of the business, so strengthening the presumption of partnership.

A creditor, if the section is satisfied, will not be regarded as a partner. In *Re Megevand; Ex parte Delhasse*,[80] Delhasse agreed to advance money to two others. Conditions of the advance stressed that the advance was a loan only and did not make the lender a partner. However, provision was made for Delhasse to share in the profits, have a right to inspect the accounts and the option of dissolving the partnership in specified circumstances. Further, the advance was not to be repayable until after dissolution and it represented all the business capital. The Court of Appeal held that this arrangement constituted a partnership. According to James LJ at 526:

> If ever there was a case of partnership this is it. There is every element of partnership in it. There is the right to control the property, the right to receive profits, and the liability to share in losses. But it is said that there are other provisions in the contract which prevent its having this operation, and which show clearly that the parties meant the relation of lender and borrower, and not the relation of partners, to subsist between them. And for this purpose reliance is placed on the recital of . . . the agreement for a loan . . . and the declaration . . . that the 'advance does not and shall not be considered to render Delhasse a partner in the business.' Can those words really control the rest of the agreement? Do they really show that the intention was not in truth that which it appears to be by all the other stipulations? To my mind it is clear that they do not. When you come to look at all the other stipulations, they are utterly inconsistent with the notion of a loan by the one to the two, so as to make the two personally liable in respect of it in any event or under any circumstances whatever. The loan is said to be made to the two, but, when you read the whole of the agreement together, it is impossible not to see that it was not a loan to the two upon their personal responsibility by the person who is said to be the lender but that it was a loan to the business which was carried on by the two for the benefit of themselves and him, and was to be repaid out of the business, and out of the business only, except in the case of loss, when the loss would have to be borne by the three in the proportions mentioned in the agreement. The use of the word 'lend', and the reference to the Act, are, in my opinion, mere sham—a mere contrivance to evade the law of partnership.'[81]

It falls to be considered whether one who lends without a written and signed contract is *prima facie* to be deemed a partner. No doubt it is difficult to give any meaning to the proviso unless its effect is in the

---

[80] [1878] 7 Ch D 511.
[81] [1878] 7 Ch D 511 at 527.

affirmative. Ivamy[82] asserts that this is not the correct interpretation. He notes that this would negate the express words of s 2 that 'receipt of profits is not of itself sufficient' and goes on to observe that its import remains obscure. Finally, he submits that it may not amount to more than that a lender who receives a rate of interest varying with the profits of the borrower's business or a share of those profits, the contract not being in writing, is called on to explain the absence of a written agreement.

(e) A person receiving by way of annuity or otherwise a portion of the profits of a business in consideration of the sale by him of the goodwill of the business is not by reason only of such receipt a partner in the business and liable as such. In *Pratt v Strick*[83] a doctor sold his practice to a colleague and as part of the contract of sale agreed to stay on at the house for some months to introduce this colleague to patients and assist in running the practice. During that time, profits and expense were to be shared. It was held that they were not partners, and the practice belonged to the colleague who had purchased it alone.

3.13 DEFERRED CREDITORS

Section 2(3)*(d)* and *(e)* indicates that persons who receive a share of the profits either (1) as repayment of loans to the business, or (2) in consideration of sale of goodwill, are not necessarily partners thereby; consequently, they are not usually liable as partners for the debts of the firm. Unhappily, their position is weakened by s 3, which provides that they do not enjoy the advantages of being ordinarily creditors of the firm either; they are deferred creditors, that is to say, they are not entitled to payment of the amounts due to them out of the profits 'until the claims of the other creditors of the borrower or buyer for valuable consideration in money or money's worth have been satisfied'.

If the borrower in s 2(3)*(d)* or the purchaser of good will in s 2(3)*(e)* is adjudge bankrupt or arranges to pay his creditors less than 20 pence in a pound or dies insolvent, then the claims of the lender or the vendor are deferred to the claims of all other creditors for valuable consideration.

3.14 THE RELATIONS BETWEEN PARTNERS AND OUTSIDERS

The relation between partners and persons dealing with them is for the most part based on the adaption of agency law to partnerships. This is simply

---

[82] ER Hardy Ivamy *Principles of the Law of Partnership* (1981).
[83] [1832] 17 Tax Cases 459.

because a partnership business will be conducted or managed by one or some of the partners who, for this purpose, will act as agents for the firm. An act done by a partner on behalf of a firm—and within the parameters of the actual authority given by the firm to that partner—will generally bind the firm. An act done by a partner (within the ordinary course of partnership business) will bind the firm—even if the partner is acting outside the authority granted by the firm—unless the third party concerned actually knows of this lack of authority.

The rules of agency as they apply to partnerships are entrenched in s 5 of the Partnership Act, which provides:

> [E]very partner is an agent of the firm and his other partners for the purpose of the business of the partnership; and the acts of every partner who does any act for carrying on in the usual way business of the kind carried on by the firm of which he is a member binds the firm and his partners, unless the partner so acting has in fact no authority to act for the firm in the particular matter, and the person with whom he is dealing either knows that he has no authority, or does not know or believe him to be a partner.

It follows that a partnership carries onerous legal responsibility, including, just by way of an example, liability for the negligent acts of other parties or liabilities to third parties with whom other partners have entered into contracts for business loans or overdrafts. The partnership will be bound by anything which an individual partner was expressly authorised to do. The partner also has implied authority, and the firm is bound even if the partner so acting has exceeded his actual authority. Under s 5, the implied authority will not exist where two conditions are present, namely *(a)* the partnership articles (if any) restrict or negate the implied authority, and *(b)* the transaction done by the partner is not one which is or appears to be in the ordinary scope of the firm's business, or to use the language of the section, which is not 'business of the kind carried on by the firm'. The firm will not be bound if the outsider either knows that the partner has no authority, or does not know or believe him to be a partner. As Scrutton LJ explained in *Lloyd's Bank v Chartered Bank of India and China*:[84]

> [A] third party dealing in good faith with an agent acting within his ostensible authority is not prejudiced by the fact that as between the principal and his agent the agent is using his authority for his own benefit and not for that of the principal.

As far as certain transactions in trade are concerned, subject to some limitations, which will be discussed, every partner may bind the firm by many acts, including the following:

---

[84] [1929] 1 KB 56.

(a) selling any goods or personal chattels of the partnership or firm;

(b) borrowing money on the credit of the firm;

(c) pledging for purposes of borrowing any goods or personal chattels belonging to the partnership;

(d) purchasing on account of the partnership such goods as are necessary for or usually employed in the partnership business;

(e) receiving payments of debts due to the partnership and give receipts or releases for them; and

(f) engaging servants for the partnership business.[85]

Of course, this is not an exhaustive list of instances of a partner's implied authority. Perhaps an instructive summary of the general powers of a partner is in a passage by Story,[86] which was adopted by the Judicial Committee of the Privy Council in *Bank of Australia v Breillat*[87] as follows:

> Every partner is in contemplation of law the general and accredited agent of the partnership, or as it is sometimes expressed, each partner is *praepositus negotiis societatis*, and may consequently bind all the other partners by his acts in all matters which are within the scope and objects of a general commercial nature, he may pledge or sell the partnership property; he may buy goods on account of the partnership; he may borrow money, contract debts, and pay debts on account of the partnership; he may draw, make, sign indorse, accept, transfer, negotiate, and procure to be discounted promissory note, bill of exchange, cheques and other negotiable paper in the name and on account of the partnership.[88]

Section 5 imposes almost strict liability. Its effect can be onerous; the most prudent and intelligent of the partners may be lumbered with unexpected liabilities incurred in the course of the partnership business by the least intelligent and most reckless of the partners. It is not open for such a partner to plead ignorance or absence of approval of what the co-partner was doing. Provided that what the partner did falls within the provisions of s 5, all the other partners are bound.

In *Mercantile Credit Limited v Garrod*[89] two partners were carrying on the business of repairing motor cars and letting lock-up garages. In an express agreement between them, they agreed not to sell cars. Without the knowledge of one partner, the other partner sold a car to the plaintiff for £700. It later transpired that the partner who sold the car did not have title to the car. The plaintiff brought an action for the return of the purchase price. When the seller partner failed to pay the £700, the other (innocent) partner

---

[85] See *Re Bourne* [1906] 2 Ch 427, 430 per Vaughan Williams LJ.
[86] Joseph Story *Commentaries on the Law of Agency* (1839).
[87] [1847] 6 Moo. P.C at 193.
[88] [1847] 6 Moo. P.C at 193.
[89] [1962] 3 All ER 1103.

was held liable as his partner. The court noted that on the facts there was nothing to cause the plaintiff to suspect that the two partners had restricted the nature of the business to be conducted under their partnership. Both partners were therefore liable.

It must, however, be emphasised that it is not every act done by a partner for the benefit of the firm that will be binding upon the partnership. Unless there are restrictions as aforesaid, every partner is a general agent of the partnership and is capable of binding the firm by all acts within the *usual course of business* of the firm. The key question as regards the unauthorised acts of a partner is what sort of thing is necessary for the usual conduct of the partnership business? The acts of a partner done in the name of the firm will not bind the partnership merely because they are convenient or prudent, or even necessary, for a particular occasion. A power to do what is usual does not include a power to do what is unusual, however urgent or expedient it may be. The question of what is usual is a question of fact to be determined by the nature of the business and by the practice of persons engaged in it.

Notwithstanding that a partner has entered into a transaction which is within the scope of the kind of business carried on by the partnership, the transaction will not be binding if it is carried out in an unusual way. The reasoning for this is that the outsider is put on notice that the partner with whom they are dealing may lack the requisite authority to bind the other partners. Furthermore, for an act to be usual in the business of the firm, it must be reasonably necessary and not merely convenient for the carrying out of that type of business. In ascertaining whether the partner's action was 'carried out in the usual way' courts will look at the particular business and at other people's actions in similar businesses. Thus, even if the action by the partner is within the scope of the business carried on by the firm, if it is carried on in an unusual manner, the other partners may not be bound. An illustration is *Goldberg v Jenkins*.[90] In that case, a partner purported to borrow money on behalf of the firm at over 60 per cent interest when at the time the comparable rates were between 6 per cent and 10 per cent. It was held that such borrowing was beyond 'the usual way' of the firm and thus the firm was not bound to the transaction. According to Hodges J:

> A person conducting his transactions in the ordinary way in the year 1888 would have been able to obtain all the advances which he could reasonably require at rates varying from 6 to 10 per cent; but in this case, referring to the last transaction, the interest was something over 60 per cent and the person lending money on those terms knows that the

---

[90] [1889] 15 VLR 36.

person borrowing is not conducting an ordinary business transaction, and that, therefore the partner borrowing would have no power to bind his co-partners.[91]

However, where a partner has not entered into a transaction in his capacity as a partner, he cannot bind the firm even though the transaction relates to a matter which is within the scope of the partnership business and within that partner's usual authority.

Although each partner is an agent of the firm, he is not entitled to full indemnity or to reasonable remuneration as are most agents under ordinary agency principles.

Notwithstanding the implied authority of a partner to bind the firm, a partner cannot without express authority bind the firm by deed. As is well established under the general law of contract, any such authority must be under seal and a provision giving such power in a partnership deed will not be sufficient.[92]

While partners are deemed to be agents of the firm, the firm itself is not presumed to be the agent of the partners. A payment to the firm of a separate debt owed to a partner does not discharge the debt unless it is shown that the firm was empowered to receive the payment.

Under s 6, partners are bound by acts done on behalf of the firm relating to the business of the firm. It provides that an act or instrument *relating to the business of the firm* and done or executed in the firm name, or in any other manner showing an intention to bind the firm by any person thereto authorised, whether a partner or not, is binding on the firm and all the partners, provided that this section shall not affect any general rule of law relating to the execution of deeds or negotiable instruments.

The difference between s 5 and s 6 is significant. While s 5 confines itself to the implied agency of the partners as far as transactions within the usual business of the firm are concerned, s 6 deals with transactions which are not necessarily 'usual' and applies to partners and other persons, provided such other persons have authority.

Under s 6, therefore, the firm will only be bound where the transaction is either done in the firm's name or is effected in some other manner showing an intention to bind the firm. The authority in s 6 extends to non-partners.

Under s 23(2) of the Bills of Exchange Act of 1882 it is provided that the signature of the name of a firm upon a bill is equivalent to the signature, by the person so signing, of the names of all persons liable as partners in that firm.

---

[91] [1889] 15 VLR 36 at 38–9.
[92] *Harrison v Jackson* [1797] 101 ER 935.

Section 7 provides:

> Where one partner pledges the credit of the firm for a purpose apparently not connected
> with the firm's ordinary course of business, the firm is not bound, unless he is in fact
> specially authorized by the other partners, but this section does not affect any personal
> liability incurred by an individual partner.

What s 7 does is to amplify the meaning of s 5. The implied agency given
by s 5 will not be relied upon in aid of a claimant against a firm if he has
relied on a partner's authority in a transaction which does not even appear
to be connected with the firm's ordinary course of business. The latter part
of the section echoes a claimant's right against the partner he deals with
personally. Assume that Chibumba and Chimutunzi are partners in a tea
growing and processing firm called Chai Tea Mixers. In terms of s 5 of the
Act, each of the two will be the unlimited agent of Chai Tea Mixers and his
other partner *for the purpose of the business of the partnership*. Aside all
considerations premised on corporate social responsibility, if Chibumba
pledges the credit of Chai Tea Mixers for purposes of financing a netball
team in his constituency, Chai Tea Mixers will not be bound because clearly
netball is not apparently connected with the firm's ordinary course of
business, being tea growing and processing. Chibumba will therefore be
personally liable for the transaction in these circumstances. Chai Tea
Mixers will, however, be bound if Chimutunzi agrees to the pledge of the
firm's credit.

Under s 8 the firm is not bound by the acts of a partner in excess of his
powers where the third party has notice of the restriction on the partner's
authority. It is important to note that any restriction in the partnership
agreement or articles on the apparent authority of a partner will not bind a
third party unless he has actual notice of it.

3.15 THE LIABILITY OF PARTNERS IN CONTRACTS

Partners do not have limited liability. Under s 9 every partner in the firm is
jointly liable for all debts and obligation of the firm incurred while he is a
partner; and, after his death, his estate is also severally liable for such debts
and obligations, so far as they remain unsatisfied (but subject to the prior
payment of his separate debts).

Each partner is liable for the full amount due but can apply to the court to
have the others joined as co-defendants. In practice, claimants usually sue
the firm in the firm's name, but proceed to enforce the full judgment, once

obtained, against any partner. This is often done to circumvent the rule in *Kendal v Hamilton*[93] (explained below).

A partner's liability in contract is similar to that of a principal for contracts entered into on his behalf by an agent. As Tindal CJ put it in *Fox v Clifton*:

> Each individual partner constitutes the others his agents for the purpose of entering into all contracts for him within the scope of the partnership concern, and consequently is liable to the performance of all such contracts in the same manner as if entered into personally by himself.[94]

Liability of partners in contract is joint. This means that a creditor has only one right of action. He may choose to sue either the firm jointly or any individual partner separately. He has only one right to action, so that if he, for instance, chooses to sue one partner alone, he waives his right of action against the other partners and will not be allowed to later sue those others even if it turns out that the partner sued is unable to satisfy the claim owing to impecuniosity.

In *Kendal v Hamilton*,[95] a lender lent money to two partners who failed to repay the loan. The lender obtained judgment against the partners which remained unsatisfied as both of them were insolvent. In due course the lender discovered that a financially well-to-do man had been a secret partner of the two known partners. He sought to proceed in legal action against this third partner. It was held that since the firm's liability was joint, the lender had only one right to action, which he had used to no avail. He had no right to proceed against the third partner who was discovered belatedly. It must be observed that the common-law rule that a judgment against one partner was a bar to a subsequent action against other partners jointly liable (*Kendall v Hamilton*) was abrogated by s 3 of the Civil Liability (Contribution) Act of 1978, which provides that a judgment recovered against any person liable in respect of any debt or damage shall not be a bar to an action, or to the continuance of an action, against any other person who is (apart from such bar) jointly liable with him in respect of the same debt or damage. It is needless to point out that the Civil Liability (Contribution) Act does not apply in Zambia.

Under s 9 the estate of a deceased partner is severally liable for the contractual obligations incurred during his lifetime. Such debts or obligations are, however, subordinate to the deceased partner's separate debts. In

---

[93] [1879] 4 App Cas 504.
[94] [1830] 6 Bing 17.
[95] [1879] 4 App Cas 504.

this regard, a claimant against a firm could sue the firm, and if his debt remains unsatisfied in full, he could sue the deceased partner's estate for the sum outstanding. If a partner settles a firm's indebtedness to a third party from his own resources, he is entitled to indemnification by his co-partners under s 24(2) unless otherwise agreed.

3.16 LIABILITY OF THE FIRM IN TORT

The Partnership Act provides in s 10 that 'where, by any wrongful act or omission of any partner acting in the ordinary course of the business of the firm, or with the authority of his co-partners, loss or injury is caused to any person not being a partner in the firm, or any penalty is incurred, the firm is liable therefore to the same extent as the partner so acting or omitting to act'. Under this section, therefore, where one partner commits an act which is wrong in itself, as opposed to merely being outside his authority, the firm will be civilly liable for any harm caused, and criminally liable for any penalty incurred if either:

(1) the act in question was done with the actual authority of the co-partners; or

(2) the act was within his 'usual' authority, in the ordinary course of the firm's business.

Thus, in *Lloyd v Grace, Smith and Co*,[96] a clerk in a firm of solicitors preferred fraudulent advice for his own enrichment and not for the benefit of the firm. In an action for damages against the firm, the solicitors argued that giving fraudulent advice could never be considered as part of the ordinary course of a solicitor's business. It was held that the firm was liable since the clerk was doing wrongfully what he was employed to do lawfully. Obviously, no partnership can lawfully exist for the purpose of committing torts. The test applicable in determining whether the firm is or is not liable for the tortuous acts of one of its partners is the vicarious liability test, namely whether the wrongful act was committed by a person when acting in or about the business for which he was employed.

In *Hamlyn v Houston and Co*,[97] it was held that it was 'usual' for a partner to obtain information about a rival business. Part of the partnership business in that case was obtaining, by legitimate means, information about competitors' business activities. One of the partners bribed a competitor's clerk to provide such information about the clerk's employer's business. The employer sued both partners together for damages. It was held that

---

[96] [1912] AC 716.
[97] [1903] 1 KB 81.

both partners were liable since the one partner acted (improperly) in the course of the firm's business. Notwithstanding the *Hamlyn* and *Lloyd* cases, in *Arbuckle v Taylor,* the court held that the firm is not liable for torts that fall outside the scope of the firm's usual business activities.

Section 11 deals with misapplication of moneys and it compliments s 10. It provides the following:

(a) Where one partner acting within the scope of his apparent authority receives the money or property of a third person and misapplies it; and

(b) When a firm in the course of its business receives money or property of a third person, and the money or property so received is misapplied by one or more of the partners while it is in the custody of the firm; the firm is liable to make good the loss.

The section deals solely with the particular case of liability of the firm in cases of misapplication of money by a partner. The problem envisioned in s 11 may arise in two ways. First, a partner may receive money or property belonging to a third party and misapply it before it reaches the firm. In this case, the firm is liable if it was within the scope of the partner's usual or apparent authority to receive the property. It is no defence for the firm to show that it did not receive the money or the property involved, or that the co-partners had no knowledge or were not complicit to their co-partner's fraud. This situation is dealt with under s 11(1). Secondly, the firm may already have custody of someone else's money or property, and a partner then takes it from the firm and misapplies it. In this case, so long as the money or property was in the firm's custody in the ordinary 'course of its business', the firm and all its partners are liable. This situation is dealt with in s 11(2).

Section 12 caps off the liability under ss 10 and 11 by declaring that every partner is jointly and severally liable with his co-partner for any tort for which the firm as a whole becomes liable under ss 10 and 11. While liability for contracts is joint, liability for torts is joint and several. A claimant can bring successive actions against successive partners (or sue them jointly) if he so wishes.

In *Rhodes v Moules*,[98] Mr Rew was a solicitor in partnership with Messrs Hughes and Masterman. Mr Rhodes was a client of the firm which had acted for him on previous occasions. Rhodes wanted to borrow some money on a property and asked Rew as his solicitor to assist him to effect the mortgage. Some clients of the firm, the Moules, were willing to lend the

---

[98] [1895] 1 Ch 236.

money. As security for the mortgage, Rhodes gave Rew some share certificates, and these were misappropriated by Rew.

One of the questions the court had to determine was whether the other two partners were liable for Rew's actions. The court held that the partners were jointly and severally liable for the value of the shares under both sub-ss *(a)* and *(b)*. According to Lindley LJ:

> The only conclusion at which I can arrive is that the plaintiff's certificates came into Rew's hands when acting within the scope of his apparent authority. The case is thus brought within the first half of s 11 of the Partnership Act, 1890. But it is also, I think, brought within the second half.[99]

The judge said that 'the inference that the plaintiff's certificates were received by the firm in the course of its business' was justified.

Section 12 provides that the liability for wrongs is joint and several:

> Every partner is liable jointly with the partner's co-partners and also severally for everything for which the firm while the partner is a partner therein becomes liable under either of the last two preceding sections.

Thus, liability for both civil wrongs and crime is covered by these sections. In order for liability to be established it must be shown that the wrongful act or omission of the partner occurred in the ordinary course of the business of the firm (usual authority) or was authorised by the co-partners (actual authority).

Section 13 deals with improper employment of trust property. For breaches of trust by a partner, liability attaches individually.

In *Walker and Others v Stones and Another*[100] Sir Christopher Slade gave an instructive elaboration of the law thus:

> Sections 10, 11 and 13 have recently been given close consideration by this court in *Dubai Aluminium Co Ltd v Salaam* [2000] 2 Lloyd's Rep 168. In that case the claimants sought to make the partners of a solicitor, Mr Amhurst, who was alleged to have dishonestly assisted a Mr Livingstone in a fraudulent scheme to defraud the claimants and to have thereby constituted himself a constructive trustee, vicariously liable under s 10 for the acts of Mr Amhurst. It was argued on behalf of the Amhurst partners by way of defence that: (1) the words 'wrongful act or omission' in s 10 were to be construed as being confined to torts and therefore did not include the pleaded acts of knowing assistance; (2) the pleaded acts were not done in 'in the ordinary course of the business of the firm'. As to (1), the court held by a majority (Evans and Aldous LJJ, Turner J dissenting) that the reference to 'any wrongful act or omission' is not limited to torts, but is wide enough to include the accessory liability of a person for giving dishonest assistance in a breach of trust or fiduciary duty. As to (2), the court by the same majority held that, on the particular facts, the allegedly wrongful acts of Mr Amhurst went

---

[99] [1895] 1 Ch 236 at 249.
[100] [2000] 4 All ER 412.

outside 'the ordinary course of the business of the firm', so that the firm incurred no liability for such acts . . .

In my judgment ss 10, 11*(a)* and 13 are all drafted on the assumption that individual trusteeships which a partner may undertake are not undertaken 'in the ordinary course of business of a firm'. Support for this view is to be found in a helpful analysis of the three sections made by Rix J at first instance in the *Dubai Aluminium* case, in a passage expressly approved (at 184) by Aldous LJ in the Court of Appeal:

'Section 10 itself is in the widest terms: it refers to "any wrongful act or omission" causing "loss or injury" or the incurring of a penalty. I do not see why that language cannot extend beyond torts properly so called [to] wrongs such as accessory liability in equity. *To confine it solely to torts is to construe the section with excessive formalism, and I do not see what there is in the language of the section to suggest such formalism. Section 11 provides that the firm is liable to make good loss caused by the misapplication of a third person's money or property received by either a partner "acting within the scope of his apparent authority" or by the firm "in the course of its business". That section only applies therefore in the case of receipt of property. It does not seem to me to follow that in a case otherwise within s. 10 it matters whether or not a third party's property has been received by a partner or the firm. Section 11 rather seems to me to be saying that in the case of the misapplication of property received by a partner or the firm, it is only where the property is received in the ordinary course of the firm's business that the firm can be made liable for the misapplication of any partner. The underlying principle is therefore consistent with s. 10.* Finally, s. 13 deals with the position where a partner accepts the responsibility of being a trustee ("If a partner, being a trustee") and states that liability will only attach beyond the partner in question for misuse of trust funds in the partnership business where the funds can be traced or a partner has notice of the breach of trust. That section, however, appears to assume that the individual trusteeships which a partner may undertake are not something undertaken in the ordinary course of business, otherwise it would be inconsistent with s. 11: (see *Lindley and Banks On Partnership* (17th edn, 1995) para 12–136). That seems to me to leave open the situation where a partner, not being a trustee, nevertheless so conducts himself as an accessory to a breach of trust, that he is visited in equity with the remedies available against a constructive trustee; I do not see why that situation cannot be dealt with under the general principle enunciated in s. 10. I therefore see nothing in the terms of the Partnership Act 1890 itself to limit the application of s. 10 to torts alone, even though they may have been the primary focus of the section in its origin.'[101]

This passage clearly explains the difference between the case where a firm is sought to be made vicariously liable for breaches of trust by a trustee-partner and the case, such as the *Dubai Aluminium* case itself, where a partner, not being already a trustee, conducts himself as an accessory to a breach of trust in such manner as to constitute himself in equity a constructive trustee; in the latter case only s 10 leaves open a finding of vicarious liability.

The assumption that individual trusteeships which a partner may undertake are not something undertaken in the ordinary course of the business of a firm might nowadays appear somewhat outdated, at least in the case of solicitors' partnerships. However, it is important to note that ss 10 to 13 apply to all partnerships, not merely solicitors' partnerships. Furthermore, it appears that, at least in the mid-nineteenth century, even a solicitor was not regarded as having the implied authority of his co-partners to accept

---

[101] Own emphasis.

office as a trustee and so make his co-partners liable for a misapplication of the trust property . . .

I would accordingly accept the argument advanced on behalf of Wiggin & Co that the legislature, in enacting s 10 of the 1890 Act, treated breaches of trust committed by a trustee-partner as falling outside the ordinary business of any partnership and correspondingly incapable of giving rise to vicarious liability under that section. I see no other way of reconciling ss 10 and 11 with s 13, as a matter of construction, without an interpolation of additional words to s 13 which would in my judgment be unnecessary and unjustified. For these reasons, I would hold that, even if the appellants were to establish liability against Mr Stones, they could not succeed in establishing liability against his firm, Wiggin & Co, because s 10 of the 1890 Act could not on any footing render the firm vicariously liable for his wrongdoing as a trustee-partner. If that conclusion were wrong, it would be necessary for the court at a trial to consider whether the acts and defaults of Mr Stones complained of were committed 'in the ordinary course of the business of the firm'. This would be primarily a question of fact. The acts and defaults complained of essentially amount to alleged participation in the dishonest milking of the Bacchus trust for the benefit of BWG, Birdcage Walk and Mr Walker. As is common ground, the mere fact that such acts or defaults were dishonest would not by itself preclude their being held to have been committed in the ordinary course of the business of the firm. Nevertheless, the decision of the court in the *Dubai Aluminium* case illustrates its reluctance to hold innocent partners liable for the dishonest conduct of a co-partner except in favour of third parties who reasonably believed that he was acting with their authority. As Evans LJ pointed out ([2000] 2 Lloyd's Rep 168 at 178):

> 'The principles of vicarious liability underlying s. 10 were those developed in connection with the vicarious liability of a principal for wrongdoing by his agent, and they are comparable with those governing the liability of an employer for wrongs committed by his employee in the course of his employment. The principal is liable "not only for the authorised acts of his agent but also for such unauthorised acts as fall within the scope of the authority apparently conferred upon him" (Lindley and Banks p 332, para 12–88 per Lord Lindley). Vicarious liability extends to fraudulent acts and omissions provided they were committed in the course of employment or within the scope of apparent authority, even if they were against the interest of the employer or principal . . .'

3.17   LIABILITY OF NON-PARTNER FOR THE DEBTS OF THE FIRM

Section 14 imposes liability on a non-partner under specified circumstances. Subsection 1 provides that anyone who represents himself, or knowingly allows himself to be represented, as a partner is liable as a partner for any of the firm's debts incurred through the creditor relying on such representation, and it makes no difference that the person made liable may have been unaware that such representation has been communicated to the creditor in question.

In *Re Buchanan & Co*,[102] it was held that the section places liability upon a person who represents himself, or allows himself to be represented, as

---

[102] [1876] 4 QSCR 202.

a partner—not upon actual partners. Thus, to incur liability under this section, three tests need to be fulfilled:

(1)   A representation must be made that the person is a partner. The person himself or any partner can do this. It will be a question of fact whether a representation has been made. Further, the representation need not have been made directly to the person who acts upon it. As was held by William J in *Martyn v Gray*:[103] '[I]f the defendant informs AB that he is a partner in a commercial establishment and AB informs the plaintiff, and the plaintiff, believing the defendant to be a member of the firm, supplies goods to them, the defendant is liable for the price.'

(2)   A third party who believes the representation to be true must provide credit. Credit would include the receiving of property or the incurring of an obligation.

(3)   The third party must rely upon the representation. In *Tower Cabinet Co Ltd v Ingram*[104] a partnership between C and I, carrying on business as household furnishers under the name 'Merry's', was dissolved by agreement. I gave notice of the dissolution to the firm's bankers and arranged with C to notify those persons who dealt with Merry's, but he did not advertise it, or procure an advertisement of it, in the *London Gazette*. C procured new notepaper for the purposes of the business, omitting I's name from the heading. In January 1948, S, a representative of the T Co, which had not previously had dealings with Merry's, obtained an order from the new firm of that name, and this order, in breach of the arrangement made with I and without his knowledge or authority, was confirmed by C by a letter on headed notepaper which had been in use by the partnership before the dissolution and bore I's name as well as C's name. On an application by the T Co for the issue of execution against I on a judgment obtained against Merry's for the price of the goods supplied pursuant to the order obtained by S, it was held that I had not represented himself or knowingly suffered himself to be represented as a partner in Merry's within s 14 of the Act of 1890, and his negligence or carelessness in not seeing that all the notepaper of the partnership firm had been destroyed when he left the business did not bring him within the terms of that section. Lynskey J said:

> It is clear on the master's finding that in January and February, 1948, when the goods were ordered and delivered Mr Ingram was not in fact a partner in this

---

[103] [1863] 143 ER 667 at 674.
[104] [1949] 2 KB 397; [1949] 1 All ER 1033.

business. The question is whether the company are able to make him liable as a partner by reason of the provisions of the Partnership Act, 1890, dealing either with holding out . . . Before the company can succeed in making Mr Ingram liable under this section, they have to satisfy the court that Mr Ingram, by words spoken or written or by conduct, represented himself as a partner. There is no evidence of that. Alternatively, they must prove that he knowingly suffered himself to be represented as a partner. The only evidence of Mr Ingram's having knowingly suffered himself to be so represented is that the order was given by Mr Christmas on notepaper which contained Mr Ingram's name. That would amount to a representation by Mr Christmas that Mr Ingram was still a partner in the firm, but on the evidence and the master's finding that representation was made by Mr Christmas without Mr Ingram's knowledge and without his authority. That being the finding of fact, which is not challenged, it is impossible to say that Mr Ingram knowingly suffered himself to be so represented. The words are 'knowingly suffers'—not being negligent or careless in not seeing that all the notepaper had been destroyed when he left.

The court therefore held that Mr Ingram had not knowingly allowed himself to be represented as a partner. Further, the court held that Tower Cabinet Co Ltd did not know Mr Ingram was a partner before the dissolution and therefore he was not liable for the debts contracted after the partnership was dissolved.

In the case of *Nationwide Building Society v Lewis and Another*[105] L, a sole principal, invited W to join him as a 'salaried partner' in his firm of solicitors. W accepted the offer and, although his name was added to the firm's notepaper, he remained a 'salaried partner' and was not entitled to a share of the profits. The firm subsequently acted for the plaintiff building society in a mortgage transaction. The matter was handled solely by L, but the final report was sent together with a letter on the firm's notepaper giving the names of L and W. Thereafter, the plaintiff commenced proceedings for damages for negligence against L and W, contending that it had suffered loss as a result of the firm's negligence. W contended that, although he was held out as a partner in the firm, he was not in fact a partner and was not therefore liable for L's negligent acts.

The judge ordered the trial of certain preliminary issues, including whether W was liable on the basis that he was held out as L's partner. It was held that by virtue of s 14(1)(*a*) of the Partnership Act 1890, anyone who represented himself as a partner in a firm was liable as a partner to anyone who had given credit to the firm on the faith of that representation, whether or not that representation had been made with the knowledge of the apparent partner. In the circumstances, the

---
[105] [1997] 3 All ER 498.

plaintiff had instructed the firm to obtain advice from it in respect of the mortgage transaction. That advice was supplied together with a letter on the firm's notepaper, showing the name of the firm alongside the names of L and W and, consequently, the plaintiff was entitled to regard the enclosed report as being the advice of that two-partner firm. Since the court would therefore presume that the plaintiff had relied on it as being a report which carried with it the implied imprimatur of both partners, it followed that W was estopped from denying responsibility for the report. Rimer J dealt with the issue thus:

> For Mr Williams, Mr Parker concedes that he was held out as a partner. His name was on the notepaper alongside that of Mr Lewis and there was no accompanying explanation suggesting he was other than Mr Lewis's partner. But Mr Parker submits that that is not enough to make Mr Williams answerable to Nationwide . . .
>
> In talking only in terms of 'giving credit', that subsection may perhaps be viewed as expressed somewhat restrictively, although in *Lindley and Banks on Partnership* (17th edn, 1995) para 5.52, the editors say of 'the giving of credit' that: 'This expression is not defined in s 14 of the Partnership Act 1890, and it is submitted that it should not be construed in a technical or restrictive sense but as describing any transaction with the firm.' I do not have to decide whether that view is correct, because neither counsel argued that s 14(1) should be construed restrictively and Mr Parker was content to accept that the Lindley view was correct . . .
>
> Before coming to the facts, I should refer to the authorities on which Mr Parker relies for the principle which he says is applicable. He referred me to *Re Fraser, Ex p Central Bank of London*,[106] where Lord Esher MR said: 'But it is said that John Fraser is liable on the bill because he held himself out as a partner in the firm. The doctrine of 'holding out' is a branch of the doctrine of estoppel. If a man holds himself out as a partner in a firm, and thereby induces another person to act upon that representation, he is estopped as regards that person from saying that he is not a partner. The representation may be made either by acts or by words; but the estoppel can be relied upon only by the person to whom the representation has been made in either way, and who has acted upon the faith of it.'
>
> Mr Parker also relied on *Hudgell Yeates & Co v Watson*.[107] Waller LJ said: 'The doctrine of holding out only applies in favour of persons who have dealt with a firm on the faith that the person whom they seek to make liable is a member of it.'[108] The fact, if it be the fact, that Mr Smith was held out as being a partner might well make the other partners liable for his actions in contract because they were holding him out as a partner. Similarly, insofar as he was holding himself out as a partner he would be making himself liable for the debts of the firm. But in each case this would not be because he was a partner but because on the facts he was being held out.'[109]

---

[106] [1892] 2 QB 633 at 637; [1891–4] All ER Rep 939 at 941.
[107] [1978] 2 All ER 363; [1978] QB 451.
[108] See N Lindley, B Lindley & EH Scamell *Lindley on Partnership* 13 ed (1971) 108.
[109] See [1978] 2 All ER 363 at 372–73; [1978] QB 451 at 467.

Megaw LJ said: 'But what is the effect of a holding out of someone as being a partner? A holding out is relevant, and relevant only, as an estoppel. As it is put in *Lindley on the Law of Partnership* (13th edn, 1971) p 100: "The doctrine that a person holding himself out as a partner, and thereby inducing others to act on the faith of his representations, is liable to them as if he were in fact a partner is nothing more than an illustration of the general principle of estoppel by conduct." For an estoppel to exist it is necessary to show, not only that there has been an unequivocal representation (here the holding out), but also that the person seeking to assert an estoppel has acted on the faith of the representation: *Freeman v Cooke* (1848) 2 Exch 654, [1843–60] All ER Rep 185. This requirement is stressed by Lord Blackburn in his speech in *Scarf v Jardine*[110] where he says: "I put emphasis on those last words 'against those who acted upon the faith that the authority continued'." . . . So though there was a holding out, a continued holding out, of Mr Smith as being a partner when he was not, there is no estoppel in favour of the defendant on the facts of this case. It is not that the defendant is estopped from alleging the holding out. He is not. It is that the holding out was irrelevant because the defendant's own assertion as to his state of mind involves that he did not rely on it. We are not here concerned with any question as to the burden of proof, or as to presumptions, in relation to reliance on a holding out.'[111]

That case was, therefore, one where there was a holding out of Mr Smith as a partner, but where no estoppel arose since the defendant's own case was that, in instructing the firm, he retained one particular partner, Mr James, personally and, as Megaw LJ said, his case was that—'he was in contract with Mr James, and Mr James alone, or at least that that was his intention and understanding, and that Mr James had broken that contract, personal to him, by handing over the conduct of the defendant's business to others in the firm.'[112]

I accept that there will be circumstances in which it may be presumed that the claimant has acted on the faith of the holding out as a partner of someone who is not a partner. But there must be a factual basis justifying such a presumption . . . Nationwide's problem is the absence of any evidence that, on 8 May 1991, it even knew that Mr Williams had joined the firm, let alone that he was shown on its notepaper as apparently a partner . . .

In my view, however, whilst 8 May 1991 is an important date, it is not the only important one. All that happened then was that Nationwide instructed the firm to act for it. That was the beginning of the relationship, not the end of it. The purpose of instructing the firm was to obtain advice from it as to the title to the property and as to whether the offered mortgage security was sufficient for Nationwide's purposes. That advice came back with the firm's letter of 10 May when it thanked Nationwide for its instructions and enclosed a favourable title report. The letter was on the firm's notepaper, showing the firm name of 'Bryan Lewis and Company' with alongside it the two names 'Bryan Lewis BA (Hons) Law' and 'Alyn Williams BA (Econ)' . . .

In my judgment, however, that letter was not one by which Mr Lewis was acknowledging a personal retainer of himself alone in the matter, or was offering his personal opinion on title. It may well be that the report was exclusively his work and I am prepared so to assume. But the letter was a response from what was apparently

---

[110] [1882] 7 App Cas 345 at 357; [1881–5] All ER Rep 651 at 657.
[111] See [1978] 2 All ER 363 at 374–75; [1978] QB 451 at 470–71.
[112] See [1978] 2 All ER 363 at 375; [1978] QB 451 at 470.

a two-partner firm, enclosing that firm's report on title. Correspondingly, when Nationwide received the letter, it was entitled to regard the enclosed report as being the advice of that two-partner firm. I find no difficulty in presuming in its favour that it relied on it as being a report which carried with it the implied imprimatur of both partners. If reliance of this sort was not precisely what Mr Lewis and Mr Williams intended by putting the latter's name on the notepaper, I cannot see why they did it. It may be that any presumption that Nationwide so relied on the title report is rebuttable and that it could be shown that it in fact relied on it only as being the advice of Mr Lewis. But Mr Williams has not attempted to show that. One of the ways Nationwide puts its case is, in effect, that the firm negligently failed to advise it of matters which materially qualified the advice contained in the title report. It is ultimately of the essence of Nationwide's case that it relied on that report. In my judgment, Mr Williams is estopped from denying responsibility for it . . .

The effect of s 14(1) is that a person may be held liable by holding out if two factors are satisfied:

(1) He represents himself to be a partner or knowingly allows others to represent him as a partner.

(2) The creditor making the claim relied on this representation.

A person who has held himself out as a partner, or allowed himself to be represented as a partner, but who is in fact not a partner, may be held liable as though he were a partner.[113] However, a person who is admitted as a partner into an existing firm does not thereby become liable to the creditors of the firm for anything done before he became a partner (s 17(1)).

Section 14(1) appears to be a statutory application of the doctrine of estoppel which precludes a person who holds out that a certain state of affairs exists from denying their existence.

Section 14(2) contains a proviso to the effect that where, after a partner's death, the business is continued in the old firm's name, the continued use of that name (or of the deceased partner's name as part of it) shall not of itself make his estate liable for partnership debts contracted after his death, but the estate might be liable if the executors or administrators allowed the deceased to be represented as still being a partner.

Section 14 refers to liability for credit (ie contractual debts) and therefore a partner cannot be made liable under this section for the firm's torts. Section 14 makes a person who has made a representation liable as a partner, but it does not make him a partner.

Section 15 provides that an admission or representation made by any partner concerning the partnership affairs in the ordinary course of its business is evidence against the firm. Though the section states that admissions are evidence against the firm, it is important to note that these

---

[113] See *Re Fraser* [1892] 2 QB 633.

admissions are not conclusive evidence. It is always open to a person who has made an admission to withdraw what he said.

Under s 16, notice to any partner habitually acting in the partnership business, of any matter relating thereto, operates as notice to the firm, except in the case of a fraud on the firm committed by or with the consent of that partner.

In terms of s 49 of the Bills of Exchange Act of 1882, notice of dishonour of a bill of exchange to any partner of a firm will operate as notice to such firm.

3.18 NEW PARTNERS/RETIRING PARTNERS

In terms of s 17(1) a new partner is not liable for transactions done before he assumes partnership. A retiring partner, however, remains liable for debts incurred before his retirement (s 17(2)). He could, however, be discharged if a contract of novation (s 17(3)) is made between himself, the other partners and the creditors. This is a prudent thing to do and is an advisable course for a retiring partner to insist on.

A retiring partner may also be liable for debts incurred after his retirement. Third parties dealing with the firm after a change in its membership composition are entitled to treat all apparent members of the old firm as still being partners until notice to the contrary is given. It is advisable for any retiring partner to protect himself by notifying all clients of his retirement; normally, this should be done by an advertisement.[114]

3.19 RELATIONS OF PARTNERS TO ONE ANOTHER

The relationship between partners is one of utmost good faith and trust and loyalty. This includes a duty to act honestly, not to make 'secret' profits, not to compete against the business and not to act in a manner that conflicts with the interests of the business. As will be seen in the part dealing with the duties of a partner, there is a general duty to account to the firm for any benefit derived by a partner from any transaction concerning the partnership or from the use of the firm's property, name or business connection (s 29(1)).

Transparency, accountability and honesty are values that should characterise any partnership arrangement. Thus, for example, a partner who received a secret commission from a partnership transaction would be obliged to account for that to the firm. On the other hand, a partner is entitled to retain

---

[114] See *Tower Cabinet Co v Ingram* [1949] 2 KB 397.

the benefit of transactions completely outside the scope of the partnership business, even though this involves the use of information acquired in the partnership.[115] A partner is under a duty not to compete with the firm and if he, without the consent of is co-partners, carries on any business of the same nature as, and competing with, that of the firm, he must account for and pay over to the firm all profits made by him in that business (s 30).

Subject to any agreement express or implied between the partners, all the partners are entitled to share equally in the capital and profits of the business (s 24(1)). A partner continuing the business with the partnership assets after dissolution must account for the profits up to the final winding up of the concern. In the absence of express or implied agreement, partners must contribute equally towards losses, whether of capital or otherwise, sustained by the firm (s 24(1)). Where there is an agreement, express or implied, as to the proportions in which profits will be shared, losses are, in the absence of an agreement to the contrary, to be borne in the same propositions. Each partner is entitled as against the other partners to true accounts and full information of all things affecting the partnership (s 28) and to inspect and copy the partnership books (s 24(9)).

Each partner is entitled to be indemnified out of the assets of the firm or by way of contribution from his partners in respect of payments made and personal liabilities incurred by him in the ordinary and proper conduct of the partnership business, or in or about anything necessarily done for the preservation of the business of the firm (s 24(2)). The right of indemnity does not extend to sums paid by a partner for which the partnership is not liable, or to losses due to the fraud or culpable negligence of the partner concerned.[116] In many respects, the fiduciary duties of an agent towards his principal apply with equal force in partnerships.

Section 19 echoes the position that a partnership is essentially a relationship anchored on the agreement of the members and that the intentions of those members are paramount. It provides that the mutual rights and duties of the partners, whether contained in an agreement or defined in the Partnership Act, may be varied by the consent of all the partners. The intentions of the partners (expressed or implied) will override both (1) detailed provisions of the partnership articles (if any) and (2) the provisions of the Act itself where they conflict with the partner's intention. There are three significant points to note about s 19:

---

[115] *Aas v Benham* [1891] 2 Ch 244.
[116] See *Thomas v Atherton* [1878] 10 Ch D 185.

(1) The consent of the partners must be unanimous. The Act speaks of *all* the partners' consent before a variation can be effective. It seems the rule by the majority here does not have room. The minority cannot be forced to accept a variation against their will.

(2) Partners are entitled to vary the terms of their association at will and at any time without any express agreement. This is so even where the partnership articles are definite in their provision of a matter which is the subject of a variation. As Langdale MR remarked in *England v Curling*:[117]

> Partners, if they please, may, in the course of the partnership, daily come to a new arrangement for the purpose of having some addition or alteration in terms on which they carry on business, provided those additions or alterations be made with the unanimous concurrence of all the partners.

(3) Once a partner has expressly or impliedly consented to a variation, the same will be binding on personal representatives of the partner after his death.

In *Coventry v Barclay*[118] the articles of a partnership contained a provision prescribing a certain method of asset valuation on an annual basis. Years later, and without amending the articles, the partners adopted another mode of valuation which they used for several years. It was held that their course of dealing showed an intention to alter the articles, and the alteration was binding upon the partners unless they by unanimous mutual consent agreed otherwise.

Section 20(1) defines partnership property in the following terms:

> All property, and rights and interests in property, originally brought into the partnership stock, or acquired on account of the firm or for the purposes and in the course of the partnership business, are known as 'partnership property' and must be used exclusively for the purposes of the partnership.

Unless the contrary intention appears, property bought with money belonging to the firm is deemed to have been bought on account of the firm (s 21). If it is land that is held by the partnership, it becomes personal property (s 22). Such land is usually conveyed to the partners on trust for sale and to hold the proceeds of sale and the rents and profits until sale as part of the partnership property. The principle behind s 22 is that *prima facie* all the property of the firm, real and personal, must be sold on the dissolution of the partnership. Consequently, in equity it is deemed to have been already converted into personal estate and therefore devolves as such.

---

117 [1844] 50 ER 51.
118 [1864] 12 WR 500.

A writ of execution levied against partnership property can only be issued if judgment has been obtained against the firm.[119] The only remedy of a creditor in respect of a partner in his private capacity, and not as a member of the firm, against the partnership property is to obtain an order charging that partner's interest in the partnership property and profits with the amount of the debt.[120] This may be followed by an order appointing a receiver of the debtor partner's share of the profits. Other partners may redeem the interest charged or purchase it;[121] they also have an option to dissolve the partnership.[122]

The Partnership Act also provides that every partner is entitled to have the property of the partnership applied in the payment of the debts and liabilities of the firm and to have any surplus assets after the payment applied in the payment of what is owing to the partners.[123]

In the case of *Don King Productions Inc v Warren and Others*,[124] W and two other defendants appealed, contending inter alia that the benefits of certain management and promotion agreements were not assets of the partnership or partnership property within the meaning of s 20(*a*) of the Partnership Act of 1890. It was held that for the purposes of s 20 of the 1890 Act, property which was not assignable might, nevertheless, be partnership property, and similarly whether an asset was 'brought into the partnership stock or acquired ... on account of the firm ... or for the purposes and in the course of the partnership business' did not depend on whether it was assignable at law.

Thus, partnership property within the meaning of the section included that to which a partner was entitled and which all the partners expressly or by implication agreed should, as between themselves, be treated as partnership property, and it was immaterial, as between the partners, whether it could be assigned by the partner in whose name it stood to the partners jointly. Morritt LJ stated:

> The judge's reasoning and conclusions have been subjected to sustained criticism by Mr Steinfeld QC on behalf of Mr Warren. First he contended that the benefit of the management and promotion agreements was not 'property' within the meaning of that word as used in the 1890 Act. Second he argued that even if, contrary to his first submission, the benefit of such agreements was 'property' within the meaning of the 1890 Act because of their nature they could not be 'brought into the partnership stock'

---

[119] Section 23(1) of the Partnership Act.
[120] Section 23(2) of the Partnership Act.
[121] Section 23(3) of the Partnership Act.
[122] Section 32 of the Partnership Act.
[123] Section 39 of the Partnership Act.
[124] [1999] 2 All ER 218.

or 'acquired . . . on account of the firm' (s 20(1)) so as to become partnership property for the purposes of s 20 of the Act . . . Mr Steinfeld also relied on the provisions of s 39 of the 1890 Act whereby on the dissolution of the partnership the assets are applicable in payment of the debts and liabilities of the firm and of what is due to the partners. He submitted that if the item in question could not be sold then it could not be an asset of the partnership . . . I do not accept this submission . . . it is plain that property which is not assignable may, nevertheless, be partnership property. Thus in *Ambler v Bolton* (1872) LR 14 Eq 427 an inalienable government contract was a partnership asset which, in the winding up of the affairs of the partnership, was valued and debited to the share of the partner by whom it was concluded. Likewise in *Pathirana v Pathirana* [1967] AC 233, [1966] 3 WLR 666 a personal licence granted to one of the partners was a partnership asset . . .

I reject the second submission for similar reasons. The question whether, in the terms of s 20(1) of the 1890 Act an asset is 'brought into the partnership stock or acquired . . . on account of the firm . . . or for the purposes and in the course of the partnership business' does not depend on whether it is assignable at law. In both *Ambler v Bolton* and *Pathirana v Pathirana* the asset was inalienable. In both cases the inalienable asset had been acquired by the individual partner in his own name during the subsistence of the partnership but was still treated as acquired on account of the firm. In my view it would make no difference if the asset had been acquired before the commencement of the partnership but the partner in question was required by the terms of the partnership to bring it into the common stock. The reason is quite simply that partnership property within s 20 of the 1890 Act includes that to which a partner is entitled and which all the partners expressly or by implication agree should, as between themselves, be treated as partnership property. It is immaterial, as between the partners, whether it can be assigned by the partner in whose name it stands to the partners jointly.

3.20 MANAGEMENT OF A PARTNERSHIP

Partnership decisions are to be taken by a majority of partners where the decisions relate to the 'ordinary' business of the firm. If the decision is 'extraordinary', for example, to fundamentally change the kind of business to be carried on or to admit a new partner or expel an existing one, unanimity will be required.

3.21 DUTIES OF PARTNERS

The relation of partners, if founded on mutual confidence and the law, requires that a partner shall act towards the other members of the firm with the utmost good faith.

3.21.1 To render true accounts

By s 28, a partner is bound to render true accounts of the partnership. It follows that he must permit the other partners to inspect such accounts. He must also be ready to explain to them any moneys that may have come into his hands through the partnership. Section 28 also requires the partner to give full information of all things affecting the partnership.

Utmost good faith between partners is the overriding rule. Since every partner is an agent of the other partners, he is bound to communicate full information to his co-partners. If he acquires any information in the course of the partnership business, he is bound to pass it on to the other partners.

In practice, a partner is obliged to disclose partnership opportunities to all other partners or their legal representatives while the partnership is a going concern[125] and must disclose any special knowledge about the condition of the partnership when dissolution is contemplated, especially where the partner with special knowledge proposes to buy out another's interest.

3.21.2 To account for private profits

By s 29, every partner must account to the firm for any benefit derived by him without the consent of the other partners from any transaction concerning the partnership, or from any use by him of the partnership property, name or business connection. This is because partnership property belongs to all the partners and therefore a partner cannot directly or indirectly use the property of the firm for his own private purposes or gain or try to get any advantage without disclosing it.

3.21.3 To account for profits of competing business

Under s 30, if a partner, without the consent of the other partners, carries on any business of the same nature as, and competing with, that of the firm, he must account for and pay over to the firm all profits made by him in that business. The rule in s 30 may be restated thus: no partner can carry on any business which is likely to compete with the business of the partnership, except with the consent of his co-partners.

If a partner, without obtaining such consent, carries on competing business, he must account for the profits of such business to the firm. In *Tugbobo v Adelakun*,[126] the plaintiff and the defendant were carrying on a stevedoring business in partnership. The defendant also ran a solely owned firm which secured similar stevedoring contracts for the Nigerian Marketing Producing Company. The plaintiff sued the defendant for an account and payment of half of the profits arising from the stevedoring contracts secured by the defendant's firm. It was held by the Supreme Court that a partner is not allowed to derive any advantage by setting up business in

---

[125] See *Birtchnell v Equity Tnustees, Executors and Agency Co Ltd* [1929] 42 CLR 384; *Chan v Zacharia* [1984] 154 CLR 178.
[126] [1974] 1 All NLR 49.

competition with his firm. The defendant was bound to account to the plaintiff for a breach of his fiduciary duty.

3.21.4 To act within authority

Naturally, every partner is bound to act within the scope of the actual authority conferred upon him. Where such authority is exceeded, the partner is liable to compensate or indemnify the other partners for any ensuing loss, unless the other partners ratify his unauthorised act.

3.21.5 To act in the partnership business without remuneration

Section 24(6) provides that 'no partner shall be entitled to remuneration for acting in the partnership business'. Every partner is by this provision bound to attend to the business of the firm and, in the absence of any agreement to the contrary, he is not entitled to any remuneration in any form or shape for conducting partnership business. It is, however, usual in partnership for an agreement to be made that certain partners, for example, the managing partner or any other partner with additional responsibilities, are to be allowed compensation or remuneration for such additional services.[127]

3.21.6 To contribute to the losses

Under s 24(1), all partners are entitled to share equally in the capital and profits of the business and must contribute equally towards the losses of the firm. This will be the position unless there is an agreement to the contrary.

In *Garner v Murray*[128] a partnership was formed upon the terms that the capital should be contributed by the three partners in unequal shares, but that they should receive equal shares of the net profits. After all the liabilities of the firm had been paid and all advances made by the partners repaid, the assets were insufficient to repay the capital due to default by the third partner in contributing his share of the deficiency.

The question was how this deficiency was to be borne. It was held that each partner was liable to contribute one third of the deficiency because this was the proportion in which the profits were divisible. There was nothing in the Partnership Act to make a solvent partner liable to contribute for an insolvent partner who failed to pay his share.

What became known as the rule in *Garner v Murray* can be stated thus: if any partner is insolvent and unable to contribute his share of lost capital, the solvent partners are not liable to contribute it for him, but the amount

---

[127] See *Harris v Sleep* [1897] 2 Ch 80.
[128] [1904] 1 Ch 57.

available after the solvent partners have made their proper contributions is divided rateably according to the amount of capital standing to the credit of each partner (not including, of course, the insolvent partner who has failed to bear his share of the loss).

We see from the foregoing that s 24(1) means that there is no necessary connection between the proportion in which capital is contributed and that of profit and loss. *Prima facie*, partners share profits and bear losses equally, notwithstanding that the capital contributed by each may not be equal. Stated differently, profits and losses are not shared in proportion to the capital contributed by each partner. However, there is an inference that losses are to be borne in the same proportion as profits are shared (see s 44).

In the case of *Popat v Shonchhatra*[129] the plaintiff and the defendant were in partnership together in the business of a newsagent from 29 September 1989 to 10 January 1990. The business was carried on at leasehold premises, the lease having been assigned to the partners in joint names, together with fixtures and fittings and the goodwill of the business. The cost of acquiring those assets was funded principally by bank loans. The balance was funded by contributions from the partners to the capital of the partnership—£4 564 in the case of the plaintiff (£2 700 of which was funded by a loan from the defendant) and £23 064 in the case of the defendant. The partnership was at will and it was determined by the plaintiff on 10 January. From that point the defendant carried on the business on his own and subsequently purchased the freehold of the premises for £80 000. Two and a half years after the dissolution of the partnership, the premises, together with the goodwill of the business and the fixtures and fittings, were sold at a profit by the defendant for £179 758, the stock and book debts being valued at a further £7 265. Thereafter the plaintiff brought proceedings against the defendant seeking, inter alia, a declaration that the defendant held the freehold of the partnership premises, or the proceeds of the sale thereof, on trust for himself and the plaintiff in equal shares by virtue of s 24(1) of the Partnership Act of 1890, which provided that in the absence of 'any agreement express or implied between the partners' they were 'entitled to share equally in the capital and profits of the business'. The deputy judge held that s 24(1) of the 1890 Act only dealt with the position between partners up to the date of the dissolution of the partnership; he accordingly made declarations that the freehold of the partnership premises belonged to the partnership, and the post-dissolution capital profits (including the profits realised on the sale of the premises)

---

[129] [1997] 3 All ER 800.

were to be apportioned between the parties pro rata to their proportionate shares in the capital of the partnership as at 10 January 1990. The plaintiff appealed.

It was held

Where partners contributed to the capital of the partnership by funding the cost of acquiring partnership assets, those contributions were not determinative of the size of the partners' respective shares of the assets, since subject to any agreement to the contrary, the partners were entitled to share equally in the partnership property. Since, in the instant case, there had been no such agreement, the deputy judge ought to have held that the freehold was held in trust for the partners in equal shares. Furthermore, while capital profits were not 'profits' for the purposes of s 42(1) of the 1890 Act, they were 'profits' for the purposes of s 24(1), which applied equally both before and after the dissolution of the partnership. It followed, therefore, that under s 24(1) the plaintiff was entitled to share equally in the post-dissolution capital profits. Accordingly, the appeal would be allowed to that extent and appropriate declarations substituted for those made by the deputy judge.

Nourse LJ, in his judgment propounded the law thus:

The main question arising on this appeal is whether the profit realised on a sale, after dissolution, of the assets of a short-lived partnership at will is divisible equally between the partners pursuant to section 24(1) or, as has been held below, in shares corresponding to their respective shares of the capital of the partnership as at the date of dissolution. In order to answer that and other questions, it is necessary to restate basic principles as to, first, the distinction between the capital of a partnership and its assets and, second, the nature and size of a partner's share of the assets.

The relevant principles of partnership law are well settled. I start with the distinction between the capital of a partnership and its assets. As I said at first instance in *Reed (Inspector of Taxes) v Young* [1984] STC 38 at 57: 'The capital of a partnership is the aggregate of the contributions made by the partners, either in cash or in kind, for the purpose of commencing or carrying on the partnership business and intended to be risked by them therein. Each contribution must be of a fixed amount. If it is in cash, it speaks for itself. If it is in kind, it must be valued at a stated amount. It is important to distinguish between the capital of a partnership, a fixed sum, on the one hand and its assets, which may vary from day to day and include everything belonging to the firm having any money value, on the other (see generally [Lindley on the Law of Partnership (14th edn, 1979) p 442]).'

In the present case the judge treated the contributions of £4 564 and £23,064 made by the plaintiff and defendant respectively to the cost of acquiring the partnership assets as contributions to the capital of the partnership. In that he was right. But he proceeded from there to treat those contributions as determinative of the size of the partners' respective shares of the assets. In that he was wrong, although it must at once be said that it seems probable that his attention was not fully directed to the correct legal principles.

On 29 September 1989, when the leasehold premises, fixtures and fittings and the goodwill of the business were acquired, they became 'partnership property' to be held and applied exclusively for the purposes of the partnership pursuant to section 20(1) of the 1890 Act. Although it is both customary and convenient to speak of a partner's 'share' of the partnership assets, that is not a truly accurate description of his interest in them, at all events so long as the partnership is a going concern. While each partner has a proprietary interest in each and every asset, he has no entitlement to any specific asset and, in consequence, no right, without the consent of the other partners or partner, to require the whole or even a share of any particular asset to be vested in him. On dissolution the position is in substance not much different, the partnership property falling to be applied, subject to sections 40 to 43 (if and so far as applicable), in accordance with sections 39 and 44 of the 1890 Act. As part of that process, each partner in a solvent partnership is presumptively entitled to payment of what is due from the firm to him in respect of capital before division of the ultimate residue in the shares in which profits are divisible; see section 44(*b*)3. and 4. It is only at that stage that a partner can accurately be said to be entitled to a share of anything, which, in the absence of agreement to the contrary, will be a share of cash.

Having dealt with the nature of a partner's share of the assets, I turn to its size. Here a start must be made with the opening words of section 24, which generate an expectation that its subsequent provisions will prescribe the entitlement, subject to any agreement, of the partners to share in the partnership property. On a further perusal, that expectation is disappointed, subsection (1) referring only to 'the capital and profits of the business' and none of the other subsections being relevant. That makes it necessary to have resort to the rule, established well before the 1890 Act and no doubt recognised by section 24, that, subject to any agreement, all the partners are entitled to share equally in the partnership property. Lord Lindley's statement of the rule and his justification for it are set out and discussed in *Lindley and Banks* pp 540–542. In the present case, there having been no agreement to the contrary, the partners were entitled to share equally in the assets of the partnership.

I now revert to the capital of a partnership. It is implicit in what is said in the preceding paragraph that 'capital' in section 24(1) cannot be construed so as to include the partnership property. As appears from *Lindley and Banks* pp 500–501, this is a point which has occasioned some discussion in successive editions of that work. Lord Lindley's own view of it was:

'If it be proved that the partners contributed the capital of the partnership in unequal shares it is presumed that, in the absence of an agreement to the contrary, on a final settlement of accounts, the capital of the business remaining after the payment of outside debts and liabilities, and of what is due to each partner for advances, will, subject to all proper deductions, be divided amongst the partners in the proportions in which they contributed it and not equally.'

An attempt was subsequently made to justify that apparent departure from the plain words of the provision by reading 'capital' as including partnership property. However, the view of the current editor, Mr R C I'Anson Banks, is that 'capital' should be given its normal meaning and I am in no doubt that his view is correct. Equally, I am in no doubt that the slightest indication of an implied agreement between the partners that their shares of capital should correspond with their contributions to it will suffice to displace the provision that they are entitled to share equally. That could, in most cases, be expected to be the common sense of the matter. Clearly, Lord Lindley would have approved of that approach.

However that may be, the plaintiff's case on this appeal depends not on 'capital' in section 24(1) but on 'profits', which clearly includes capital as well as revenue profits.

Before coming to the individual elements of the judge's decision, I summarise the position by saying that at all material times the plaintiff and the defendant were entitled to share in the capital of the partnership in proportions corresponding to their respective contributions to the cost of acquiring the leasehold premises, fixtures and fittings and the goodwill of the business, but that they were entitled to share equally in the assets of the partnership. I suspect that the confusion arose out of a natural but erroneous assumption on the part of the judge that the entitlement of partners to the assets of the partnership was similar to the entitlement of shareholders of a company limited by shares to the assets of the company on a liquidation.

... [T]here is no authority and nothing in principle to support the view that section 24(1) was only intended to apply to revenue profits up to the date of dissolution. Like all the provisions of s 24, being entirely general in its terms, it applies equally both before and after dissolution. The true view is that section 42(1) provides for an exception to the general provision made by section 24(1) only in the 'certain cases' ... in which its requirements are satisfied.

Barclays Bank Trust Co Ltd v Bluff, the decision in which was approved by the Privy Council in *Chandroutie v Gajadhar* [1987] AC 147 at 154, is indeed authority for the proposition that post-dissolution capital profits cannot properly be regarded as profits within the meaning of section 42(1); see [1981] 3 All ER 232 at 239–240, [1982] Ch 172 at 181–183. It follows that the partners here are entitled to share equally in the post-dissolution capital profits, in this instance not because they are divisible in the shares in which they are entitled to share in the assets of the partnership, but because they are covered by the general provision in section 24(1). That is enough to dispose of this point in favour of the plaintiff and it is unnecessary to consider the further reasoning of the judge.

3.22 THE RIGHTS OF A PARTNER

A partner has several rights as a member of the firm against his co-partners. Subject to any express or implied agreement to the contrary, every partner has the following rights.

3.22.1 The right to participate in the management of the partnership

Every partner has a right to take part in the conduct and management of the partnership business. Section 24(5) provides that 'every partner may take part in the management of the partnership business'. It seems from the language of s 24(5) that all sort of partners, including sleeping partners, may participate in the management of a partnership business in the absence of an agreement to the contrary.

3.22.2 The right of access to accounts

By s 24(9) the partnership books must be kept at the place of business of the partnership and every partner may, when he thinks fit, have access to and inspect and copy any of them. Any partner, active or dormant, has a right to free access to all records, books, and accounts of partnership business and to examine and copy them.

3.22.3 The right to share profits

By s 24(1), all partners are entitled to share equally in the profits of the business of the partnership. This will be the position unless the partners agree otherwise, such as by altering the entitlement to profits of each partner. This usually occurs in partnership with senior and junior partners.

3.22.4 The right to be indemnified

In the absence of an agreement to the contrary, a partner is entitled to be indemnified by the firm in respect of payments made and personal liabilities incurred by him in the ordinary and property conduct of the business of the firm and in respect of expenses and disbursements made for purposes of protecting the firm from loss. This right is encapsulated in s 24(2)*(a)* and *(b)*.

3.22.5 Right of interest on advances

Section 24(3) provides that a partner who makes payment or advance beyond the amount of capital which he has agreed to subscribe is entitled to interest at the rate of 5 per cent per annum from the date of payment or advance. By agreement, the rate of interest could of course be raised. It is important to note that his interest is payable out of the partnership property as an item of expense and not necessarily out of the profits of the partnership business.

It should be noted that where a partner borrows money from the partnership, he is not obliged to pay back that loan with interest.

3.22.6 Co-ownership of partnership property

Section 20(1) defines partnership property to include rights and interests in property originally brought into the partnership stock or acquired on account of the firm or for the purposes and in the course of partnership business. In the absence of any agreement to the contrary, every partner is a co-owner of the partnership property and is entitled to have an equal share in the property and shall be treated as personal or movable and not heritable estate (see ss 20(3) and 22).

3.22.7 Right to consent to introduction of new partner

Section 24(7) provides that 'no person may be introduced as a partner without the consent of all existing partners'. Every partner is entitled to object to the introduction of a new partner without conduct or that of any of the co-partners unless of course there is express agreement permitting such introduction.

3.22.8 The right not to be expelled

Section 25 provides that 'no majority of the partners can expel any partner unless a power to do so has been conferred by express agreement between the partners'. This section therefore entails that a partner has a right to remain in partnership and not to be dismissed from it except where a clause in the agreement conferring a power of expulsion by the majority exists. Even where such power exists, it cannot be used unreasonably. It must be exercised *bona fide*, and not with ulterior motives. In *Re a Solicitor's Arbitration*,[130] a partnership deed stated that 'if a partner is guilty of misconduct, the others may expel him'. One partner acting alone sought to exercise the power and was held unable to do so.

3.22.9 The right to engage in competing business

Strangely, the Partnership Act does not prescribe the carrying on of rival or competing business by partners. What it does is merely to make conduct of such business conditional on the other partners' consent if the obligation to account for the profits of such business to the partnership is to be avoided. Section 30 provides:

> If a partner, without the consent of the other partners carries on any business of the same nature as and competing with that of the firm, he must account and pay over to the firm all profits made by him in that business.

In practice, agreements among partners will generally restrain a partner form engaging in other business (especially a competing business) other than the partnership as long as he is a partner.

When a partner retires or departs from the firm, the partner's common-law duty of good faith encompasses treating and maintaining as confidential all information, communications and documents received in his capacity as an employee and relating to his duties. An employer would succeed with an injunction to restrain an employee from using trade secrets or other confidential information that could harm the firm when the departing partner forms his own firm.

As a general rule, a partner's duty of faithfulness and good faith does not prevent the employee from competing with a former employer once he has left employment. However, it is possible for the firm to bind the partner to a restraint of trade agreement. Valid restraint of trade clauses or agreements can prevent an employee from engaging in a similar type of business as the former employer within a specified geographical area for a specific period. Restraint of trade clauses are linked to the common-law duty of good faith, specifically the duty to avoid soliciting customers of the firm and undermining the interests of the other partners. The restraint of trade clause is therefore a measure necessary to protect against misuse of information obtained by a partner once they leave the firm. The most recognisable and legally protectable interests are those which the court in *Faccenda Chicken*

---

[130] [1962] 1 All ER 772.

Limited v Fowler[131] characterised as the employer's trade secrets or customer connections. Therefore for a restraint of trade to be valid it must protect an interest that is at the level of client information or trade secrets. In the absence of a legally protectable interest, these agreements will not be enforced.

The law on restraint of trade in Zambia comes from the common law and the landmark case of *JK Rambai Patel v Mukesh Kumar Patel*.[132] The Supreme Court in this case held that restraint of trade clauses are *prima facie* unenforceable, unless they are reasonable. The reasonableness of the restraint of trade clause will be determined by looking at the interests of the parties concerned and the public. The duration of restraint and geographical coverage are also relevant factors. In this case, the court held that a restraint clause that did not permit the employee to seek employment in the public sector was unreasonable as the employer's trade secrets were in no way threatened.

3.22.10 The right to retire

Every partner has the right to retire or leave the partnership. Retirement is usually a matter of agreement. If it is not provided for in any agreement, a partner would still be entitled to disengage from the partnership by the consent of the other partners or by giving notice to them. Section 26(1) states that if a partnership is entered into for an undefined time, a partner may give notice of his intention to leave and this effectively determines the partnership. In the case of *Abbott v Abbott*,[133] in the partnership agreement there was no period or duration of the partnership fixed, but it was expressly provided that the death or retirement of a partner should not determine the partnership. One partner wishing to retire claimed that his retirement would necessitate the dissolution of the partnership between the remaining partners, but the court did not agree with this contention. Clauson J dealt with the issue thus:

> The plaintiff in this action is one of the sons. He is claiming that the partnership constituted by that deed was what is commonly spoken of as a partnership at will. On 8 November 1934, he gave notice claiming dissolution, or that by reason of the issue of the writ in this action the partnership is to be treated as dissolved by reason of its being a partnership at will. The father and brothers say it is not a partnership at will. If one desires to give notice and retire, he has his rights. That is the dispute between the parties, and the sole question I have to consider is whether on the true construction of the deed the plaintiff has the right, which he claims, to put an end to the partnership by notice.

---

[131] [1986] 1 All ER 617.
[132] [1985] ZR 220 (SC).
[133] [1936] 3 All ER 823.

At one time I had a slight difficulty because of the verbal difficulties of precisely reconciling the terms of the Partnership Act 1890, s 26, with the terms of s 32 of the same Act. The matter came before the Court of Appeal in the case of *Moss v Elphick* and it is authoritatively stated in the judgments in that case—I refer to the judgment of Farwell LJ, in particular, which I adopt fully—that the statement contained in *Lindley on Partnership* (7th Edn, p 142) is correct. That statement is that:

'the result of a contract of partnership is a partnership at will unless some agreement to the contrary can be proved.'

This being an agreement for a partnership, it is an agreement which each partner has a right to bring to an end at any moment, if he so desires, unless I am satisfied that there is some other agreement. The first point is that on reading cl 2 it is clear that a partner who says 'I want to go out of the partnership' does not determine the partnership by doing that. If this were a partnership at will and one partner said, 'I am determined to go out of this partnership,' the effect would be that the partnership would come to an end as between all the partners, although the others might form some new partnership amongst themselves if they so desired. So there is some limitation upon this character of the partnership; it is subject to the express agreement that a single partner cannot determine the partnership although he can determine it as between himself and the others. This involves the fact that if one intimates his desire to go out, the partnership shall continue among the remaining partners. The next question that I have to decide is how long and until when is the partnership to continue, and is there any light thrown upon that by the document? *Prima facie*, if two partners agree that they will continue indefinitely in partnership until by agreement they alter that position, that is not a partnership at will. It is a partnership for their joint lives unless they agree to terminate the relationship. That was decided in *Moss v Elphick*. Accordingly, I get this from cl 2. The partners have agreed that the partnership shall continue, notwithstanding that one partner goes out, and they have also agreed that notwithstanding that one partner dies, the partnership shall continue. That does not mean that the partnership shall continue when all but one of the partners has either died or retired, because there cannot be a partnership with one partner. But the clause seems consistent with the view that so long as there are two partners the partnership is to continue. Cl 10 seems to contemplate that there may be circumstances in which the partnership might have to be dissolved by the court. That is quite alien from the conception of a partnership at will to which a partner can put an end of his own volition. It is difficult to see in what circumstances the court could decree dissolution of such a partnership. The court could, of course, determine that the partnership had been duly dissolved. But it never discusses the grounds which justify dissolution except in the case of a partnership otherwise than at will. That clause seems to indicate that this is a partnership which is not determinable at the will of one partner as between all the partners, but it is a partnership which is to continue until there is a dissolution of it by the court or by some other event, save as against a partner who retires. In these circumstances, it seems clear that sense cannot be made of the document unless it is that this partnership shall not be brought to an end so long as two of the partners are still living and have not retired. In these circumstances, the claim of the plaintiff to dissolve the partnership as between all the partners is one which must fail, and accordingly the action must fail, and it only remains to dismiss it with costs.

3.23 DISAGREEMENT BETWEEN PARTNERS

Differences between and among the partners is bound to occur. Disagreements between partners could prove expensive and protracted to resolve, especially when there is a compelling need to preserve a continuing business or goodwill. Urgency becomes very much of the essence. The usual mechanisms of conflict resolution may have to be resorted to. These include mediation, arbitration and litigation. The remedy of last resort should be an application to court. The range of remedies available when an application to court is made includes:

(1) an order to dissolve the partnership;
(2) an order that an account be drawn to determine the parties' entitlement or liability;
(3) an order of specific performance (a court will rarely make an order for the continuation of a partnership against the wish of any partner (specific performance); such Orders are occasionally made in exceptional circumstances to enforce clear cut obligations, for example, directing the particular individuals to collect partnership debts);
(4) injunctive relief to prevent individuals from breaking obligations imposed by the Deed of Partnership or the law; and
(5) miscellaneous or other orders, including directing one partner to make records available to other partners for purposes of inspection.

3.24 DISSOLUTION OF PARTNERSHIP AND ITS CONSEQUENCES

Sections 32 to 35 set out circumstances in which a partnership may be dissolved. These are as follows below.

3.24.1 Expiration of term

Where a partnership is for a fixed term it will stand dissolved by the expiration of that term, unless there is a contrary agreement between the parties.

3.24.2 By completion of the adventure

Under s 32*(b)* where a partnership is entered into for a single adventure or undertaking, the accomplishment or termination of that adventure or undertaking brings the partnership to an end. This again is subject to any agreement to the contrary between or among the partners.

3.24.3 By notice

Where the partnership is for an undefined term, any partner may give notice to the other or others of his intention to dissolve the partnership. This is the general common-law position, which allows the termination of any agreement by notice. Where the agreement contains a provision for termination, such provision will bind the parties to it. Where, however, there is no provision, the agreement will be determinable by reasonable notice.

In *Mclead v Dowling*[133] a partner who sent a notice of termination of the partnership to the other partner died before the co-partner received the notice. It was held that the partnership was terminated by death and not by notice.

3.24.4 By death of a partner

Under s 33(1) every partnership is dissolved as regards all the partners by the death or bankruptcy of any partner. Because a partnership has no independent existence, every time there is a change in the membership of the firm, there will technically be dissolution.[134] If for instance, Chibale, Zulu and Likezo have a partnership trading under the firm name 'Chibale Likezo and Associates', the death of Zulu, in the absence of an agreement between all three partners as to the continuation of the partnership on the death of a partner, will stand dissolved in terms of s 33(1). If the surviving partners wish to continue in partnership, they would have to reconstitute their partnership. The question of agreement between the partners to continue the partnership upon the death of a partner where only two partners constitute the partnership does not arise since a partnership cannot subsist with one individual.

3.24.5 By the bankruptcy of a partner

Like death, the insolvency of a partner dissolves the partnership. Under s 33(2) a partnership may, at the option of the other partners, be dissolved if any partner suffers his share of the partnership property to be charged for his separate debt. This provision is subject to any agreement between the partners.

3.24.6 By the partnership business becoming illegal

A partnership is in every case dissolved if the partnership business is unlawful, that is to say, where the object for which the partnership was created is prohibited by law or becomes illegal as a result of some subsequent development or event, the partnership dissolves by operation of the law. This is set out in s 34 of the Act.

---

[133] [1927] TLR 65.
[134] *Hadlee v Commissioner of Inland Revenue* [1989] 2 NZLR 447.

In *R v Kupfer*,[135] the fact of a partner becoming an enemy alien was held to necessarily make the continuance of the partnership illegal since the other partners would be trading with the enemy. Lord Reading CJ said:

> We assume that the partnership came to an end by operation of law as soon as war was declared. There can be no partnership between enemies of this country and a subject of this country when war has once been declared. Commercial intercourse is prohibited, and immediately that prohibition comes into force it is impossible for the relationship of partners to subsist, at any rate during the war. The partnership was therefore at an end ... But giving full effect to the law—and we assume not only that the partnership came to an end, but that the prisoner knew that it did so because he was presumed to know the law—what is the position?

What is interesting is how the courts have interpreted the question whether a partnership may subsist between individuals who may not be conscious of the fact that they are no longer carrying on business legally. In *Hudgell, Yeates and Co v Watson*[136] where a solicitor's practicing certificate lapsed, the partnership between him and the other partners was held to automatically have been dissolved. Bridge LJ rendered a somewhat formidable dissenting opinion in the following terms:

> The second submission we have to consider rests on the application of s 34 of the Partnership Act 1890 ... The lapse of Mr Smith's certificate was an event, it is contended, which effected the automatic dissolution of the pre-existing partnership. So long as Mr Smith was uncertificated the other partners should be regarded as carrying on the business of a newly constituted firm of which he was not a member. When his new certificate was issued, the firm was once again reconstituted to include him and he should be regarded as a plaintiff in the present proceedings only in respect of the claim for costs relating to work done after 2 May 1973. This is an ingenious and, at first blush, compelling way of avoiding the harsh consequences of penalising innocent partners for an oversight by one member of their firm. It has the particular merit, in the instant case, that on the facts it was clearly a matter of complete indifference to the defendant whether or not Mr Smith was at any time a member of the firm acting for him.
>
> The operation of s 34 of the 1890 Act is easy enough to understand when the event which would make it unlawful for the members of a firm to continue their partnership is known to and recognised by them, as would occur for instance when one partner in a firm was struck off the roll of solicitors. But I find the concept of automatic dissolution and the relevant effects of s 34 much more difficult to understand when the event occasioning the statutory dissolution goes unnoticed by all the partners, being due to mere inadvertence by one of them, and consequently they all continue to act in relation to the conduct of the partnership business as if the original partnership continued in existence. It would be surprising if, in these circumstances, when the unlawfulness of continuing to operate the partnership subsequently came to light, the partners could rely on s 34 to relieve them of all the disabling consequences of having done so. However that may be, the critical question for present purposes is whether, notwithstanding that throughout the period during which Mr Smith was uncertificated the business of the

---

[135] [1915] 2 KB 321.
[136] [1978] 2 All ER 363.

firm was conducted on the footing that he was still a member of it, the other partners can rely on s 34 as leading to the conclusion that they were the sole principals for whom Miss Griffiths, as the supervising partner, Mr Frost as managing clerk, and any other employee concerned, were acting as agents in the conduct of the defendant's litigation and that consequently costs claimed in respect of work done before 2 May 1973 are not in respect of anything done by Mr Smith.

Throughout the relevant period Mr Smith was held out as being a partner in the firm. There can be no doubt, therefore, that he continued as a principal to be subject to all liabilities incurred by the firm. But equally it must have been the intention of all parties concerned that he should continue to enjoy the rights of a principal and to participate in the fruits of the labours of all the partners in the firm as well as those of its employees. This being the factual position it is not, in my judgment, possible to rely on the operation of s 34 of the Partnership Act 1890, as having terminated the vital relationship of principal and agent between Mr Smith and his partners the existence of which is decisive in determining affirmatively that, for the purpose of ss 18(2)*(b)* and 23 of the Solicitors Act 1957, the conduct of the defendant's litigation was 'done by him in the course of acting as a solicitor'.

If a solicitor, A, practised in his own name but employed B, another solicitor, as a salaried assistant, it is clear that no costs could be recovered in respect of litigation carried on at a time when A held no practising certificate, notwithstanding that B had had the entire conduct of the litigation without supervision from A and that the client had been aware of and content with this situation. A's name would be on the record as the solicitor acting. It would be clear throughout that B was acting as agent for A as principal. In these circumstances, whatever was done in the conduct of the litigation would be done by A acting as a solicitor. I find it impossible to see any valid distinction in principle between this situation and the situation where A and B are not employer and employee but are partners. In this latter case the names of A and B or the name of their firm would be on the record. Here again it would be clear that B was acting not solely on his own behalf, but on behalf of himself and A as joint principals. Here again what was done in the conduct of the litigation would be done by both A and B and thus, A, being unqualified, would fall within the disabling provisions of s 18(2)*(b)* and s 23 of the 1957 Act. B could not circumvent this by claiming, contrary to the fact that he was acting on his own account and in his own name alone.

In the words of Waller LJ:

Section 34 of the Partnership Act 1890, to which counsel for the plaintiffs drew our attention, reads as follows: 'A partnership is in every case dissolved by the happening of any event which makes it unlawful for the business of the firm to be carried on or for the members of the firm to carry it on in partnership.'

When the words of the section say 'A partnership is . . . dissolved' by the happening of an event making it illegal, does the fact that the partners were unaware of the circumstances make any difference? There are three cases to which I would refer which give some assistance about this. In *Hill v Clifford*, which was an action for dissolution of a dentists' partnership when one of the partners had been struck off the register, Sir Gorell Barnes P said (1907) 2 Ch 236 at 255): 'By s 34 of the Partnership Act, 1890, a partnership is in every case dissolved by the happening of any event which makes it unlawful for the business of the firm to be carried on or for the members of the firm to carry it on in partnership. As the Cliffords have ceased to be registered or entitled to be registered under the Act, and can no longer call themselves dentists and are liable to penalties if they do, it may perhaps be said that an event has happened which makes it unlawful for the business of the firm to be carried on by them, and that this may be so even though the defendants' names do not appear in the style of the firm . . . It is idle to say that the partners can still do work of the kind performed by dentists without calling themselves dentists. The deed is a deed for a partnership as dentists, which cannot really be carried on any longer.'

After referring to the statement of Lord Reading CJ in *R v Kupfer*, he continued:

So that Lord Reading CJ clearly took the view that the moment the partnership became illegal it was dissolved. And, inferentially, dissolved whether the partners knew or not. It is true that in that case the facts were known and knowledge of the law was to be presumed, whereas in the present case there is no evidence as to whether the facts were known or not. Nevertheless in my opinion this does not affect the principle . . . Although these cases do not decide the question they do tend to show that the knowledge or otherwise of partners does not affect the dissolution. It takes place by force of law.

If the partnership was dissolved by force of law and since it is illegal for someone who is not qualified to be in partnership with a solicitor, it is inevitable in my view that if there is a partnership of solicitors it cannot include the unqualified man. I do not find the effect of s 5 of the Partnership Act 1890 to provide any obstacle to the view that I have expressed.

I do not find the doctrine of holding out to be inconsistent with this view. 'The doctrine of holding out only applies in favour of persons who have dealt with a firm on the faith that the person whom they seek to make liable is a member of it.' The fact, if it be the fact, that Mr Smith was held out as being a partner might well make the other partners liable for his actions in contract because they were holding him out as a partner. Similarly, insofar as he was holding himself out as a partner he would be making himself liable for the debts of the firm. But in each case this would not be because he was a partner but because on the facts he was being held out. When the different question is asked, was there a partnership so that the acts of the others must have been the acts of Mr Smith, my answer is no. There was no partnership. Accordingly s 5 of the Partnership Act 1890 has no application.

Megaw LJ, forming the other half of the majority decision, stated:

The answer to the defendant's submission, on the facts of this case is, in my opinion, provided by reference, first, to the provisions of the Partnership Act 1890 to which counsel for the plaintiffs drew our attention. Section 34 of the 1890 Act, which Bridge and Waller LJJ have already read, produces the result, on the facts of this case, that the existing partnership was dissolved on 1 January 1973. Thereafter a solicitors' partnership including Mr Smith could not legally be created until he again became a qualified person by holding a current practising certificate. That does not mean that the remaining partners in the plaintiff firm could not be, or were not, thereafter partners lawfully carrying on the business of solicitors in partnership with one another. Though none of them realised it, by operation of law the old partnership was dissolved, and a new partnership came into being by conduct. Mr Smith was not a partner. By statute, the partnership, including him as a partner, was dissolved. What is dissolved by statute cannot be recreated by the courts. Though Mr Smith, no doubt unconscious of the problem, as were the remaining partners, continued to act as though he were a partner, he was not a partner, for statute precluded him; and no conduct of his could override the statute so as to bring him in again as a partner by conduct, so long as he was not a qualified person. For the strict purposes of the 1890 Act, he was not a partner.

But, of course, Mr Smith held himself out as being a partner; and the remaining partners in the new partnership, reconstituted by conduct, held Mr Smith out as being a partner. They did so in ignorance of the statutory bar on his being a partner. But that does not make it one whit the less a plain holding out.

But what is the effect of a holding out of someone as being a partner? A holding out is relevant, and relevant only, as an estoppel. As it is put in *Lindley on the Law of Partnership*:

> 'The doctrine that a person holding himself out as a partner, and thereby inducing others to act on the faith of his representations, is liable to them as if he were in fact a partner is nothing more than an illustration of the general principle of estoppel by conduct.'

For an estoppel to exist it is necessary to show, not only that there has been an unequivocal representation (here the holding out), but also that the person seeking to assert an estoppel has acted on the faith of the representation: *Freeman v Cooke*. This requirement is stressed by Lord Blackburn in his speech in *Scarf v Jardine* ((1882) 7 App Cas 345 at 357) where he says: 'I put emphasis on those last words "against those who acted upon the faith that the authority continued".'

In the present case, the defendant cannot say that he, in January 1973, instructed the plaintiff firm on the faith of the representation, the holding out, that Mr Smith was a partner; nor that he suffered any detriment. His own case, as was pointed out to us by counsel for the plaintiffs, was that he instructed one particular partner, Mr James, who has since died.

. . . So though there was a holding out, a continued holding out, of Mr Smith as being a partner when he was not, there is no estoppel in favour of the defendant on the facts of this case. It is not that the defendant is estopped from alleging the holding out. He is not. It is that the holding out was irrelevant because the defendant's own assertion as to his state of mind involves that he did not rely on it. We are not here concerned with any question as to the burden of proof, or as to presumptions, in relation to reliance on a holding out. As the defendant did not rely on the holding out and as, in law, Mr Smith was not a partner, the partners in the new partnership which had come into existence before the defendant gave his instructions, are not contaminated so as to lose their entitlement to profit costs for work done, not being work done by Mr Smith, by reason of any question of partnership between them and the temporarily unqualified Mr Smith.

. . . Mr Smith became a partner again, by the conduct of himself and the other plaintiffs, immediately on the issue, belatedly, of his practising certificate on 2 May 1973 . . .

3.24.7 By mutual consent

Since a partnership is created by consent, it could be dissolved by the mutual agreement of all the partners. This, again, is an affirmation of the general rule that mutual agreement may discharge a contract.

3.24.8 By court order

Section 35 of the Act lists instances when a partnership may be dissolved through court decree on application by a partner. These are as follows below.

(i) *Lunacy or unsoundness of mind*

Section 35*(a)* states that where a partner is found lunatic by inquisition or cognition, or is shown to the satisfaction of the court to be of permanently unsound mind, an application may be made on behalf of that partner by his next friend or person having title to intervene or any other partner for the partnership to be dissolved. What is important to note is that the lunacy and unsoundness of mind of a partner do not *ipso facto* dissolve the partnership. The lunatic partner will continue to have all the rights and obligations under the partnership until a dissolution decree is made.

Whether the lunacy or insanity of a dormant or sleeping partner could justify the granting of a decree of dissolution may not be free from doubt.

(ii) *Permanent incapacity of a partner*

Under s 35(1) permanent incapacity of a partner, other than the partner making the application, is a ground for the grant of a decree of dissolution. This rule is premised on the footing that when partnerships are created partners would attend diligently to the partnership business. Where a partner becomes permanently incapable of performing his duties as a partner, for example, through blindness, deafness or paralysis, it should be justified to dissolve the partnership. A sleeping or dormant partner who becomes permanently incapacitated would probably not be caught by this rule since he does not in any case take part in the partnership business. He should, however, be able to take his 'part of the partnership contract'.

(iii) *Partner's misconduct*

Where a partner conducts himself in a manner likely to prejudicially affect the partnership business, the court may on application of one or other of the 'innocent' partners dissolve the partnership. As in the case of permanent incapacity, the affected or guilty partner is not entitled to file the application for dissolution. This is spelt out in s 35*(c)*.

Although the nature of conduct that could persuade a court to make a dissolution order under s 35*(c)* are not mentioned or suggested, it appears that any form of misconduct which is likely to negatively affect the carrying on of partnership business may suffice. Bouncing cheques, misapplying clients' money, street fights and such conduct would probably be sufficient to persuade a court to decree the dissolution of a law practice partnership.

(iv) *Breach of the partnership agreement*

Where a partner wilfully and persistently commits a breach of the partnership agreement or he otherwise conducts himself in matters relating to the partnership business in such a manner that it is not reasonably practicable for the other partner or partners to carry on the business in partnership with him, then the innocent partner/partners could apply to court for dissolution of the partnership. Various forms of conduct could justify an application to court under this rule. For example, constant wilful refusal by a partner to perform his duties as set out in the partnership articles could be a good ground. This rule is provided for in s 35*(d)*.

(v) *Partnership business carried out at a loss*

Under s 35*(e)* the court may dissolve a partnership where it is satisfied that the business of the firm cannot be carried on except at a loss. This provision should be interpreted strictly, as was the case in *Handyside v Campbell*[137] when the Chancery Division held that for the ground mentioned in s 35*(e)* to come into operation, the practical impossibility of making a profit must be proved.

3.25 REALISATION OF THE ASSETS OF THE PARTNERSHIP

Notwithstanding the dissolution of a partnership, where assets remain undistributed, the duty of good faith between the partners continues. In the case of *Don King Productions Inc v Warren and Others*,[138] W and two other defendants appealed, contending inter alia that the rights of the partnership ceased on the date of its dissolution, so that thereafter neither the benefit nor the proceeds obtained from the exploitation of any agreement could be partnership assets. Morritt LJ stated:

> [H]e submits that the rights of the partnership, whatever they were, ceased on the date of dissolution so that thereafter neither the benefit nor the proceeds obtained from the exploitation of any management or promotion agreement nor any renewal thereof could be assets of the partnership ... he submitted that ... management and promotion agreements concluded by either partner in the period between the dissolution and the completion of the winding up with a boxer with whom there was such an agreement at the date of the dissolution were not partnership assets, whether pursuant to the rule in *Keech v Sandford* or otherwise.
>
> I agree with the statement of principle of Pennycuick V-C in *Thompson's Trustee in Bankruptcy v Heaton* [1974] 1 All ER 1239 at 1249, [1974] 1 WLR 605 at 613: 'The fiduciary relation here [between partners] arises not from a trust of property but from the duty of good faith which each partner owes to the other. It is immaterial for this purpose in which partner the legal estate in the leasehold interest concerned is vested. What then is the position when a partnership is dissolved but there remains property of the former partnership which has not been realised? The general principle I think, is correctly stated in (*Lindley The Law of Partnership* (13th edn, 1971) pp 615, 616), in the following terms: "Upon the dissolution of a partnership, and in the absence of any agreement to the contrary, it has been seen ... (4) That, for the purposes of winding up, the partnership is deemed to continue; the good faith and honourable conduct due from every partner to his co-partners during the continuance of the partnership being equally

---

[137] [1901] 17 TLR 623.
[138] [1999] 2 All ER 218.

due so long as its affairs remain unsettled; and that which was partnership property before, continuing to be so for the purpose of dissolution, as the rights of the partners require." It necessarily follows, I think, that where the property of a dissolved partnership includes a leasehold interest then, subject of any other arrangement which may be made between the partners concerning that interest, each of the former partners owes the same obligation to the other former partners in respect of that interest as he did while the leasehold interest remained the partnership property and, accordingly, he is under the same limitations with regard to the purchase of the reversion as he would have been had the partnership still been subsisting.'

His statement of principle, as well as his conclusion in that case, was further considered and upheld by the High Court of Australia in *Chan v Zacharia* (1984) 154 CLR 178. Deane J said (at 198):

'The variations between more precise formulations of the principle governing the liability to account are largely the result of the fact that what is conveniently regarded as the one "fundamental rule" embodies two themes. The first is that which appropriates for the benefit of the person to whom the fiduciary duty is owed any benefit or gain obtained or received by the fiduciary in circumstances where there existed a conflict of personal interest and fiduciary duty or a significant possibility of such conflict: the objective is to preclude the fiduciary from being swayed by considerations of personal interest. The second is that which requires the fiduciary to account for any benefit or gain obtained or received by reason of or by use of his fiduciary position or of opportunity or knowledge resulting from it: the objective is to preclude the fiduciary from actually misusing his position for his personal advantage. Notwithstanding authoritative statements to the effect that the "use of fiduciary position" doctrine is but an illustration or part of a wider "conflict of interest and duty" doctrine (see, e.g., *(Boardman v Phipps* [1966] 3 All ER 721 at 756, [1967] 2 AC 46 at 123; *New Zealand Netherlands Society 'Oranje' Inc v Kuys* [1973] 2 All ER 1222 at 1225, [1973] 1 WLR 1126 at 1129)), the two themes, while overlapping, are distinct. Neither theme fully comprehends the other and a formulation of the principle by reference to one only of them will be incomplete. Stated comprehensively in terms of the liability to account, the principle of equity is that a person who is under a fiduciary obligation must account to the person to whom the obligation is owed for any benefit or gain (i) which has been obtained or received in circumstances where a conflict or significant possibility of conflict existed between his fiduciary duty and his personal interest in the pursuit or possible receipt of such a benefit or gain or (ii) which was obtained or received by use or by reason of his fiduciary position or of opportunity or knowledge resulting from it. Any such benefit or gain is held by the fiduciary as constructive trustee . . .'

It is appropriate to consider separately each of the strands to which Deane J referred. The first question is, therefore, whether 'the renewal agreement' was obtained or received in circumstances where a conflict or significant possibility of conflict existed between the partner's duty of good faith and his personal interest in the pursuit or possible receipt of the renewal agreement. In my view the answer to that question is obviously in the affirmative. The duty of a partner to renew a management or promotion agreement for the benefit of the partnership so as to facilitate the beneficial winding up of its affairs, cf s 38 of the 1890 Act, obviously conflicts with the interest of the partner seeking to set up in business in the same field to obtain such contracts for himself. As I have observed before the benefit of such agreements is the key with which to unlock the profits to be made from those who wish to see the fights.

The second strand raises the question whether the renewal obtained by the partner for his own benefit was obtained or received by use or by reason of his fiduciary position or of any opportunity or knowledge resulting from it. In my view it is plain that, *prima facie*, that question must be answered in the affirmative too. The successful management or promotion of a boxer is likely to generate goodwill in both the legal as well as the literal sense. Such goodwill is likely to lead to a renewal with the same manager or promoter rather than another. But the goodwill and the opportunity and advantage to which it gives rise is the property of the partnership.

3.25.1 Assistance in getting partnership assets

Upon dissolution one partner is entitled by action in the firm's name to get in the firm's assets on giving the other partners an indemnity against the costs of the action. The other partners must assist. The authority of the partners continues to a limited extent even after dissolution (s 38). If the dissolution is caused by death or bankruptcy of the firm, this authority to wind up the business devolves on the surviving or solvent partners alone, to the exclusion of the bankrupt partner and of the personal representatives, or trustee in bankruptcy, of the deceased or bankrupt (s 14(2)).

The continuing authority of the partners may be taken away by the court if the parties fall out, or if special grounds are shown by the personal representatives of a deceased partner or the trustee in bankruptcy of a bankrupt partner either by the appointment of (1) a receiver to get in the outstanding assets, or (2) a receiver and manager to conduct the entire winding up. The appointment of a manager (takes over and carries on the entire business) requires a stronger case than the appointment of a receiver (takes the income and pays the necessary outgoings). The appointment of a receiver practically brings the trade to a dead stop, so if the trade is to continue a manager ought to be appointed instead.

3.25.2 Goodwill

Assets include not only the stock in trade and book debts, furniture, tools and machinery but also the 'goodwill' of the business. Goodwill has been described variously as 'the whole advantage whatever it may be, of the reputation and connection of the firm, which may have been built up by years of honest work or gained by lavish expenditure of money'. Generally, and in the absence of an agreement, the goodwill must be sold. There is said, however, to be an exception in the case of business of a very personal nature, like that of solicitors, so that on dissolution each partner retains whatever benefit may be derived from goodwill.

Sale of the goodwill does not prevent the seller from carrying on business in competition with that of the purchaser, but the former partners may be restrained from soliciting any person who was a customer of the old firm. On a purchase of goodwill, the purchaser usually obtains the premises of the old firm and the right to use the name of the old firm and, in all cases, the right to represent himself as successor of the old firm.

Goodwill is a partnership asset and, on the death or retirement of a partner, it does not pass by survival to the continuing partners but must be bought by them. If on dissolution of partnership, the goodwill is not sold, each of the partners is entitled to carry on business under the name of the old firm and canvass old customers, provided he does not expose his former partners to any risk of liability under the doctrine of 'holding out'.[139] For this reason, when there is an agreement that on dissolution the partnership assets, including goodwill, shall be taken by one partner at a valuation, the goodwill must be valued on the footing that the outgoing partner is entitled to carry on a rival business but cannot use the firm name or solicit its customers.[140]

The rights and duties between the vendor and the purchaser of goodwill, in the absence of an agreement to the contrary, are:

(1) The vendor may carry on a similar business to that sold in competition with the purchaser, but he must not use the old firm name or represent himself as continuing the old business. An executor, carrying out his testator's contract to sell the goodwill of a business, is, equally with the testator, under a duty to do nothing to destroy or deprecate the value of the goodwill which he has sold.[141] The vendor may not canvass the customers of the old firm or solicit any customer of the old firm to deal with him.[142]

(2) The vendor may advertise the fact that he is carrying on business as long as he does not offend the two preceding rules.

(3) When a partnership is dissolved on the terms that one partner will take over the assets, the other partners must not solicit the customers of the firm because assets includes goodwill.

3.25.3 Account

Where by agreement one or more members of the firm continue the business on the terms of paying off the share of the outgoing or deceased partners(s), ascertained on a certain agreed basis, no final account and distribution is necessary because the agreement is substituted for it.[143]

---

[139] *Burchell v Wilde* [1900] 1 Ch 551.
[140] *Re David and Matthews* [1899] 1 Ch 37.
[141] See *Boorne v Wicker* [1927] 1 Ch 667.
[142] *Trego v Hunt* [1896] AC 7.
[143] *Law v Law* [1905] 1 Ch 140.

But where there is a true dissolution of the firm, each partner going his own way and the partnership property being sold, then a general account is necessary, and may be claimed not only by living partners and the assignees of the shares of living partners (s 31(2)) but also by the personal representatives of deceased partners.

The remedy of taking an account is the only one available. Thus, in *Green v Hertzog*[144] a partnership was dissolved and one partner, who had lent money to the firm, sued the former partners for its return. She claimed the sum at common law and did not use the procedure of taking accounts under s 44 of the Partnership Act. The Court of Appeal held that there was no right of action at common law and the claim failed. The money could be recovered only by taking accounts under s 44.

Where there is no express agreement to the contrary, the profits of the firm must be ascertained on the basis of the sums actually paid and received in that year. The date when the work, in respect of which the sums have been received, was done is immaterial.[145]

3.26 DISTRIBUTION OF ASSETS

The right in s 39 is said to be in the nature of an equitable lien existing throughout the partnership, although it does not become active until dissolution, when it immediately attaches to what was the partnership property on that date. It is in fact a form of floating lien analogous to a floating charge created by a debenture of a limited company and is lost by the conversion of the assets into the separate property of one of the partners. The lien is enforceable, in the absence of agreement to the contrary, by a sale of the whole of the assets.

In cases where a partner has paid a premium to enter into the partnership, part of the premium may sometimes be repayable (s 40). Where a partnership is dissolved for fraud or misrepresentation, the partner defrauded is given certain rights (s 41).

An outgoing partner may be entitled to share in the profits of the partnership made after the dissolution. Section 42(1) of the Act reads as follows:

> Where any member of a firm has died or otherwise ceased to be a partner, and the surviving or continuing partners carry on the business of the firm with its capital or assets without any final settlement of accounts as between the firm and the outgoing partner or his estate, then, in the absence of any agreement to the contrary, the outgoing partner or his estate is entitled at the option of himself or his representatives to such share of the profits made since the dissolution as the Court may find to be attributable to

---

[144] [1954] 1 WLR 1309.
[145] See *Badham v Williams* [1902] 86 LT 191.

the use of his share of the partnership assets, or to interest at the rate of five per cent per annum on the amount of his share of the partnership assets.

In *Sandhu v Gill*[146] Lightman J explained this provision thus:

This is an appeal from a decision dated 24 September 2004 ('the decision') of Master Bowles. It is concerned with the construction of section 42 of the Partnership Act 1890 ('the Act') and in particular with the entitlement of an outgoing partner in respect of the profits made by a continuing partner attributable to his use of partnership assets between dissolution of the partnership and completion of its winding up . . . .

The issue between the parties focuses on the meaning of the words 'share of the partnership assets'.

It was clear and common ground that Mr Sandhu was entitled to share the capital profit of £250,000: the full proceeds of sale falls to be applied in accordance with s 44 of the Act (see *Barclays Bank Trust Co Ltd v Bluff* [1981] 3 All ER 232, [1982] Ch 172). But there was an issue as to the entitlement of Mr Sandhu to a share of the revenue profits made by Mr Gill between 12 April 1999 and the conclusion of the winding up.

[11] At common law subject to the provision of the partnership agreement each partner has a proprietary interest in all the assets of the partnership. The size of the proprietary interest is determined by the provisions of the partnership agreement, but in default of such provision each partner has an equal share. In the present case under the deed Mr Gill and Mr Sandhu had (as would otherwise have been implied by law) equal proprietary interests in the assets of the partnership. The rights attaching to the proprietary interests of the partners are severely qualified by the rights of all partners regarding the use and application of the assets and their proceeds of sale arising from the partnership relationship now contained in the Act.

[12] On the dissolution of a partnership (in default of agreement to the contrary) the partners have not only the right, but the duty, to realise the partnership property and for the purpose of that realisation to carry on the business if it is necessary so to do: see *Re Bourne* [1906] 2 Ch 427 at 430 Vaughan Williams LJ. The part of the Act headed 'Dissolution of Partnership, and its consequences' embraces sections 32–44. Section 39 of the Act provides that on dissolution of a partnership every partner is entitled as against the other partners in the firm and all persons claiming through them in respect of their interests as partners to have the affairs of the partnership wound up and in particular to have the property of the partnership applied in payment of the debts and liabilities of the firm and to have the surplus assets after such payment applied in payment of what may be due to the partners respectively after deducting what may be due from them as partners to the firm. The provisions of section 39 must be read as being subject to any agreement of the partners to the contrary. The parties may agree that on dissolution on the death, retirement or expulsion of an outgoing partner his share shall accrue or be sold to the continuing partners and that in respect of that accrual or sale a price shall be payable to the outgoing partner or his estate. In that situation (subject to any agreement between the parties) the amount due from the continuing partners in respect of the outgoing partner's share shall constitute a debt accruing at the date of dissolution. Questions have been raised as to the true construction of s 43 of the Act. In my judgment section 43 merely declares the law to this effect: see *Lindley & Banks on Partnership* (18th edn, 2002) p 579–922 paras 23–34.

[13] Section 44 of the Act sets out the rules applicable in default of any agreement to the contrary for the distribution of the assets on final settlement of accounts between the

---

[146] [2005] 1 All ER 990.

partners. The first rule provides for payment of losses. This rule has no application in this case. The second rule provides that the assets of the firm shall be applied in the following manner and order:

'1 In paying the debts and liabilities of the firm to persons who are not partners therein:

2 In paying to each partner rateably what is due from the firm to him for advances as distinguished from capital:

3 In paying to each partner rateably what is due from the firm to him in respect of capital:

4 The ultimate residue if any, shall be divided among the partners in the proportion in which profits are divisible.'

[14] The Act however recognises that winding up and discontinuance of business may not immediately follow winding up. No provision is required when the continuation of business is by agreement of the partners for the benefit of the partnership. The partnership business in such circumstances is to be treated as continuing. Where there is no such agreement, there is a limit upon the entitlement of either partner to continue the partnership business.

[15] Section 38 of the Act authorises for partners to carry on the business of the partnership after dissolution so far as this may be necessary for the beneficial winding up of the partnership and for the completion of unfinished transactions, but not otherwise. A continuing partner who carries on the business after dissolution otherwise than for this limited purpose without the consent of the outgoing partner does so without the authority of the partnership and accordingly he carries on the business on his own account and he may be held liable to account to the outgoing partner.

[16] The position in equity prior to the Act was that the continuing partner in such a situation was liable to account as a fiduciary to the outgoing partner in respect of his unauthorised use for his own benefit of the assets of the partnership. In *Willett v Blanford* (1842) 1 Hare 253, 66 ER 1027 Wigram V-C held that the quantum of the entitlement of the outgoing partner in respect of the profits made by the continuing partner must be determined by reference to what is right and equitable between the parties in all the circumstances and in particular the extent that the profits are attributable to use of the outgoing partner's share of the partnership assets. In subsequent cases there was no strict uniformity in approach to what was right and equitable in all the circumstances and cases arose when it was held right and equitable to divide the profits between the parties in accordance with their contributions to the capital of the partnership: see eg *Yates v Finn* (1880) 13 Ch D 839. This approach can on occasion be seen reflected in other authorities and the textbooks: see Pollock's *Digest of the Law of Partnership* (11th edn, 1920) p 140.

But the law in this regard was firmly established very much as stated by Wigram V-C in *Manley v Sartori* [1927] 1 Ch 157, [1926] All ER Rep 661 and by Parliament in s 42 of the Act.

[17] In *Manley's* case, the death of a partner dissolved a partnership, but the surviving partners continued the partnership business on their own account. The question arose as to the entitlement of the personal representatives of the deceased partner to a share of the profits earned between the death of the partner and the winding up. Romer J said ([1927] 1 Ch 157 at 162–166, [1926] All ER Rep 661 at 661–663):

'Where . . . the surviving partners, instead of realizing the assets and distributing the proceeds amongst the parties in accordance with their rights and interests, choose to carry on the business and make profits by virtue of the employment of any of the partnership assets, then, subject no doubt to making a proper allowance to the surviving partners for their trouble in so carrying on the business, such profits belong to all the persons interested in the partnership assets by means of which the profits have been earned in accordance with their rights and interests in those assets; that is to say, proportionately to their interests in those assets. That has been laid down in numerous cases and is affirmed by s. 42 of the Partnership Act of 1890 ... [The] profits ... were not divisible between the parties in accordance with their rights and interests in profits earned while the partnership was a going concern ... Now the rights of the deceased partner or his legal personal representatives are rights over all the assets of the partnership. He has an unascertained interest in every single asset of the partnership, and it is not right to regard him as being merely entitled to a particular sum of cash ascertained from the balance-sheet of the partnership as drawn up at the date of his death ... [as] was pointed out by Wigram V-C in *Willett v Blanford*, it does not necessarily follow that because the surviving partners have been carrying on the business the profits or the whole of the profits are attributable to the use of the partnership assets ... it may well be that in a particular case profits have been earned by the surviving partner, not by reason of the use of any asset of the partnership, but purely and solely by reason of the exercise of skill and diligence by the surviving partner; or it may appear that the profits have been wholly or partly earned not by reason of the use of the assets of the partnership, but by reason of the fact that the surviving partner himself provided further assets and further capital by means of which the profit has been earned. Those profits, so far as earned by sources outside the partnership assets, are not profits in which the executors of the deceased partner could be entitled to any share ... where surviving partners continue to carry on the business, *prima facie* they are carrying it on by reason of their possession of the assets of the partnership; and the executors of the deceased partner are *prima facie* entitled to a share of the profits proportionate to his share in the assets of the partnership. It is for the surviving partners to show, if they can, that the profits have been earned wholly or partly by means other than the utilization of the partnership assets.'

[18] The law as stated by Romer J was reaffirmed, albeit obiter, by Nourse LJ in his judgment in *Popat v Shonchhatra* [1997] 3 All ER 800 at 806, [1997] 1 WLR 1367 at 1373–4 with which the other members of the Court of Appeal agreed and by the Privy Council in *Pathirana v Pathirana* [1967] 1 AC 233 at 240–1, [1966] 3 WLR 666 at 671–672. The words in section 42 'share of partnership assets' means the outgoing partner's share in the proprietary ownership of assets belonging to the partnership. This construction is confirmed by the fact that, where in the Act reference is intended to be made to a partner's interest in 'net assets' or the surplus of the partnership assets after satisfying the partnership liabilities, this is expressly stated: see section 41(*a*).

KEY POINTS

- A partnership exists where two or more persons (natural or artificial) associate for a mutual business objective.
- The purpose of the association of the two or more persons is to make a profit.
- A partnership typically entails direct participation in the success and profits of the business and involvement (to one extent or another) in the running of the firm.

Chapter 4

CO-OPERATIVE SOCIETIES

4.1 INTRODUCTION

Co-operatives societie (co-operatives) as a form of business association have a long and rich history. They have been a natural option for business co-operation by communities desiring to achieve common economic social and cultural needs while the members retain democratic control of the business entity. They are generally viewed as voluntary and autonomous associations of people open to all persons able to use their services and willing to assume and accept the responsibility which goes with member-ship without discrimination on the basis of gender, social, political, racial or other status.

Co-operatives have occupied Zambian business life for many years. It cannot be denied that, though the idea of formalised co-operatives was one that originated elsewhere and was imported into Zambia as part of the colonial heritage, some form of community co-operation short of co-operatives existed long before the white settlers came to Northern Rhodesia.

To fully appreciate the factors that inspired the development of co-operatives, one must examine the types of economy which facilitated the development of these organisations. A historical account of the changes in policies is necessary to provide an understanding of the origin of some of the problems that confront co-operatives today. This will be considered later. First, it is imperative to consider the definition and the nature of the business enterprise itself.

4.2 DEFINITION, NATURE AND THEORIES OF CO-OPERATIVE SOCIETIES

A co-operative is a business organisation owned and operated by a group of individuals for their mutual benefit.[1] The word co-operative derives from the idea of co-operation. Co-operation is itself a vague concept and has a wide range of meanings. Back in the 1890s it could mean anything from a harmonious relationship between capital and labour to 'amicable' industrial

---

[1] Arthur O'Sullivan and Steven M Sheffrin *Economics: Principles in Action* (2003).

relations procedures and profit sharing. It could also stand for the replacement of capitalism through worker-owned and managed production enterprises or the organisation of consumers in co-operative stores.

Defined as an autonomous association of persons united voluntarily to meet their common economic, social and cultural needs and aspirations through a jointly owned and democratically controlled enterprise, co-operatives present a unique vehicle or business association guided by a set of co-operative principles, values and ethics. These principles, values and ethics provide the co-operative identity, making co-operatives different from other forms of business enterprises.

Co-operative principles form the bedrock of co-operative societies and will be examined in a little more detail below. As regards values of the members of a co-operative society these should always manifest in the members of the co-operative. They signify the bond trust and unity of the co-operators. They include honesty, openness, social responsibility and caring for others, while the values that animate a co-operative society include self-help, democracy, equality, equity, and solidarity. Self-help entails the will and capability to improve living standards through joint action, while democracy refers to the right of the members to participate in decision making. Equality refers to equal rights and opportunities amongst the members. Equity means fair distribution of income and power in the co-operative society. Solidarity entails strength in self-help and collective responsibility. These virtues are closely linked to the co-operative principles.

The International Co-operative Alliance (ICA) defined the term 'co-operative' in its Statement on Co-operative Identity as an autonomous association of persons united voluntarily to meet their common economic, social and cultural needs and aspirations through a jointly owned and democratically controlled enterprise.[2] As will be seen later this is an important institution one of whose objectives is to encourage and promote co-operation among co-operatives.

Section 2 of the Zambian Co-operative Societies Act 20 of 1998 defines a co-operative as 'any enterprise or organisation owned collectively by its members and managed for their joint socio-economic benefit and whose activities are not prohibited by law'.

A co-operative society is defined in the same section as a co-operative registered under the Act as such. Arising from the foregoing, a co-operative society as we conceive it today is a form of business association available

---

[2] ICA Statement on Co-operative Identity.

for any group of persons wishing to set up business in Zambia. Whether it is the most suitable vehicle through which a business should be operated will depend on various factors which the persons behind the business have in mind. Like any other form of business association, co-operatives have their own advantages and limitations. It is therefore important that clarity of thought and purpose should characterise the promotion phase of such enterprises.

The co-operative idea is not one single idea, but a combination of several ideas and concepts. It is easy to conceive of a co-operative as a communal group of mutually dependent individuals who come together for the purpose of exploiting their strength of numbers to achieve a set economic goal. Charles Gide,[3] a leading French economist and historian of economic thought, was a tireless supporter and champion of the co-operative movement. He was at the centre of support for the progressive development of both agriculture and consumer co-operatives in the early parts of the twentieth century. His works culminated in the book *Consumer Co-operatives* which was first published in French in 1904 and in English in 1921 and is largely viewed as a classic in the field of co-operative economics. He remarked that 'a co-operative organization is a group of people working for mutual, economic, social and educational goals through a business-company'.[4]

It is evident from various definitions given of the term co-operative that the active involvement of people (members) is the foundation of a co-operative society or organisation. This involvement springs from a mutual need which can be satisfied through collective self-help. Self-reliance and self-help are in fact hallmarks of co-operatives.

Co-operatives have existed primarily to serve the interests of their members. They were originally generally modelled on socialistic rather than capitalistic principles. They aim to improve the economic conditions of their members. It is for this reason that they are at times laconically referred to as 'poor men's businesses'. As co-operatives are owned by their members, all the economic benefits generated by their activities are kept within the community.

4.3 THE EARLY CO-OPERATIVE MOVEMENT

As already mentioned, co-operatives have existed for a long time in the history of business associations. In fact, they can be traced as far back as

---

[3] (1847-1932).

[4] Quoted in I Johanson & G Nygren *Do Rural Zambian Multipurpose Co-operatives Function Beneficially for their Members? Case studies of six primary co-operative societies in the Northern Province of Zambia. Report from a minor field study* (1988).

human beings have been associating together for their mutual benefit. In Great Britain as far back as 1761 the Fenwick Weavers' Society was formed in East Ayrshire, Scotland principally to sell oatmeal to the local working community. Eventually it offered an expanded range of services to include savings and provision of loans and education to its members.

Other notable co-operatives that emerged include that introduced by the Welsh social reformer Robert Owen who in 1810 purchased New Lanark Mill and introduced better labour standards including discounted retail shops where profits were passed on to his employees.[5] Other co-operative communities were set up in Glasgow, Indiana and Hampshire, although ultimately they were unsuccessful.[6] One of the earliest successful consumer co-operative societies was the Rochdale Society of Equitable Pioneers which was founded in 1844 by a group of 28 flannel weavers and other artisans in Rochdale, England, near Manchester. This movement, which followed an unsuccessful strike in that year, was started to combat low wages, high prices, and poor-quality goods. The co-operators desired to supply better quality basic commodities such as sugar, oil and other consumables to their members at fair prices. This was in the wake of the industrial revolution which was increasingly forcing skilled workers out of employment into the fringes of poverty. These men and women decided to associate together and open their own shop to sell consumer food items which they could otherwise not afford. Their interest in co-operation was built upon the foundations laid by Robert Owen, who believed that ideal communities based on co-operation rather than competition would eliminate unemployment and pauperism and create a prosperous and harmonious community.[7] Needless to say that this view contrasted sharply with that held by that proponent of absolute economic liberalism, the founder of modern economics, Adam Smith, who canonised the theory that free competition was a fundamental assumption in any market economy and that effective competition brings about superior economic performance which is a prerequisite for a satisfactory social policy.

The Rochdale co-operators contributed £1 per person over a period of four months. With this capital of £28 they opened their store on 21 December 1844, with a very small selection of consumer items like candles, salt, butter, sugar, flour, and cereals. In a matter of months, they expanded significantly,

---

[5] 'Co-operative' available at http://en.wikipedia.org/wiki/co-operative (accessed on 22 October 2018).

[6] Ibid.

[7] See N Balnave 'Rochdale consumer co-operatives and Australian labour history' Conference Proceedings, University of Western Sydney Greg Patmore, University of Sydney.

and their stock and selection improved. They soon gained a reputation for stocking high quality consumer goods.

The Rochdale movement in England, despite several legal and economic obstacles, grew from strength to strength. Private retailers attempted to limit competition from the co-operatives by persuading wholesalers to stop or restrict supplies to the co-operatives. There were also concerns about relying upon private manufacturers more concerned with profits than product quality. So, the retail co-operatives established a Co-operative Wholesale Society (CWS) in England in 1863 and in Scotland in 1868.

Although indeed there were other co-operatives before and after the Rochdale Society of Equitable Pioneers, this particular co-operative is credited in the history of co-operatives as a prototype in the United Kingdom and the Commonwealth. The most memorable innovation brought about by this co-operative was the designing of the now famous Rochdale Principles which will be considered below. The formulation of these principles of co-operation was informed by the lessons learnt from previous unsuccessful attempts to sustain co-operatives. The Rochdale Principles have to this day formed the foundation upon which co-operatives the world over operate.

The wholesalers in England and Scotland who formed the CWS also operated on Rochdale principles such as a fixed rate of interest on capital. The wholesale societies ultimately became global enterprises with purchases of primary products from countries such as Australia and Canada and tea plantations in Sri Lanka and India. The English CWS also moved into banking and insurance. The retail co-operatives formed a Co-operative Union in 1872 for education, legal, propaganda and political purposes. A notable outcome of the Co-operative Union activities was the formation in 1883 of the Women's Co-operative Guild, which aimed to promote an interest by women in the co-operative movement and also protect female employees. Retail co-operatives even formed a Co-operative Party in 1917, which formally affiliated with the British Labour Party in 1927. By 1948 there were 1 030 retail co-operatives in the United Kingdom with 10 162 000 members.[8]

---

[8] Balnave quoting AMG Carr-Saunders, P Sargant Florence & R Peers *Consumers' Co-operation in Great Britain. An Examination of the British Co-operative Movement* 3 ed (1940) 156–7; DH Cole *The British Co-operative Movement in a Socialist Society* (1951) 24; H Heaton *Modern Economic History* (1921) 300–3; M Hilson 'Consumers and Politics: The Co-operative Movement in Plymouth, 1890-1920' (2002) 67(1) *Labour History Review* 7–27.

The Rochdale co-operative principles included the provision of capital by members at a fixed rate of interest; unadulterated, high quality or pure food to be supplied; cash purchases only and no credit; management based on democratic principles with 'one member one vote' rather than 'one vote one share'; and that a share of profits should be allotted to education.

4.4 THE CO-OPERATIVE PRINCIPLES

In 1895, the ICA was formed in Geneva-Switzerland. Arising from the experience of the Rochdale Society of Equitable Pioneers, the ICA conceived of principles which it prescribed for all organisations defining themselves as co-operative societies. These principles, otherwise known as the Rochdale Co-operative Principles, form the basic philosophical foundation which guides the development and operation of co-operative societies all over the world. These principles can be summarised as follows:

4.4.1 Voluntary and open membership

Membership of a co-operative is voluntary and open to anyone who can make use of its services without discrimination whatsoever on any ground. Potential members must however be ready to accept the responsibility of membership.

4.4.2 Democratic control

Co-operatives are based on democratic ideals and therefore their affairs are administered by persons elected by the members, or at least the directors must have been appointed in an agreed manner. All members enjoy equal voting rights, that is to say, one man one vote. Members actively take part in the formulation of the policies of the co-operative and in the decision-making process.

4.4.3 Members' economic participation

Members contribute equitably to, and democratically control, the capital of their co-operative. As a condition of membership, share capital invested in the co-operative society should receive only a strictly limited rate of interest with members normally receiving limited compensation, if any, on capital subscribed. Part of that capital will normally form the common property of the co-operative. Surpluses will be allocated for, among others, the development of the co-operative, through setting up reserves, some of which would be indivisible; and supporting other approved activities of the co-operative.

4.4.4 Autonomy and independence

Co-operatives are autonomous, self-help organisations controlled by their members. If they enter into agreements with other organisations, including governments, or raise capital from external sources, they do so on terms that ensure democratic control by their members and maintain their co-operative autonomy.

4.4.5 Education for members

The provision of education and training for its members, elected representatives, employees, and managers should be a key consideration for any co-operative. All co-operatives should make a clear position for the education, training and information of their members as well as the general public.

4.4.6 Co-operation among co-operatives

Naturally, co-operatives should be able to co-operate with others at local, national and international levels. In fact, the ICA was formed with the facilitation of this principle as one of its objectives.

4.4.7 Concern for the community

Co-operative societies must aim at serving and advancing the common interests of their members. The sustainable development of its community should be one of the chief goals of a co-operative. Such development should be carried out through policies approved by the membership.

4.5 CO-OPERATIVE DEVELOPMENT POLICY IN PRE-INDEPENDENT ZAMBIA

Most people in Africa live in rural areas and farming is the dominant means of earning a living. It is a truism that most rural subsistence farmers lack formal education and their income is generally low. It is therefore generally difficult for them to access loans, inputs and other related facilities. As a result, co-operatives, from inception, were seen as being an organised method to change this situation for most people, especially rural farmers.

The introduction of formal co-operatives in former British-controlled African societies is closely linked to the colonial period. The colonisers organised farmers in co-operatives to increase the production of food, to improve marketing, and quite often to provide for the workers in commercial industries. When most African countries attained independence, the co-operative movement continued to be pursued by the new African authorities.

These authorities saw co-operatives as a means of developing the continent. African governments greatly influenced the development of these institutions.

Whilst the rise of co-operatives in Europe resulted from voluntary engagement, it would appear that in Africa, this is attributed to public authorities. As Northern Rhodesia (as Zambia was called then) was under British rule for many years it is not surprising that the legal system in the territory was almost an extension of the legal system that obtained in the United Kingdom. The same applies to the co-operative legislation. Britain's first legislation on co-operatives was the Industrial and Provident Societies Act of 1852 and with that, co-operative societies were officially recognised.[9]

The success story of co-operatives in Britain moved the British government to think that co-operatives could be the solution to socio-economic problems in their colonies. Organised co-operatives in Northern Rhodesia (as it was then) did not develop by themselves, as they had done in Britain by the beginning of the nineteenth century, and the British government therefore felt it necessary to promote them by initiating and sponsoring self-help co-operatives. The co-operative rules in Northern Rhodesia like many other colonies, followed the British model of co-operative law with minor amendments relating to governmental involvement.

The promotion of co-operatives was also being advanced in India and the Indian Co-operative Societies Acts of 1904 and 1912 were already in place. These co-operative laws together with Britain's Industrial and Provident Societies Act, 1852 came to be applied in Northern Rhodesia. The Indian Acts were intended for the function of self-reliant co-operatives where the government provided technical knowledge and initiative. A government department was soon to be created in Northern Rhodesia for initiating, teaching and registration of co-operative societies.[10]

The driving force behind all this was the desire by the colonial government to provide cheap food for workers in the mines and other commercial enterprises in urban areas while also facilitating the marketing by white settler farmers of their agricultural produce.

The first co-operatives in this country can be traced as far back as 16 October 1914 when the North West Rhodesia Farmers' Co-operative Society was registered. This co-operative society was formed to serve the interests of white settler farmers as a means of marketing their agricultural produce to the Copperbelt region of Northern Rhodesia and the newly

---

[9] Johanson & Nygren *Do Rural Zambian Multipurpose Co-operatives Function Beneficially for their Members?* 16.

[10] The Department of Marketing and Co-operatives (1948).

developing copper mines in the Katanga region of the then Zaire (now Democratic Republic of Congo). Not surprisingly, colonial policy then was predominantly to protect the interests of the white settler community in Northern Rhodesia. This accounts for the initial trend which saw the emergence of co-operative societies amongst white settlers only. Inevitably, however, some co-operatives of small-scale African farmers also emerged. These African co-operatives were essentially renegade associations as they could not be formed under existing legislation. The formation of agricultural co-operatives by Africans was not permissible as Africans were not legally recognised as farmers.

Under the law[11] as it then stood, a farmer was defined as any person other than:
(a) an African; or
(b) any company or body of persons where Africans held the controlling interest.

As farming activities became more organised amongst the indigenous African communities and the need for organised marketing arrangements inevitable, the colonial administration was forced, in 1947, to recognise co-operatives amongst indigenous Africans. An effort by the British government to promote co-operatives in Northern Rhodesia moved the colonial office to publish, in 1946, a model Co-operative Societies Ordinance and a draft model of co-operative society rules to be used in the colony, based on the British Indian oo-operative law.

This ordinance was accepted with some amendments in 1948. The Department of Marketing and Co-operatives was established under the Ministry of Agriculture and Water Development for the registration and regulation of co-operative enterprises. The new Ordinance and the creation of a government department to register and regulate co-operative societies paved the way for the development of co-operative societies. The first indigenous African Co-operative Society, which was Chilenje African Town Store Co-operative Society, was registered on 10 February 1948. In that year alone, the number of co-operatives rose to 27. By 1958, there were 227 co-operatives.

Africans continued, however, to face obstacles in forming agricultural co-operatives. The biggest farmers' co-operative, the Northern Rhodesia Farmers' Union (NRFU), the forerunner to the Zambia National Farmers Union (ZNFU) was, not unexpectedly, essentially a union for the European

---

[11] Farmers Licensing Ordinance 30 of 1946 as amended in 1953.

commercial farmers at independence in 1964. It was recognised as the only representative organisation for the farming community in the territory.

4.6 CO-OPERATIVES IN THE POST-INDEPENDENCE PERIOD: 1964 TO 1991

At independence, the new government of President Kaunda under the United Independence Party (UNIP) viewed the creation of co-operatives as a tool for social and economic development. The newly independent Zambia embarked on a vigorous campaign to stir the formation of co-operatives to stimulate rural development. In 1965, President Kaunda appealed to the unemployed and small-scale farmers to form co-operatives. The operation of s 3 of the Farmers Licensing Ordinance which defined a 'farmer' was suspended by statutory instrument 381 of 1965 and in 1966 the Northern Rhodesia Farmers Union Incorporation (Repeal) Act was passed and came in operation on 7 October 1966. In 1966 a new Act abolished the colonial definition of a 'farmer' and all assets, liabilities and obligations of the NRFU were transferred to the Commercial Farmers Bureau of Zambia (CFB). This organisation was later to change its name to the Zambia National Union of Farmers. By 27 November 1964, there were seven agricultural producers, co-operative societies, one labour recruiting co-operative society, one consumer co-operative society and one rural credit co-operative society.

Still in 1965, on 17 January, a declaration, popularly known as the Chifubu Declaration, was made by the government encouraging the formation of co-operatives countrywide. This declaration resulted in the registration of an additional 468 co-operatives by the end of 1965. The rise continued, with 1 121 societies existing by the end of 1969.

The UNIP government continued to promote co-operative societies as an important stage of Zambia's economic revolution. Dr Kenneth Kaunda, addressing the National Council of UNIP at Mulungushi on 9 November 1968, explained the importance of co-operatives. For what it was worth, Dr Kaunda's speech on that occasion deserves to be reproduced in some detail. In his words:

> [V]ery often some of our people have believed that the co-operative approach to life was simply a way of earning more and more money through collective effort.
>
> True, this is important, but I think over and above this is the importance of the principle of collective effort in itself. Where people understand this, where people understand the value of this, they will be able to evolve a democratic system that was second to none. They will realize that individually the harshness of life, human or otherwise, will find them easy victims, but collectively it would take a lot of doing to exploit them.

Collectively, almost nothing is impossible [to attain]. We, in fact, like the old biblical saying, could move mountains into the seas.[12]

The President called upon all leaders to join co-operatives societies. These leaders included Members of Parliament, diplomatic envoys, public officers and other civil servants, as it was now 'obligatory':

[T]he next stage is that of involving every Member of Parliament. Those of you who are going to be nominated as candidates will have to sign a document to testify that you understand and accept that it is now obligatory for anyone of us who wants to be a Member of Parliament to be a member of a co-operative society, either in his own constituency or wherever he will be asked to serve.

May I add that this extends to the Foreign Service. Everyone, who becomes an Ambassador, Deputy Ambassador, or Counselor, must in future be a member of a co-operative society. All these will be required to help, if they are overseas, with the growth of their co-operative societies, or if they are Members of Parliament, actually lead their respective co-operative societies to success . . .

We will study how the civil service, the Army and the Police will in future participate in this as they are beginning to do now successfully and effectively in cultural and sporting activities. I expect the leadership amongst workers to form co-operatives. If you don't do that, we will not accept your leadership, comrade . . .

In fighting to establishing a fair and just society, we must continue to be as revolutionary as we were during the struggle for independence. What I am telling you is that we must experiment with the best methods we can think of spreading wealth to all our people in as short a time as possible so that our aim in all this is to implement Humanism. It is the surest guarantee to continued peace, stability and progress. In this old and tired world we need something more revolutionary to achieve a fair and just society.[13]

The wisdom displayed by the first Republican President is admirable and the import of the reasoning in these co-operatives can be fully appreciated if no attempt is made at paraphrasing what he said in his opening address at the 1965 UNIP National Council:

If the co-operatives movement in Zambia is meant to be a way of life and not just a way of solving our unemployment problems then it is desirable that all of us shall give it a serious thought. In trying to philosophize on co-operative activities as they affect us, we should recall that from the cradle to the grave, most Zambian people of old lived in the co-operative way. This had been accepted as a way of life without philosophizing the pundits and there is no earthly reason why we should not be proud of it, because it was employed by our ancestors.

The foregoing policy position and resulting government-sponsored initiatives led to multiplication in the number of co-operative, societies. Primary societies were formed in all parts of the country. From a total of about half a thousand co-operatives at independence the number approximately doubled in less than 10 years to about 1 000 in 1973. Many

---

[12] See K D Kaunda *Zambia's Guideline for the Next Decade* (1968).
[13] Ibid.

secondary co-operatives, in the form of co-operative unions, also sprang up in many parts of the country, notably in the Southern, Central and Eastern Provinces.

As the number of co-operatives multiplied, it became clear that there was need to create a national apex organisation to oversee these societies and also make regulations. The reluctance in doing so made the country pay heavily. Most of these co-operatives faded into oblivion for lack of economies of scale, training and direction.

Following the demise of many co-operative societies, a nationwide research study was commissioned to investigate what went wrong and recommend solutions. The result of the research was a document called the 'Co-operative Development Plan'. The document, among other issues, recommended that feasibility or viability studies should precede the formation of a co-operative. This document was later presented to the *First National Co-operative Conference* which was held in Lusaka in January 1970. The Conference identified the following problems:

(1) Communal farming, which was being promoted by the government, was found to be unsuitable for Zambian society.
(2) Excessive government assistance defeated self-reliance.
(3) Lack of education and training for co-operative members and staff.
(4) Lack of proper planning at the initial stages of co-operative formation.
(5) Single-purpose co-operatives, which did not provide sufficient economies of scale.

At the same conference, President Kaunda introduced some principles to be followed in the co-operative movement. These principles constituted some requirements that a proposed society must fulfil, for example, economic resources, competence in management and education for members.

But perhaps the most important achievement of this conference was the enactment of the Co-operative Societies Act of 1970 and creation of Zambia Co-operative Federation (ZCF) Limited as the apex organisation to spearhead co-operative development as well as to assume the representation and spokesmanship roles for the co-operative business in the country. ZCF Ltd was registered on 13 April 1973.

In 1983, co-operatives were declared a mass movement by UNIP, the only party at the time. The movement was referred to as 'the co-operative movement'. In the same year, President Kaunda formed the Ministry of Co-operatives as a base for co-operative policy formulation. The Ministry took over the Department of Marketing and Co-operatives (DMC) as well and the Co-operative College from the Ministry of Agriculture and Water

Development. This college, situated in Lusaka near Bauleni compound, was established through donor funding (SIDA) in 1979. It was the major institution conducting co-operative education and training. The only other institution which was involved, though on a much smaller scale, in co-operative education and training was the President's Citizenship College in Kabwe. The Co-operative College ran residential, long distance and field training courses aimed at educating co-operative members, elected co-operative leaders, and co-operative staff in the areas of co-operative organisation, leadership and management. In 1990 the government agreed to transfer the Co-operative College to the co-operative movement, in line with the original intention of the donor.

Agricultural co-operatives therefore dominated the co-operative movement during the UNIP government's rule. Consequently, it is not surprising that in 1984 the government adopted a deliberate policy to create provincial co-operative unions (PCUs) in all the nine provinces of Zambia. These PCUs had as their main function agricultural marketing, initially as agents of the National Agricultural Marketing Board (Namboard).

These PCUs did not obviously operate under the known co-operative principles. They were in the first place a result of external initiatives. Primary or producer co-operative societies were furthermore obliged to buy shares in these PCUs. Consequently, there was no co-operative autonomy and self-reliance. UNIP and its government were 'calling the shots' so to speak.

The UNIP government continued to believe that co-operatives in Zambia should succeed because after all the traditional way of living in Zambia has always reflected some sort of co-operation. Before the modern forms of co-operatives, village societies were based on mutual aid, that is to say, everybody helped to satisfy the basic needs of all the members of the village. This society was well-described by President Kaunda in his opening speech at the Fourth National Co-operative Conference held at Mulungushi Hall in Lusaka on Tuesday, 4 March 1986:

> The traditional community was a mutual aid society. It was organized to satisfy basic human needs of all its members and, therefore, individualism was discouraged. Most resources, such as land, might be communally owned, administered by chiefs and village headmen for the benefit of everyone. If for example, a village required a new hut, all the men would turn to forests and fetch poles to erect the frame and bring grass for thatching. The women might be responsible for making the mud plaster for the walls and two or three of them would undoubtedly brew some beer so that all workers would be refreshed after a hot but satisfying day's work.
>
> In the same spirit, the able bodied would accept responsibility for tending and harvesting the gardens of the sick and infirm.

Human need was a supreme criterion of behaviour. The hungry stranger could, without penalty, enter the garden or village and take, say some peanuts, a bunch of bananas, mealie cob or a cassava plant root to satisfy his hunger. His action only became theft if he took more than was necessary to satisfy his needs. For then he was depriving others

'Obviously, social harmony was a vital necessity in such a community where almost every activity was a matter of teamwork.'

The above description of the traditional way of life in Zambia was largely accurate but there are obviously questions to be answered as to whether this alone could be the basis for a successful co-operative movement in the country.

In 1988 the government decided that as a means of finance for co-operatives all marketing functions were to be performed by co-operatives only, while Namboard would be responsible for importation of fertiliser and maintenance of strategic maize reserves. Before this, the government-controlled Namboard was the monopoly buyer of maize at prices set by the government.

An important milestone in the development of co-operatives came in July 1989 when the National Agriculture Marketing Act was adopted stipulating the dissolution of Namboard and the transfer of its function to ZCF Ltd and Nitrogen Chemicals of Zambia (NCZ). This was the consummation of the lobbying efforts that ZCF had employed. For some time, it had been actively advocating this course of action. The result was that ZCF Ltd came to be a mammoth organisation.

Other developments during 1988/1989 include the merger of the Ministries of Agriculture and Rural Development and that of Co-operatives; the creation of District Co-operative Unions (DCUs) to help in decentralising PCUs; and the registration of multi-purpose co-operatives societies.

The non-exhaustive listing below of co-operative societies in Northern Province alone speaks volumes of the popularity of the idea of co-operatives in the First and Second Republics in Zambia. This example illuminates the larger national scene.

- Northern Co-operative Union Limited (NCU). It was registered in 1954 in Northern Province for Agricultural Marketing.
- Makumba Multi-purpose Co-operative Society in Luwingu District. It was founded in 1965 for marketing agricultural products; it had a hammer mill and communal farm. It was affiliated to NCU.
- Buwa Multi-purpose Co-operative Society in Chinsali District, founded in 1972 to enhance marketing, and install a hammer mill for members and a consumer shop.

- Twime Self Reliance Multi-purpose Co-operative Society in Kasama District. Established in 1974 for marketing, hammer mill, and consumer shop.
- Kalanga Multi-purpose Co-operative Society Limited was established in Isoka District in 1975. Its activities included marketing, consumer shop, three hammer mills, and a communal farm.
- Musombezi Multi-purpose Co-operative Society was created in Mbala District in 1975 by government as a rural construction centre. Its activities included marketing, a consumer shop, hammer mill, women's club, poultry farm, and fish ponds.
- Lukashya East Young Farmers Club in Kasama District. It was founded in 1984. It was essentially for vegetable growing.
- Kabangwe Multi-purpose Co-operative Society, founded in 1986 in Chinsali District, for marketing and a consumer shop.

The factors responsible for the desire on the part of the UNIP government to lay so much emphasis on co-operative development until its removal from office by the Movement for Multi-party Democracy (MMD) in 1991 are not hard to appreciate. They have a lot to do with the performance of the economy as a whole. It is instructive that in order to give a clear picture of these factors reference is made to the economic performance of the country, albeit succinctly.

4.7 THE ZAMBIAN ECONOMY

By about 1991, Zambia was ranked as one of the poorest countries in the world, exhibiting an economy which was heavily dependent on production of a single commodity—copper—and perhaps it was because of this that the economy continued to be one of the weakest. Copper exports generally accounted for not less than 85 per cent of the total exports, contributed to the Gross National Product and represented an important source of budgetary revenue.[14] This is not to say the country lacked other resources; the country has always been rich in agricultural, forestry, tourism, fishing and human resources.

Zambia's economy in the early 1960s was fairly good. There was economic growth between 1960 and 1970, but this progress came to a stop in 1975 when the country experienced a sharp decline in its economy owing to a decline in copper production coupled with some 80 per cent deterioration in the terms of trade. In anticipation of a recovery in copper

---

[14] Zambia Co-operative Federation Limited *Co-operatives in Zambia: A Background Information and Policy Document* (1991).

exports, financial policies of the Kaunda government were still geared towards maintaining consumption levels and living standards of the people. The anticipated recovery was however never attained leading to large budgetary and external deficit and a rapid build-up of external debt which has tormented the country up until the recent debt cancellations by developed countries and multilateral agencies.

Zambia had since then been striving for diversification in the economy by moving from heavy dependence on copper exports, but this effort has been hindered by various factors including insufficient incentives for non-traditional exports, price controls, and trade restrictions, to mention but a few.

It is no wonder that by 1985, the economy was performing so badly that the country launched an economic programme which involved macro-economic and structural reforms. Domestic financial policies were tightened, and market determination of the exchange rate was replaced by determination of the exchange rate through an auction mechanism. These policies, sadly, failed to yield anticipated results, largely because of the shortfalls in copper exports, rapid increase in money supply and sharp currency depreciations. The sum total effect of these developments was that performance in all key sectors of the economy was poor. To salvage the situation, the New Economic Recovery Programme (NERP) was launched in May 1987.

The NERP provided for a major shift in the orientation of the economic policy in Zambia. The NERP was regarded as the first phase of the development plan which was to be continued as phase two in the five-year 'Fourth National Development Plan' (FNDP). The NERP was different from the previous programmes due to its emphasis on foreign exchange rationing, seeking to combat inflation by stabilising the exchange rate and interest rates, reintroducing price controls and giving emphasis to recovery through the use of domestic resources.[15] This programme saw the improvement in the economic performance of Zambia in 1988 recording a growth rate of 6.7 per cent compared with 2.2 per cent in 1987.

The second phase of the NERP was outlined in the FNDP, 1989 to 1993. The FNDP was a medium-term plan and it focused on the need to adhere to the economic policies outlined in the NERP. Its emphasis was on industrial 'economic and financial viability' and hence constituted the basis for all operational plans by co-operative societies. The government came to realise

---

[15] Zambia Co-operative Federation Limited *Co-operatives in Zambia* 3.

that the subsidy policy was not only expensive to maintain, but also distorted the economy.[16]

The Policy of the UNIP government on co-operatives was further reflected in the FNDP which stated:

> It has always been the policy of the party and its government to ensure that a strong co-operative movement is created in Zambia, as the basis for the establishment of a Zambian Humanistic Society, devoid of exploitative tendencies in which political and economic power is equitably distributed among all the people.[17]

The FNDP further stated the overall objective of the Co-operative Development Programme as perceived in the NERP:

> The overall objective of the Co-operative Development Programme 1989–1993, is to improve the standard of living and quality of life of the people of Zambia, especially the disadvantaged groups in both rural and urban areas, including women and youths through the successful practice of participatory democracy, equitable distribution and mutual self-help.[18]

Clearly, the government of Kenneth Kaunda viewed the development of co-operatives as a means of achieving a humanistic society. The government deliberately targeted co-operative development at the poor or the disadvantaged groups.

From the foregoing explanation of the historical factors under which co-operatives developed in Zambia, one would conclude that co-operatives emerged through the encouragement and support that the government gave to them. They in turn depended largely on the government. This dependence of co-operatives on the government was probably due to the important role that the co-operatives were given, and aspired to, in the national economy. Co-operatives were viewed as a significant movement towards rural social mobilisation and agricultural development. As co-operatives largely involved themselves in maize production and marketing, government found itself inevitably under the obligation to ensure that the production and marketing the staple food had appropriate management and regulation.

Co-operatives were not primarily seen as business enterprises. This perception of co-operatives also led to their incorporation in national development plans that were drawn up by the government with co-operative input and participation. Rural and agricultural economic development fuelled by co-operatives was the overriding consideration. The obligation toward their members was generally relegated to a secondary position. This significantly undermined their co-operative identity and

---

[16] Zambia Co-operative Federation Limited *Co-operatives in Zambia* 3.
[17] K D Kaunda *Zambia's Guideline for the next Decade* (1968).
[18] Ibid.

resulted in their being viewed, by the general public and to some extent also by their members, as part of the government sector.

This is the background that animated the official policy and management of co-operatives in Zambia in the First and Second Republics. In a nutshell, co-operative policy and practice were characterised by the controlling role of government in the affairs of these organisations. The government set the agenda and economic parameters for co-operatives and invariably involved itself in the financial and other operations of the co-operatives at all levels, including making organisational and personnel changes in these entities. Ultimately the resulting situation as regards co-operative management, economic performance, democratic control by the members and other co-operative principles was unsatisfactory.

4.8   CO-OPERATIVE DEVELOPMENT IN THE THIRD REPUBLIC: 1991 ONWARDS

The wind of change in both the political and economic arenas which swept through Zambia in 1990 brought about its own challenges for the co-operative movement. An economy which had hitherto been commandist was liberalised following the change of government in 1991. This shift proved to be the *coup de grâce* to the development of co-operatives in Zambia.

The Movement for Multi-Party Democracy (MMD) government reflected its policy on co-operatives in its election manifesto which provided that co-operatives should be business organisations, formed and controlled by their members, and that they should operate independently of the government. The MMD manifesto specifically stated that it

> will insist that the spirit of the Co-operative Societies Act is implemented where the motivation for forming and managing co-operatives is from the individuals concerned and not forced from government.

Government policy on co-operatives was thus radically changed with the coming of the MMD. The new policy was that of non-interference in co-operatives and their operations as business organisations in the private sector. The role of government was confined to providing a legal basis for the registration of co-operatives, as is the case with other business associations.

Agricultural marketing, which used to be the exclusive domain of co-operatives, was now liberalised. The new government created, in 1995, the Food Reserve Agency (FRA) which assumed the functions and assets of the defunct Namboard from ZCF Ltd. Although the liabilities were supposed to be taken over by the government in accordance with the 1995

Food Reserve Act, these liabilities continued to lumber ZCF Ltd until only early in 2003 when the New Deal Government of President Levy Mwanawasa started to honour its obligation to ZCF Ltd.

In 1998 there was a change in the legal framework in which co-operatives developed. The Co-operative Societies Act of 1970 was repealed by the Co-operative Societies Act 20 of 1998 which now governs the formation, registration and organisation of co-operatives in Zambia. Co-operative development which was ranked among the top governmental policies in the UNIP government is not reflected in the current Act. Government intervention is restricted to mere 'encouragement' of the development of co-operatives by the Minister. Section 3(1) provides that 'the Minister shall adopt policies, as the Minister considers necessary, to encourage the development and sustainability of co-operatives and co-operative societies'.

The aforementioned changes had some telling consequences not only on ZCF Ltd, but also on the co-operative movement as a whole. The movement, as it were, could not cope with the fast pace of change and sudden loss of its major source of income, namely agricultural marketing, which had now been invaded by smaller, fitter and more aggressive dealers from the private sector. As a result, many co-operatives established in the First and Second Republics have become moribund because they cannot effectively compete with more stable and effective enterprises in the private sector without government intervention.

It is for this reason that ZCF Ltd embarked on a major restructuring exercise in 1996 aimed at scaling down its operations. This entailed not only doing away with its divisional structure by abolishing some divisions but also placing its subsidiary companies like ZCF Finance Services Ltd under voluntary liquidation.

The MMD government's economic policies introduced in the early 1990s represented a radical departure from the policies of its predecessor. In its *Policy Framework Paper* (1992)[19] the new President Frederick Chiluba emphasised the need to transform the country into a liberal market economy. The new measures introduced the removal of all subsidies, low inflation, and extensive privatisation of parastatal or state-owned or controlled companies.

Today, almost all parastatal companies have been privatised, but the country is still wallowing in poverty with more than 70 per cent of the people still living on less than a dollar per day. The 'New Deal government'

[19] K D Kaunda *Zambia's Guideline for the Next Decade* (1968).

of President Levy Mwanawasa who came into office in 2001 strove to transform the economy from dependence on a single commodity to other sectors such as tourism and agriculture. The latter was to be promoted by laying emphasis on the efficient operation of the fertiliser support programme and the encouragement of the production of winter maize. The fertiliser support programme was to be implemented essentially through co-operatives. This position does not seem to make any change to the MMD policy as President Mwanawasa was implementing the MMD manifesto. There are however many political pronouncements that have been made of late to the effect that the government is committed to the development of co-operatives through the Ministry of Agriculture and Co-operatives. But the reality does not seem to support this.

The law on the development of co-operatives, like many other branches of Zambian law, originated from the United Kingdom. The law has however undergone significant changes over the years, influenced by the policies of subsequent governments.

Evidently, the history of co-operatives in this country is a long one and one cannot point to a single event which triggered their development. Zambian society, as evidenced by rural communities, has been organised on the concept of co-operation and it was therefore not difficult for the UNIP government to encourage people to form co-operatives. All that was needed were good policies and government commitment. Government involvement in the setting up, operation and management of these co-operatives, however, flew in the face of the established Rochdale co-operative principles.

The apparent collapse of co-operatives in Zambia is attributed to the unfavourable policies of the MMD government. Co-operatives grew rapidly after independence because Dr Kaunda recognised that most people were unemployed and also uneducated small-scale farmers. He therefore encouraged them to form co-operatives as a means of earning a living. The nature of co-operatives is such that they are modelled on socialist principles and it is normally the poor or the unemployed who can make use of them. This does not seem to have been appreciated by the MMD government because notwithstanding the fact that there are high unemployment levels, the government liberalised the economy. This made it difficult for poor people to compete favourably with other enterprises, as liberalisation reflects capitalism.

Co-operatives can flourish well in a socialist economy which the Kaunda government advanced. People are willing to form the organisations, but without government intervention they are likely to fail as the Zambian experience reveals. The dream of effective co-operatives is not farfetched where the majority of the people are poor and unemployed, and the government is committed to their development.

Data on co-operative registration[20]

Following are estimated data on co-operative registration under various pieces of co-operative legislation in Zambia:

CO-OPERATIVE LEGISLATION	PERIOD	NUMBER OF CO-OPERATIVES REGISTERED	CUMULATIVE NUMBER OF CO-OPERATIVES
Registrar of the High Court	Before 1948	23	23
Co-operative Ordinance	1948 to 1970	1 270	1 293
Co-operative Societies Act Cap 689 of 1970	1970 to 1998	2 573	3 886
Co-operative Societies Act 20 of 1998	1998 to December 2006	9 308	13 194
	January 2007 to June 2009	3 363	17 744
	July 2009 to December 2010	5 575	23 319
	January 2011 to June 2012	6 980	30 299
	July 2012 to December 2013	3 509	33 818

4.9 LAW APPLICABLE TO CO-OPERATIVE SOCIETIES

The Co-operative Societies Act[21] is the principal piece of legislation that governs the formation and regulation of co-operatives in Zambia. The Act, which repealed and replaced the 1970 Co-operative Societies Act, contains detailed provision, dealing with registration and organisation, rights and liabilities of members, administration, amalgamation, transfer of engagements and divisions, co-operative unions and federations and winding up and cancellation of co-operative societies.

As co-operatives involves person associating together for purposes of achieving set economic or business objectives, it is inevitable that some contractual arrangements are implicit in the set-up of these organisations. Principles of contract law, therefore, have a significant place in the governance of co-operatives. The Companies Act[22] also governs certain aspects of

---

[20] Source: Department of Co-operatives, Ministry of Agriculture and Livestock (2014).
[21] 20 of 1998.
[22] 10 of 2017.

co-operative societies. For example, there is considerable reference to the Companies Act and the role of the Registrar of Companies in ss 11 and 13 of the Co-operative Societies Act relating to conversion of a limited company registered under the Companies Act into a co-operative society. Other areas of overlap between co-operatives and companies include matters to do with winding up of co-operatives with the Co-operative Societies Act stating in s 82(3):

> Subject to the provisions of other provisions of the Act, the Companies Act shall apply, with the necessary modification, to any winding up under this Act.

There are many similarities between the legal natures of co-operatives and companies. They both become corporate entities when registered and have members who hold a stake in the entity upon contribution of equity capital and are essentially the owners. They both have boards of directors who direct the affairs of the entity subject to the rules, these being the articles in the case of registered companies and the by-laws in the case of co-operatives; they are both required to have registered offices and to keep registers of members which should be open for inspection; they should file annual returns and must register charges, etc. These similarities entail that the modus operandi of these entities are materially similar. Principles of company law which are not expressly excluded by the Co-operative Societies Act or the by-laws of the society will naturally apply to co-operatives.

Co-operatives are of course not exempt from the operation of all other laws and regulations, such as those relating to taxation, licensing and environmental control, so that in addition to complying with the provisions of the Co-operative Societies Act under which they are set up, it is necessary for them to be conversant with the legal milieu in which they operate and to ensure they comply with all the other laws and regulations.

Regrettably, co-operatives as a form of business association in Zambia have not attracted the level of litigation that other business associations have. This accounts for the paucity of case law around the various provisions of the Co-operative Societies Act, prior or current. Fortunately, due to the striking similarities between co-operatives and companies, many company law principles apply to co-operatives.

4.10 REGISTRATION AND ORGANISATION OF CO-OPERATIVE SOCIETIES

Co-operatives are formed by way of application in the prescribed form to the Registrar of co-operatives. Any 10 or more persons wishing to form a co-operative society may apply to the Registrar for registration of their association as a co-operative. The application should, in accordance with s 9 of the Co-operative Societies Act, be accompanied by four copies of the by-laws of the co-operative society to be registered, and a statement by the applicants that the capital to be furnished initially by the applicants and other persons expected to become members is sufficient for the commencement of the operations. Furthermore, a notice of the location of the registered office of the proposed co-operative should be submitted.

The by-laws of a co-operative form the constitution of the association, which covers virtually every aspect of the life of the co-operative beginning from the name of the co-operative to the geographical area of operation of the co-operative. Other matters covered in the by-laws are as diverse and as detailed as the place and postal address of the registered office, the objects of the co-operative, the value of each share in the co-operative, the qualification for membership, the entrance fee, if any, the annual membership fee, if any, terms as to withdrawal of membership, provision on directors, the composition of the board of directors, the qualifications, tenure of office, and remuneration of directors, to the dates of the financial year of the co-operative society.

One would assume that the by-laws of a co-operative society are the same as the regulations of the co-operative society so that the two terms could be used interchangeably to mean the rules by which a co-operative is governed. In the case of a registered company the articles of the company are understood to be the same as the regulations of the company. Any such assumption, however, should be cautioned by s 21 of the Act which seems to suggest that the by-laws and regulations are distinct and separate. That section reads:

> A co-operative society shall keep a copy of *its regulations, by-laws and list of members* open to inspection by any member free of charge or any member of the public on payment of a prescribed fee, at all reasonable times, at the registered office of the co-operative society [emphasis added].

The term 'regulation' is not defined anywhere in the Act. A perusal of the Act also shows that the term is not mentioned anywhere else in the Act, except in s 83 which empowers the Minister to make regulations for the better carrying out of the purpose of the Act. Doubtless these are not the regulations envisioned by s 21. Regulations made by statutory instrument under the Act are part of the law generally available to the public and need not be a subject for a search at the registered office of a co-operative society. One wonders, therefore, whether in fact this was not another slip by the draftsperson.

Upon receipt of the application for registration, the Registrar scrutinises same and is obliged to register the co-operative if it complies with the provisions of s 9(2) as regards the documentation and the details which should, under the Act, be furnished together with the application. Furthermore, the Registrar should satisfy herself that the by-laws of the proposed co-operative make adequate provision for regular audits to be carried out and for the education, training and provision of advisory services to its members. The by-laws must not be *ultra vires* the Act or any other written law. Upon registration, a certificate of registration is issued to the society.

Quiet clearly, s 9(2)(*b*) on contribution of share capital and s 10 which obliges the Registrar to register a proposed co-operative society satisfying the requirements as laid down in the Act take into account at least two of the established co-operative principles namely, members' economic participation and their education and training.

Under s 15(11) the Registrar may refuse to register any proposed co-operative if she is not satisfied with the application submitted. She is, however, under an obligation to give reason for her refusal to register within 30 days of receipt of the application.

The Act provides for the right of appeal against any refusal to register a co-operative first to the Minister responsible for co-operatives and thereafter a further appeal to the High Court. One assumes that the purpose for the Act providing for an initial appeal to the Minister is to encourage an administrative settlement in the first place. Ultimately, aggrieved applicants for registration who are unhappy with the decision of the Registrar and that of the Minister on appeal can access the court.

4.11 CO-OPERATIVES THAT ARE ABLE TO REGISTER UNDER THE CO-OPERATIVE SOCIETIES ACT

The Act, unlike its counterpart dealing with companies, does not set out the types of co-operative societies that could be registered under it. Section 13 of the Companies Act lists the types of companies that could be incorporated under that Act as:

(*a*) public companies; and

(*b*) private companies being—

     (i) private companies limited by shares;

     (ii) companies limited by guarantee; or

     (iii) unlimited companies.

There is no similar or equivalent provision in the Co-operative Societies Act. This would immediately give one the impression that perhaps co-operative societies that could be registered in Zambia are of one type only, namely, private limited co-operatives. It is inconceivable that any group of people would wish to set up something called a public co-operative, nor indeed are the rules applicable to public flotation of shares applicable to co-operative societies. The possibility of setting up an unlimited co-operative would appear to be farfetched if one examines the language of certain sections of the Act such as s 12 which requires that 'the word "limited" shall be the last word in the name of every co-operative society upon its registration'; s 14 which states that 'a co-operative society shall be a body corporate with perpetual succession, a common seal and limited liability and shall have power'; s 79 which provides that 'a co-operative union or a federation, registered under this Act, shall be a body corporate with perpetual succession, a common seal and limited liability'. It is inconceivable that the Act intended to allow the registration of unlimited co-operatives or public limited co-operatives. If the intention of the Legislature was to allow for the creation of unlimited co-operatives or public limited co-operatives, the Act would expressly have so provided in the same way as the Companies Act.

Furthermore, the Co-operative Societies Act would not have set out categorically as it does in the sections quoted above that all co-operative societies which are registered under the Act shall use the word 'limited' as part of their name. It is important to observe that in as far as companies are concerned, s 37(1) provides that a public company shall have a name the last word of which is 'Plc' while s 37(2) requires that a private company limited by shares or a company limited by guarantee shall have a name the last word of which is 'Limited'. While s 36 of the Companies Act imposes an obligation on all limited companies to include the word 'limited' as part of their name, there appears to be no equivalent provision requiring unlimited companies to have the word 'unlimited' at the end of their name. It is unclear why the Companies Act has this omission. The position becomes even more confusing when one considers s 364(2) of the Companies Act which provides:

> A person who, not being a body corporate trades or carries on business in Zambia under a name or title which includes the word 'Limited', 'Plc', 'Corporation' or any contraction or imitation thereof, or any equivalent in a language other than English commits an offence and is liable, on conviction, to a fine not exceeding one thousand penalty units for each day that the person trades or carries on business under that name or title.

It is apparent that an unlimited company which uses the word limited as part of its name would be in contravention of s 364(2) of the Companies

Act though in the present formulation it may use its name without both the words 'limited' and/or 'unlimited' forming part of its name.

It has already been pointed out that s 19(1) requires that the by-laws of a co-operative should include the matters specified in the Schedule. Clause II of the Schedule provides that:

> The by-laws of a co-operative society may, inter alia, deal with the following matters:
> *(a)* the liability of members, whether limited by shares, guarantee or unlimited . . .

The implications of this provision are compelling. There is clearly a suggestion implicit in this clause that it is possible to form a co-operative whose members' liability is limited by shares or by guarantee or is indeed unlimited. Assuming that this view is correct, it is still very difficult to envision an unlimited liability co-operative registered under the Co-operative Societies Act whose members' liability is unlimited but whose name should still end with the word 'limited' as required of all co-operatives under ss 12, 14 and 79 as discussed above.

4.12 LIMITED LIABILITY CO-OPERATIVE SOCIETIES

As already discussed above, a co-operative society's liability is limited. This means in effect that the liability of the members is limited, ie the members are liable up to a limited amount, and beyond that limit, they cannot be called upon to contribute towards the payment of the co-operative society's liabilities. Thus, assuming that the co-operative society has to be wound up for any reason and the assets of the co-operative society are not sufficient to pay its liabilities, the private property of the members of the co-operative cannot be attached or used for the payment of the company's liabilities. This is set out in s 17 of the Act which provides:

> The liability of the members for debts and liabilities of a co-operative society shall be limited to the amount, if any, unpaid on the shares respectively held by them, or on the membership fee, as the case may be.

Thus, it is clear from the foregoing provision that the liability of the members of a co-operative may be limited in two ways: by shares or by membership. A co-operative limited by shares is one in which the liability of its members (ie the shareholders) is limited to the amount, if any, unpaid for those shares. Section 26(2) envisages payment for shares by members of a co-operative society in instalments. It reads:

> Where a co-operative society is registered with share capital and each member is obliged to take up shares in the co-operative society as a condition for being, or remaining a member of the co-operative society, the shares may be paid for in installments at the times and in the manner prescribed by the by-laws; but no share certificate shall be issued to a member until the shares to which it relates have been fully paid for.

Where a member pays for her shares in full then the liability of such a member is nil. Where a co-operative has no share capital and the members are only required to pay a membership fee, their liability will be limited to the amount unpaid, if any, on such membership fee.

4.13   CAN A CO-OPERATIVE BE LIMITED BY GUARANTEE?

It has been pointed out already that the Co-operative Societies Act does not contain any provision for the creation of a co-operative society limited by guarantee, though there is some vague reference to co-operatives by guarantee in the Schedule to the Act. To clear any doubts as to whether or not a co-operative by guarantee may be formed it is important to draw useful analogies from a co-operative society's closest sibling, the company.

Companies limited by guarantee are provided for in s 10 of the Companies Act. In a company limited by guarantee, s 51(2) of the Corporate Insolvency Act[23] provides that the liability of the members is limited to such amounts as the members undertake to contribute to the assets of the company in the event of the company being wound up. Section 10(1) of the Companies Act requires each subscriber to an application for incorporation of a company limited by guarantee to sign a declaration of guarantee specifying the amount that such subscriber undertakes to contribute to the assets of the company in the event of its being wound-up. As in the case of companies limited by shares, the liability of members of companies limited by guarantee is therefore limited. Two points must be emphasised: first, the guaranteed amounts may differ from member to member or they may be fixed by the articles. Secondly, the liability of the members can only be enforced during the winding up of the company. Members cannot be called upon to pay the guaranteed amounts during the normal existence of the company.

While in some jurisdictions, companies limited by guarantee may or may not have a share capital, in Zambia, companies limited by guarantee have no share capital. This necessarily means that such companies do not obtain their initial capital from their members. In terms of the provisions of s 19(5) of the Companies Act, a company limited by guarantee is prohibited from carrying on business for the purpose of making profits for its members or anyone concerned in its promotion or management. It is for this reason that this form of business association is confined almost exclusively to charitable or philanthropic causes and ordinarily sources its funding from endowments, grants, subscriptions, fees etc. Such a company would never

---

[23] 9 of 2017.

be a public company. In accordance with the provisions of s 37 of the Companies Act, the Registrar may, on the application of a company limited by guarantee grant the company permission to dispense with the word 'Limited' in its name. This provision is often invoked.

There are no similar restrictive provisions in the Co-operative Societies Act. The whole essence of forming a co-operative society is in fact to make an income for the member, to better their economic well-being. The definition of a co-operative in s 2 refers to the 'joint economic benefit' of the members. The Act talks about net surplus (ie profit) in defining patronage bonus (see ss 2 and 22), envisages dividends on the shares held by the members and share of net surplus (s 37(5a)(*b*)). It is obvious, therefore, that co-operative societies are incorporated for purposes completely inconsistent with and in a manner totally different from those of companies by guarantee and it is inconceivable that an attempt to set up a co-operative by guarantee under the Co-operative Societies Act would be feasible.

4.14 AN UNLIMITED CO-OPERATIVE?

So much has already been said about the provisions stating that a co-operative society must have the word 'limited' in its name, meaning in effect that an unlimited co-operative is not in the contemplation of the Co-operative Societies Act. Again, if appropriate inferences can be drawn from the position of unlimited companies and juxtaposed with the position applicable to co-operative societies, we would note that unlimited companies are those having no limit on the liability of their members.

The members of such companies are personally liable for the companies' debts and liabilities. Where, for instance, in the event of winding up of such a company, it is established that the assets of the company are not sufficient to pay its debts, then the members' private property can be attached for the purpose of settling the company's obligations. The Companies Act provides for such companies in s 11. That section directs that an unlimited company shall have a share capital. There is no mandatory requirement for a co-operative to have a share capital. The conclusion one makes from all this is that setting up an unlimited co-operative is not a practical option available under the Co-operative Societies Act.

4.15 EFFECT OF REGISTRATION

Section 14 indicates the effects of registration of a co-operative society. It states:

> A co-operative society shall be a body corporate with perpetual succession, a common seal and limited liability and shall, subject to the other provisions of this Act and its bylaws have power to do all such acts and things as a body corporate may by law do or perform.

This provision is materially similar to s 22*(b)* of the Companies Act. The capacity of a co-operative once registered is similar to that of a company. It has among the unstated powers, the power to sue and be sued in its own name, to own property in its name and to enter into contracts. In fact, it is capable of doing all things and acts which it is not precluded by its corporate nature from doing or performing, provided always that such acts or things are within the provision of the Act, the law generally, and the by-laws of the co-operative society. The same rules as regards to *ultra vires* acts as applied to companies will apply to co-operative societies. By s 17 liability of the members for debts and liabilities of a co-operative society shall be limited to the amount, if any, unpaid on the shares respectively held by them or on the membership fees as the case may be.

4.16 NAME OF A CO-OPERATIVE SOCIETY

Once registered, a co-operative society acquires the status of a limited liability entity. In terms of s 12(2), the world 'limited' shall be the last word in the name of every co-operative society and the word 'co-operative' shall also form part of the name. The section reads as follows:

> The word 'limited' shall be the last word in the name of every co-operative society and except as otherwise provided in this act, the word 'co-operative' shall form part of the name of every co-operative society.

This section in and of itself appears fairly harmless. What is more, s 12 says nothing about the fate of a co-operative or its officers where there is failure to comply with its provisions. It is, however, easy to appreciate that a co-operative that does not comply with this particular provision will, in the first place, probably not be registered by the Registrar in exercise of her power under s 15 for failure to comply with s 9(1) of the Act. It is when s 12 is read together with s 18 that some issues of concern begin to emerge. Section 18 reads as follows:

> (1) A co-operative society shall—
> (a) Cause its registered name to be painted or affixed, in a conspicuous place and in letters which are easily legible, at its registered office and at every other office or place at which the business of the co-operative society is carried on; and
> (b) Engrave its registered name, in legible characters, on its seal; and shall emboss its registered name—
>   (i) On all notices, advertisements and other official publications of the co-operative society;
>   (ii) On all business letters of the co-operative society; and

> (iii) On all bills of exchange, promissory notes, endorsements, cheques, and orders for money or goods, purporting to be signed by or on behalf of the co-operative society.

This section equally contains no penalty clause for failing to observe its provisions. In the event, s 84 provides for a general penalty to apply. Under that section any person who contravenes the provisions of the Act where no penalty is specifically provided shall be liable on conviction to a fine not exceeding six hundred penalty units, or to imprisonment for a term not exceeding six months, or to both. The question one would ask is whether payment of such a penalty by a guilty co-operative absolves the officers of the co-operative from personal liability.

The Zambian High Court had occasion to consider a similar issue in *S.J. Patel (Zambia) Limited v D.V. Cinamon (Male).*[24] The court in that case considered a similar but not identical provision in the Companies Ordinance to s 18 of the Co-operative Societies Act. Section 8(1)(*a*) of the Companies Ordinance[25] requires that the memorandum of association of every company must state the name of the company with 'Limited' as the last word of the name. Section 80 of the Ordinance provided:

> Every company shall paint or affix and shall keep painted or affixed its name on the outside of every office or place in which the business of the company is carried on, in a conspicuous place and in letters easily legible, and shall have its name engraved in legible characters on its seal and shall have its name mentioned in legible characters in all notices, advertisements, and other official publications of the company, and in all bills of exchange, promissory notes, endorsements, cheques and orders for money or goods purporting to be signed by or on behalf of the company, and in all bills of parcels, invoices, receipts and letters of credit of the company.

Section 81 of the Ordinance prescribed the penalties and sanctions for non-compliance with the requirement to publish a company's name and further provided:

> If any director, manager or officer of the company or any person on its behalf, uses, or authorises the use of any seal purporting to be a seal of the company whereon its name is not so engraved as aforesaid, or issues or authorises the issue of any notice, advertisement, or other official publication of the company, or signs or authorises to be signed on behalf of the company, any bill of exchange, promissory note, endorsement, cheque, order for money and goods, or issues or authorises to be issued any bill of parcels, invoice, receipt, or letter of credit of the company, wherein its name is not mentioned in the manner aforesaid, he shall be liable to a penalty of fifty pounds sterling, and shall further be personally liable to the holder of any such bill of exchange, promissory note, cheque or order for money or goods for the amount thereof, unless the same is duly paid by the company.

---

[24] [1970] ZR 63.
[25] Chapter 216 of the Laws of Zambia.

In that case the plaintiffs supplied goods to Longacres Stores Limited and three cheques were drawn in their favour signed by the defendant in his capacity as managing director of the company over a rubber-stamp bearing the inscription 'Longacres Store', without the word 'Limited' appearing on the cheques. Subsequent to the issue of these cheques the company went into voluntary liquidation and on presentation of the cheques they were dishonoured. The court had to consider the issue of whether the defendant was liable for the amount claimed by the plaintiff. It was held that failure to comply with the provisions made the person who signs the documents personally liable if the company fails to pay. By not complying with the statutory provisions the defendant rendered himself liable to the plaintiffs for the amount payable in respect of the three cheques.

This case is, of course, distinguishable from the situation that would arise if a co-operative society failed to comply with the provisions of s 18 principally on grounds that the Companies Ordinance, which was a subject of interpretation in that case, expressly provided for the personal criminal liability of the officers of a defaulting company as well as their civil liability to the injured third party which s 18 of the Co-operative Societies Act does not do. While it appears desirable that a third party who suffers loss as a result of the failure by a co-operative society to comply with s 18 of the Act should have recourse to the officers of the co-operative personally for redress, it appears that the wording of the Act does not provide for such a possibility and one has to be extremely clear as to why a sanction additional to that prescribed in the Act should be imposed on either the co-operative or the officers in disregard of the concept of the corporate personality of the co-operative.

Under s 68 a savings and credit co-operative may be registered as a credit union under the Act for the promotion of savings among its members and for the creation of a source of financing for its members and it shall be a co-operative society for purposes of the Act. Such a co-operative society should have in accordance with s 69 one or more of the words 'savings', 'thrift' or 'credit' as part of the name of that co-operative society.

As regards the need to have the word 'co-operative' form part of the name of a co-operative society two points need to be noted: first, that unlike the case with the word 'limited' which by s 12(2) must be the last word in the name of the co-operative, no order in which the word 'co-operative' should appear in the name of the co-operative is prescribed, and, secondly, under s 78 the Registrar may exempt a co-operative union or a federation from the requirement that the word 'co-operative' shall form part of the name of that union or federation, if it is clear to the public that it is a co-operative society.

4.17 MEMBERSHIP OF A CO-OPERATIVE SOCIETY

A co-operative society may be made up of persons, natural and/or artificial, who in essence own the co-operative society. Since upon registration a co-operative society acquires a distinct legal personality, the persons who own the co-operative society will be different from the co-operative society itself, and vice versa. Persons who come together to form a business association called a co-operative or who join an existing co-operative society are referred to as the 'members' or 'shareholders' of the co-operative society. Although the terms 'member' and 'shareholder' are often used interchangeably, it is possible to have a member who is not a shareholder. This is because it is possible to have a co-operative without share capital and based on membership fees only or with a share capital and no membership fees, or both.

Section 2 of the Act defines a member as 'an individual who, or a body corporate which, has been admitted to the co-operative society as a member in accordance with the by-laws'.

As already pointed out, in terms of s 8 of the Act a co-operative must have a minimum of 10 members. Section 23 states that in no case shall the by-laws of a co-operative society fix any limit to the number of its members. The members could either be natural persons or bodies corporate or a mixture of these two. It would appear from s 2 of the Act that an unincorporated association such as a partnership would not qualify to be a member of a co-operative society since it is neither an individual nor a body corporate.

4.17.1 Minors as members of a co-operative society

As regards contracts the position is that minors generally have no legal capacity to contract and all contracts with minors, save for necessaries, are void. This is clearly set out in s 1 of England's Infant Relief Act of 1874 which is applicable in Zambia by virtue of the English Law (Extent of Application) Act.[26] However, so as far as membership of a co-operative society, which invariably concerns entering into a contract of sorts, is concerned, the Act makes specific provision totally contrary to the known common-law position. Interestingly, s 24 of the Act specifically entitles minors to form or join co-operative societies. It provides:

(1) Notwithstanding anything contained in any other law, a minor may form or become a member of a co-operative society.

---

[26] Chapter 11 of the Laws of Zambia.

(2) Notwithstanding anything contained in the by-laws or any other law, where any member has not reached the age of eighteen years, that member may execute or cause to be executed any instrument under this Act; and any contract entered into by that member with the co-operative society shall be valid whether as principal or as surety, and shall be enforceable at law.

This provision removes all the contractual restrictions imposed by the law of contract on the minor's capacity to contract. It is possible for minor's to form a co-operative society without the involvement of persons of full age. Since by s 38 of the Act the members of the board of directors of a co-operative society are to be elected from the members of the co-operative society, it follows that ninors can be directors in a co-operative. This contrasts sharply with the Companies Act which specifically disqualifies minors from directorship of a company in s 92(3)*(a)*.

4.17.2 Persons with legal disabilities

The position of persons of unsound mind, and persons with undischarged debts or alcoholism is not referred to in the Act. The common-law position will therefore apply in respect of the membership of these categories of persons.

4.17.3 By-laws and membership

Both ss 2 and 23 refer to the by–laws in respect of the question of membership. Section 2 states that members are admitted to a co-operative society in accordance with the by-laws while s 23 provides that member-ship of a co-operative society shall be governed by its by-laws. Section 19 directs that the by-laws of a co-operative society shall include provisions relating to matters specified in the Schedule. As far as they relate directly to members, the matters in the Schedule affecting membership are the following:

Clause I*(e)* stating that the by-laws should deal with the qualification for membership, clause I*(f)* requiring the by-laws to indicate the minimum number of shares to be subscribed for by each member as a condition of being admitted to membership, clause I*(g)* requiring the by-laws to state the terms of membership if the co-operative society has no share capital, clause I*(h)* which requires the member's entrance fee if any to be stated in the by-laws, clause I*(i)* which equally directs that the annual membership fee should be dealt with by the by-laws if any, clause I*(m)* regarding the condition of a member's withdrawal from membership and II*(a)* dealing with the liability of members whether limited by shares, guarantee or unlimited. It is important to point out that any provision dealing with membership or any other matter in the by-laws which is in conflict with the provisions of the Act and any other written law will be regarded as *ultra vires* the Act or such other written law and will contravene section 10*(c)* of the Act and thereby justify the refusal by the Registrar to register the co-operative society under section 15(1) of the Act.

4.18 RIGHTS OF A MEMBER OF A CO-OPERATIVE SOCIETY

A member of a co-operative society is entitled to a number of rights. These rights will ordinarily be detailed in the by-laws of the co-operative society. They will, however, only be available to a member who has paid to the co-operative society the amount required for membership of that co-operative society or has acquired such interest in the co-operative society as may be prescribed in the Act or in the by-laws (s 25). Though the detailed rights will be a matter for the by-laws, there are some rights which are set out or discernible from the provisions of the Act. These include the following:

4.18.1 The right to be issued with a certificate of membership

A member of a co-operative society is entitled to be issued with a certificate evidencing her membership of the co-operative society. Where the co-operative has a share capital, a member will be entitled to be issued with a share certificate evidencing her interest in the co-operative. Under s 26(2) no such share certificate will be issued to a member unless the share to which the certificate relates has been paid for in full. In terms of s 26(1) on the other hand, where a co-operative society does not have any share capital, a member who has paid the membership fee, as set by the co-operative society, in full, shall be issued with a certificate of member-ship.

4.18.2 The right to pay for membership in instalments

A member is entitled to pay for her membership in instalments. Although the conditions for membership are by s 23 a matter for the by-laws, it should also be recalled that the by-laws must conform with the provisions of the Act so that if they are not in conformity with the provisions of the Act they could be possibly *ultra vires* the Act. Section 25 provides that a member shall not be entitled to exercise any right of membership unless she has paid the amount required for membership. This is amplified by s 26 which requires full payment before a share certificate, or a certificate of membership is issued. The clear implication here is that payment in instalments is permissible, and a member is therefore entitled to opt to pay in instalments.

4.18.3 The right to attend meetings of the co-operative society and to vote at such meetings

Every member has the right to attend the duly convened meetings of the co-operative society of which she is a member and to vote thereat in accordance with the provisions of the by-laws. This is aptly summarised in s 29 of the Act. These meetings include the general and the special meetings of the co-operative society. The subject of the meeting is discussed in a separate section.

4.18.4 The right to transfer, assign, redeem or repurchase shares

Subject to the conditions laid out in the by-laws and the Act a member is entitled to transfer, assign, redeem, or repurchase shares in the co-operative society. A member of a co-operative society is therefore entitled as a starting point to sell or assign her shares when she so desires. Such sale or transfer may however be subject to such reasonable conditions as the co-operative may set in its by-laws. The one condition set forth by s 31*(b)* of the Act is that such transfer will not be valid unless approved by the board; except that the board shall not give the approval if it would reduce the total number of members below the minimum required by the Act (ie 10) for the registration of a co-operative society.

4.18.5 The right to elect and be elected to board membership of the co-operative society

Every co-operative society should have a board of directors to manage and direct the affairs of the co-operative society. These directors are elected by the members from amongst their number at an annual meeting of the co-operative held in accordance with the provisions of the by-laws. Every member is entitled to attend these meetings, and to elect and be elected to membership of the co-operative (s 38). Unless there are good reasons specified in the by-laws or determined by the general meeting, this right to attend meetings and to elect and stand for elections to board membership cannot be denied a member who has paid her dues in full. Furthermore, persons whose names appear in an application for the registration of a co-operative society shall: upon registration, be deemed to have all the powers and duties of directors; and shall direct the affairs of the co-operative society until directors have been elected at the first general meeting of the co-operative society.

4.18.6 The right to elect and be elected to membership of committees of the co-operative

In terms of s 39(1) a co-operative society shall, at an annual general meeting, establish such number of committees as it may consider necessary for the purpose of assisting the board carry out its functions as set out under the Act. Members of a co-operative society are entitled to elect from amongst its members at least three persons, who are not employees of the co-operative society, to constitute each committee.

4.18.7 The right not to have one's shares attached

Under s 32(1) a member has the right not to have her shares or other interests in the capital of a co-operative society attached or sold under decree or order of any court in respect of any debt or liability incurred by the member. A member's interest in a co-operative society's capital is therefore insulated or immune from attachment for separately and privately contracted debts of the member.

4.18.8 The right to have one's estate paid one's entitlement from the co-operative society

A deceased member of a co-operative society is entitled to have her shares or other interests transferred to a person nominated according to the rules made in that regard and where there is no person nominated to the legal representative of that deceased member, or to pay to any nominee or legal representative a sum representing the value of such member's share or interest. Furthermore, a deceased member is entitled to have her estate paid all moneys due from a co-operative society (s 33).

4.18.9 The right to withdraw membership

A member of a co-operative society has the right, at any time, to withdraw from a co-operative society, subject to the other provisions of the Act and the by-laws. If the withdrawal is premised on grounds of illness, disability, permanent removal from the area or district served by the co-operative society or death, then payment of the shares or other interests of the member shall be made in such order or priority as the by-laws may prescribe; or where not so prescribed, in such order or priority as the board may approve (s 36(1)).

In terms of s 36(3), where it appears that the financial stability of a co-operative society would be impaired if the co-operative society made payment for the shares held by a member who has withdrawn from the co-operative society, at their par or paid-up value, or of any other interests of such a member at the value shown on the books of the co-operative society, the directors may suspend payment for such period as may be approved by the annual general meeting, except that, such period shall not exceed one year from the time the member withdrew from the co-operative society. This provision is no doubt intended to strike a balance between the interests of the departing member and those of the co-operative society.

4.18.10 The right to defend oneself from allegations

Section 37 contains somewhat interesting, if not altogether clear, provisions. It states that upon any complaint arising against a member, the secretary shall, upon the instructions of the board, provide the member with a written notice of the particulars of the complaint and of the date, time and place of the meeting of the board at which the complaint shall be considered. The board may, after having given the member against whom the complaint has been made the opportunity to make representations or submissions, orally or in writing, or both, in rebuttal or in mitigation, recommend to the general meeting, in a report detailing the complaint and the opinion of the board, that the member be expelled. The general meeting may, after considering the report submitted by the board, expel a member by a resolution passed by at least a two-thirds majority vote of the members of the co-operative society.

First, it is not clear as to who could make a complaint against a member. Secondly, it is equally not stated what the complaint would be about, and thirdly, the whole procedure seems to fall short of natural justice requirements. What is clear is that the member concerned will have the right to exculpate herself, or at least to answer to the allegations against her before the board refers the matter to the general meeting for a decision.

4.18.11 The right to a refund upon expulsion

Section 37(5) of the Act provides that a member who has been expelled from a co-operative society, under that section shall forfeit all rights to shares in the net surplus or other benefits of the co-operative society from the date of such expulsion but shall be entitled to be refunded her share capital or other interest held in the co-operative society, together with such dividend as may later be declared and calculated up to the date of expulsion.

4.18.12 The right to inspect any instrument creating a charge created by a co-operative society

Part VI of the Act relates to the creation of charges by co-operative societies on their property or undertaking. Such charges must be registered in the manner directed by the Act under s 53, a member is entitled to have access for purposes of inspection any instrument creating any charge requiring registration under that part of the Act. Whether s 53 adds any substantial value to the general provision on inspection as contained in s 59 is a matter for debate.

14.18.13 The right to inspect records of the co-operative society

Section 59 of the Act confers a right on any member to inspect the records of a co-operative society at the registered office of the co-operative during working hours. It is argued that this provision adds nothing more to s 53 since one would like to believe that co-operative societies' instruments creating charges are part of the records of the co-operative society.

14.18.14 The right to be availed of a copy of the audited annual statement on request

Under s 62(1) of the Act, a co-operative society must, within six months after the end of each financial year, make available to any member, on request, an audited statement of the receipt, expenditures, assets and liabilities of the co-operative society.

14.18.15 The right to appeal against cancellation of the co-operative society

Under s 81 the Registrar is empowered under specified circumstances to cancel the registration of a co-operative society. When this happens, a member is entitled to, within 30 days from the date of the cancellation; appeal to the Minister responsible for co-operatives against the cancellation.

4.19 CONVERSION OF A REGISTERED COMPANY INTO A CO-OPERATIVE SOCIETY

A company registered under the Companies Act may convert into a co-operative society. It is not immediately obvious why a company enjoying corporate status under the Companies Act may opt to take this course of action. One would assume, however, that there may be instances when the business outlook of the incorporated company has to be changed, or owing to changes in circumstances, it may be necessary for the members making up the company to take advantage of benefits which come with co-operatives which may not be available to a company.

The procedure for conversion of a registered company into a co-operative society is set out in s 11 of the Co-operative Societies Act. First, such company must take a resolution to convert from a company to a co-operative. In terms of s 11 such resolution should be made in accordance with the Companies Act. Secondly, the company then applies to the Registrar of Co-operatives for the registration of the company as a co-operative society. Such application must be accompanied by:—

(*a*) the resolution made by the company converting itself into a co-operative;

(*b*) copies of the proposed co-operative's by-laws in quadruplicate, signed by ten members and the secretary of the company;

(*c*) a further resolution authorising the ten members and the secretary of the company to sign the by-laws and also authorising those members and the secretary to accept any alterations made by the Registrar without further consultations with the company or authorising such members to submit to the company in general or extraordinary meeting any alteration made by the Registrar;

(d) a resolution which confirms that the capital to be furnish initially by the members of the company, is sufficient for the commencement of operations as a co-operative society; and

(e) a notice of situation or registered office. Under s 57 of the Act, every co-operative society shall have a registered office to which all communications and notices may be addressed.

Where the Registrar is satisfied that the application complies with the law, she shall register the co-operative as a co-operative society and issue a certificate of registration in accordance with s 12 of the Act.

Section 12(2) of the Act provides that

the word 'limited' shall be the last word in the name of every co-operative society and, except as otherwise provided in the Act, the word 'co-operative' shall form part of every co-operative society.

Naturally, the former company now registered as a new co-operative society will cease to operate as a company under the Companies Act. The question of an entity operating both as a company and a co-operative society does not arise. It has already been mentioned that the resolution required to convert a company to a co-operative society is a special resolution. Such resolution will require to be filed with the Registrar of Companies under the Companies Act. The Registrar of Companies is responsible for striking out companies that cease to operate as such. Presumably therefore, the Registrar will be alert to and will take note of companies that have passed resolutions to convert and will strike them off the Register of Companies.

In fact, in terms of s 13 of the Co-operative Societies Act, after registering a company as a co-operative, the secretary of the company must submit a copy of the resolution, together with the certificate of registration as a co-operative society to the Registrar of Companies 'who shall register the resolution and the certificate; and the company shall cease to be a company registered under the Companies Act and the provisions of this Act shall apply, in all respects to such co-operative society, as from the date of such registration with the Registrar of Companies'.

Section 13 of the Co-operative Society Act contains some troublesome provisions. Section 13(b) states that from the date the Registrar of Companies receives from the company secretary a copy of the resolution converting the company to a co-operative society as well as a copy of the certificate of registration of the former company as a society, and she registers them, the company shall cease to be a company registered under the Companies Act.

However, s 13*(c)* of the Act declares that the registration shall not affect any right or claim subsisting for or against the former company or any liability incurred by the former company. Section 14*(d)* goes further to provide that for the purpose of enforcing any right, claim or liability, the former company may be sued and proceeded against in the same manner as if it had not been registered as a co-operative society under the Act.

Difficult questions may arise around these provisions. Consider, for example, that Masalamusi Trading Company Limited, which is registered under the Companies Act, wishes to convert to a co-operative society under the Co-operative Societies Act. Assume that the company desires to retain the name 'Masalamusi' in its new corporate identity so that its new name is now 'Masalamusi Trading Co-operative Society Limited' to comply with s 12(2), and it ceases to be governed by the Companies Act in accordance with s 13*(b)*. Assume further that Masalamusi Trading Company Limited owes Makwacha Bank Limited a large unsecured loan. Under s 13*(d)*, for purposes of enforcing its rights and claim against Masalamusi Trading Company Limited, Makwacha Bank could sue the former company and proceed 'against it in the same manner as if it had not been registered as a co-operative society under this Act'. If Makwacha Bank sued Masalamusi Trading Company Limited and later discovered that Masalamusi Trading Company Limited is unable to pay the judgment debt, strictly speaking and theoretically so, Makwacha Bank could then bring winding up proceedings against Masalamusi Trading Company Limited under the Companies Act. The question is; what good would that course of action be if the company ceased to operate under the Companies Act as clearly stated in s 13*(d)*? In truth, the Companies Act would be inapplicable. The immediate reaction would probably be that the winding up could then be in accordance with the Co-operative Societies Act, which also by the way has provisions for winding up of co-operatives. Section 80 of the Act provides that 'a co-operative society shall be wound up only in accordance with this Act'.

That provision, which is in fact in Part XI, then proceeds to lay down the grounds upon which a co-operative may be wound up, namely:

(1) when the Registrar cancels the registration of a co-operative society than she appoints a liquidator of that co-operative society (we shall revert to the grounds for cancellation of registration of a co-operative); and

(2) when a co-operative society, by special resolution, resolves to wind up its affairs and requests the Registrar to cancel the registration.

The one point that is clear is that the provisions of the Act can cause unnecessary confusion in as far as procedure is concerned. The provisions of s 82(3) to the effect that '[s]ubject to the other provisions of this Act, the Companies Act shall apply, with the necessary modification, to any winding up under this Act,' do not help to clear up matters either.

4.20 THE REGISTERED OFFICE OF A CO-OPERATIVE

Every co-operative society is required under the law to have a registered office. Under s 9(2)*(a)* the application for registration of a co-operative society shall be submitted with four copies of the by-laws, while under sub-s (2)*(c)* a notice of situation of registered office must be filed together with the application for registration.

In terms of s 19(1) the by-laws of a co-operative society shall include provisions relating to matters specified in the Schedule. The Schedule itemises the matters which the by-laws of every co-operative society shall deal with. Under clause I*(b)* of the Schedule is stated 'the place and postal address of the registered office of the co-operative society.' These provisions reinforce the requirement for a registered office to be given at the time of registration of a co-operative society.

The purpose of the registered office is stated in s 57, which states:

> A co-operative society shall have a registered office to which all communications and notices may be addressed.

This is, however, only one of the purposes of a registered office. The other purposes will be clear from the further sections which mention the registered office directly. The registered office is referred to in at least nine other sections of the Act, namely ss 11, 18, 21, 28, 48(10), 53, 54 and 59(1) and (2).

Section 11 makes provision for the various requirements that must be satisfied if a company registered under the Companies Act wishes to convert to a co-operative society. Among the documents that must be filed with the Registrar is the notice of situation of registered office (s 11(3)*(e)*).

Under s 18 a co-operative society is required to display its name in a conspicuous place at its registered office and at every other office where it conducts its business. In terms of s 21:

> A co-operative society shall keep a copy of its regulations, by-laws and list of members *open to inspection by any member free of charge or any member of the public on payment of a prescribed fee*, at all reasonable times, *at the registered office* of the co-operative society [emphasis added].

By virtue of s 28, a co-operative society must keep a register of its members and of the shares held, if any, by each member or any membership fee paid, by its members. Interestingly, under s 28(2):

> A co-operative society shall furnish the Registrar with a list of its members; and such list shall be open for inspection, by any person, at the office of the Registrar, on payment of a prescribed fee [emphasis added].

It is quite unclear why ss 21 and 28 should differ so significantly in the accessibility of essentially the same document (list of members) kept at the registered office. In s 21 a copy of the by-laws and the list of members are open to inspection by *any person* on payment of a fee *at the registered office* while under s 28 the same list of members is available for inspection on payment of a fee *at the Registrar of Co-operatives*. What is discernible from these two sections is that a member of the public could access the list of members of a co-operative on payment of the prescribed fee from either the registered office in accordance with s 21, or from the Registrar's office on payment of a fee.

However, for members of the co-operative society, they can access the list free of charge at the registered office in accordance with s 21, or on payment of a fee at the Registrar of Co-operatives in accordance with s 28. It is rather unclear why the Act should have two separate sections both dealing with inspection of the list of members but setting quite different conditions. The two provisions could have been married so as not to create two unnecessary parallel processes to achieve the same end. It is probable that this was a drafting lapse.

Another section which refers to the registered office is s 48 which deals with charges other than agricultural charges by co-operatives. Section 48(10) requires that a co-operative society causes a copy of every instrument creating a charge, requiring registration under that section, to be kept at the registered office of the co-operative society.

In terms of s 59(1) of the Act the board of every co-operative society shall cause to be kept proper books of account and other records relating to the accounts of the co-operative society. Under sub-s 2:

> The records of the co-operative society shall be open for inspection, at the registered office of the co-operative society, by any member or delegate during office hours; except that no person who is not an officer of the co-operative society or who is not specifically authorized by a resolution in that behalf of a general meeting, shall have the right to inspect the accounts of any other member without the written consent of that member.

The final section that refers to the registered office of a co-operative directly is s 59. Under that section the registered documents of the co-operative society must be kept at the registered office and open to inspection. That section reads:

(1) The board shall cause to be kept proper books of account and other records relating to the accounts of the co-operative society.

(2) The records of the co-operative society shall be open for inspection, at the registered office of the co-operative society, by any member or delegate during office hours; except that no person who is not an officer of the co-operative society or who is not specifically authorized by a resolution in that behalf of a general

meeting, shall have the right to inspect the accounts of any other member without the written consent of that member.

The general wording of s 59(2) would mean that all records of a co-operative society must be kept at the registered office. This should include agricultural charges under s 53, auditors' records under s 60, yearly and other returns under s 61. Section 53, without directly referring to the registered office, states:

(1) A co-operative society shall keep a register of charges and agricultural charges and enter therein all charges specifically effecting the property of the co-operative society and all floating charges on the undertaking or any property of the co-operative society, giving in each case a short description of the property charged, the amount of the charge, and the names of the persons entitled thereto.

Section 54 on the other hand provides:

A copy of any instrument creating any charge requiring registration under this Part and the register of charges required to be kept under section fifty-three, shall be available at all times for inspection by any creditor or member of the co-operative society free of charge; and

(b) be open for inspection by any other person on payment of a fee, not exceeding fifty fee units, for every inspection, as the co-operative society may prescribe.

Sections 53 and 54, without making direct reference to the registered office, do in fact imply that the documents they refer to shall be kept at the registered office.

What then is the value of a registered office for a co-operative society? As already pointed out at the beginning of this section and as s 57 clearly proclaims, as in the case of a registered limited company, though a co-operative society has a legal existence it does not have a physical existence. It is imperative that those dealing with the co-operative society in its day-to-day activities should know where the co-operative can be found, where formal communications and notices could be addressed and above all where documents, particularly of a legal nature, could be served on it. This is probably the key reason for the requirement for a co-operative, like a company, to have a registered office. Again, in much the same way as a company a co-operative society's registered office indicates its nationality and domicile. A corporation's place of incorporation is also its place of domicile, and as was pointed out in *Gasque v IRC*[27] it cannot easily change its domicile.

The *lex domicilii* of the company will ordinarily determine such questions as whether or not the company was duly incorporated, its powers and duties, whether it has been validly dissolved, etc. This applies with

---

[27] [1940] 2 KB 80.

equal force to co-operative societies which acquire a separate legal personality upon registration and are for all intents and purposes treated as if they were companies registered under the Companies Act.

Another reason for co-operative societies is that they are the place for keeping the records of the co-operative society to have a registered office as well as for inspection of the various documents that may lawfully be inspected under the Co-operative Societies Act.

A registered office is the place at which documents such as writs of summons may be served. This is, at least in the case of companies, firmly established. It will be appreciated that since the company has a legal existence but does not have a physical existence, it is necessary that persons dealing with the company should know where the company can be found, where formal communications and notices can be addressed and above all where documents, particularly of a legal nature, can be served on it. This is perhaps the key reason for the requirement for a company to have a registered office.

The registered office for a company serves the purpose of the service of court process and this applies equally to the registered office of a co-operative society.

4.21 MEETINGS OF A CO-OPERATIVE SOCIETY

Being an artificial person, the business of a co-operative society is carried out either by its members or the representatives of those members, called the directors. In either case, decisions are taken at duly convened gatherings or meetings of these persons. Every gathering of the members or the directors of a co-operative society will constitute a meeting and it must be held in accordance with prescribed rules and regulations as set out in the by-laws. The Co-operative Society Act makes it plain in s 29 that meetings and the procedure at such meetings are a matter for the by-laws when it provides as follows:

> (1) Subject to the other provisions of this Act, the by-laws shall provide for the holding of general and special meetings of the co-operative society, for the procedure at such meetings and the keeping of minutes at such meetings.

Ideally, all the shareholders or members of a co-operative society must meet as and when there is need for a decision to be taken on any matter. While this may be feasible for small co-operatives with a bare minimum number of shareholders or members, it often is not practical for big co-operatives. Even to get all 10 members of a co-operative to come together every time a decision must be taken may be a tall order. This explains why, for practical purposes, the day-to-day business of the co-operative is often entrusted to a small body of persons called the board of directors, who periodically meet and perform this responsibility. The members of the co-operative society still meet to exercise the ultimate control over the co-operative society's affairs.

4.22 KINDS OF MEETINGS A CO-OPERATIVE MAY HOLD

Although, as has already been pointed out, s 29 leaves the issue of meetings to the by-laws of a co-operative society, there are several types of meetings that the Act refers to explicitly. In broad terms these meetings of a co-operative society may be classified into two types: meetings of the members or the shareholders, and meetings of the board of directors of the co-operative society.

Notwithstanding the absence of a definition of the word 'meeting' in the Act, the Co-operative Societies Act refers to meetings and resolutions in various sections of the Act. As far as meetings of the members are concerned, three kinds of meeting are mentioned in the Act, namely *(a)* an annual general meeting; *(b)* a general meeting; and *(c)* a special meeting.

In a general sense all these meetings could be viewed as general meetings in the sense that they are meetings of the general membership as opposed to being class meetings. The last of the two mentioned meetings are in fact mentioned as such in s 29.

4.22.1 Annual general meeting

Every co-operative, whether with a share capital or mere membership by subscription, must hold an annual general meeting, otherwise known in the world of business as the 'AGM', once every year. This requirement is not set out in the Act, but it is widely expected that every co-operative society will hold at least one meeting every year, to wit, the annual general meeting. Among the many things which the by-laws must provide for as directed in the Schedule to the Co-operative Societies Act is 'the holding of annual general meetings, notices, agendas, voting etc' (clause I*(p)*). There should be no doubt, therefore, that the by-laws of every co-operative must provide for the holding of annual general meetings.

It is also expected that the by-laws will indicate the nature of the business to be transacted at the annual general meeting. Such meetings, however, generally provide an opportunity to the members of the co-operative to express their views on the management of the company by the directors and would deal with other matters such as the consideration of the directors' reports, the declaration of dividends where the co-operative has a share capital, the election of the board of directors and consideration of the accounts and balance sheet of the co-operative for the ensuing year, report of the auditor etc. It is probable that the by-laws will prescribes the period between the annual general meetings of a co-operative society linked to the end of its financial year.

The Co-operative Societies Act makes reference to the annual general meeting in only three sections, namely, ss 38, 39 and 41. In accordance with s 38(1) a co-operative society shall elect a board of directors consisting of such number of persons as shall be prescribed in its by-laws at its annual general meeting. Persons whose names appear in the application for registration of a co-operative society shall upon registration be deemed to have the powers and duties of directors 'until directors have been elected at the first general meeting of the co-operative society'.

Under s 39, a co-operative society is obliged at an annual general meeting to establish such number of committees as it may consider necessary for purposes of assisting the board of directors carry out its functions. Section 41 deals with the functions of the board of directors of a co-operative society. One of such functions is to prepare and present to the annual general meeting an income and expenditure report for the previous financial year and the budget requirement for the forthcoming year in accordance with the by-laws and the provisions of the Act. Section 41(3)(*f*) directs that the board shall present audited accounts to the annual general meeting.

4.22.2 General meeting

Members of a co-operative society will normally not manage to deal with all its business at the annual general meeting. In between annual general meetings directors or shareholders or members of the co-operative will seek to deal with certain matters affecting the co-operative society in a general meeting.

A general meeting, other than an annual general meeting, called to deal with regular business of the co-operative society, is known simply as a general meeting. It is of course arguable whether the term general meeting does or does not also include the annual general meeting. There is no intention to get into that argument and for the present purpose the two will be considered as distinct in keeping with the deliberate use of both terms in the Act.

A general meeting is referred to as such in a number of sections in the Act. In terms of s 20(1) for example, a general meeting of a co-operative society may amend the by-laws of the society by a resolution passed at such meeting with a two-thirds majority. Section 37(2) and (3) refers to a general meeting of a co-operative being held to consider a report of the board of directors after it has considered a complaint arising against a member of a co-operative society. After considering such report in a general meeting, the co-operative may expel a member from a co-operative society. In s 41, which relates to the functions of the board of directors of a co-operative society, there is reference in sub-s 2*(c)* to a general meeting. It states that the board shall exercise such powers of the co-operative society as are not by the Act or the by-laws required to be by resolution of the co-operative society in a general meeting.

Section 47(1) of the Co-operative Societies Act provides that a co-operative society may remove a director at a general meeting by resolution passed by at least two thirds of the members or delegates present. Section 47(2) states that in a similar meeting and by a similarly passed resolution a co-operative society may authorise the Registrar of Co-operatives to appoint officers to provide management and administrative support services to a co-operative for a period not exceeding one year.

In terms of s 44(1), where a vacancy on the board occurs, otherwise than by expiration of the term of office, the remaining directors may fill the vacancy until the next general meeting of the co-operative society. Under s 64(1), any two or more co-operative societies may by special resolution of each of the co-operative societies at a general meeting become amalgamated without dissolution or division of the funds of those co-operative societies.

4.22.3 Special meeting

This is the third kind of meeting which a co-operative society is entitled to hold in terms of the provisions of the Act. Like the other kinds of meeting these are neither defined nor elaborated upon in the Act. These are meetings, as the name suggests, convened to discuss special items or matters that may not regularly feature in the co-operative society. It appears that special meetings may be held by either the members of the co-operative society as a whole, or by the board. They are referred to in a number of sections.

To begin with, s 29 of the Act, which leaves the issue of meetings for the by-laws, specifically states that the holding of general and special meetings of a co-operative society as well as the procedure at such meetings will be provided for in the by-laws. In s 44(2) there is reference to a special meeting to be convened by the directors when the number of directors is reduced to less than the number required by the by-laws to constitute a quorum for a meeting of the board for purposes of filling a casual vacancy on the board. This is a meeting of the members and not the board.

According to s 46(2), the board of directors of a Co-operative society may call a special meeting of itself where the urgency of any particular matter does not permit the giving of the requisite seven days' notice to hold a meeting of the board. Under s 63 of the Act, the Registrar may, in order to safeguard the interest of the members, or the rights of creditors, order an investigation to be made by a person authorised by her into the affairs of the co-operative society. A report of such an investigation shall be tabled for consideration by a special meeting of the co-operative society or the board.

4.22.4 Directors' meeting

As far as the meetings of directors are concerned it is important that directors' meetings are often held more frequently than general meetings. In practice, the directors act collectively as a board unless the powers have been delegated to an individual director or directors. As with meetings of the co-operative society, meetings of the board may be very much a function of the provisions of the by-laws of the co-operative society. The board has the prerogative to regulate its own procedure. The material terms of s 46 read as follows:

(1) Subject to the other provisions of this Act and of the bylaws, a board may determine its own procedure.

(2) Upon giving notice of not less than seven days, a meeting of a board may be called by the chairperson and shall be called if not less than one-third of the directors so request in writing; except that if the urgency or any particular matter does not permit the giving of such notice, a special meeting may be called upon giving a shorter notice.

(3) Notwithstanding the provisions of the by-laws, the quorum at any meeting of a board shall be not less than one half of the number of directors.

(4) A board shall cause minutes to be kept of every meeting of the board.

It is important to note that s 46(2) refers to special meetings of the board to be convened at shorter notice than prescribed. This can only mean that the board holds and should hold other ordinary or regular board meetings upon normal notice being given.

4.23 THE BOARD OF DIRECTORS OF A CO-OPERATIVE SOCIETY

The directors of a co-operative society are responsible for the overall supervision and control of the co-operative society's affairs. Part V of the Act makes provision for directors. Section 38 proclaims that every co-operative society shall have a board of directors whose number shall be prescribed in the by-laws and who shall be elected by the members at an annual general meeting. Section 41(1) states that the board shall represent the co-operative society subject to the provisions of the by-laws. The section then lists the functions of the board, being to:

(a) direct and supervise the business of a co-operative society;

(b) be the custodian of the property of the co-operative society; and

(c) exercise all such powers of the co-operative society as are not required by or under the Act or the by-laws to be exercised by resolution of the co-operative society in a general or special meeting.

Furthermore, and more specifically, the board shall:

(a) be provided with, and examine, reports from officers of the co-operative society as the board directs in order to determine the operations and financial status of the co-operative society;

(b) keep the members informed of progress being made in the operations of the co-operative society;

(c) render advice to the members, on any matter relating to co-operatives as the members may require;

(d) prepare and present to the annual general meeting an income and expenditure report for the previous financial year and the budget requirements for the forthcoming year, in accordance with the other provisions of this Act and the by-laws;

(e) make a report to the annual general meeting of the work of the board during the preceding financial year including the activities undertaken by the co-operative society during the preceding financial year, together with such recommendations as it may consider necessary for the maintenance or improvement of the services provided by the co-operative society to its members; and

(f) present audited accounts to the annual general meeting.

The directors' basic function is to manage the co-operative society for other people. They are agents of the co-operative society. They are in the same position as directors of companies. Expectedly therefore the body of common-law rules which prohibits company directors from feathering their own nests at the expense of the company and its members applies with equal force to co-operative societies.

In performing their functions as a body, the directors are under an equitable duty to act bona fide in the interest of the company and, one may add, a co-operative society.

As individuals, directors are in a fiduciary position in relation to the body for which they are directors. This means they have a duty to act in good faith. In the words of Centlivres CJ in *Rex v Milne and Erleigh*:[28] 'It is of course clear that the duty of all agents including directors of companies is to conduct the affairs of the business in the interest of the principals and not for their own benefit.'

The fiduciary position of the directors with regard to the co-operative entails certain consequences in equity. Any matter in which a director has interest averse to that of the company is voidable in the absence of disclosure to the co-operative society. This is the position of the common law regarding contracts involving directors of companies and should apply to directors of co-operative societies too.

In *Hely-Hutchinson v Brayhead Ltd*,[29] a case which involved a breach by the director of the duty to disclose his interest in a contract with the company, Lord Denning said:

> It seems to me that when a director fails to disclose his interest, the effect is the same as non-disclosure in contracts *uberrimae fide*, or non-disclosure by a promoter who sells to the company property in which he is interested. Non-disclosure does not render the contract void or a nullity. It renders the contract voidable at the instance of the company and makes the director accountable for any secret profit which he has made.

A contract made by a co-operative society with one of its directors or with a company or firm in which such director is interested is voidable at the instance of the co-operative. Thus in *Aberdeen Rly Co v Blaikie Bros*,[30] where the respondent who had agreed to manufacture iron chairs for the appellant railway company sued to enforce the contract, it was held and upheld on appeal by the House of Lords that the railway company was not bound by the contract because at the time when it was made, the chairman of the board of directors of the railway company was also managing partner of the respondents.[31]

Regarding co-operative societies, this position crystallised in s 46(5) of the Co-operative Societies Act which provides:

> If a director is present at a meeting of a board at which any matter is the subject of consideration and in which matter the director or the director's spouse is, in a private capacity, interested, the director shall, as soon as is practicable after the commencement of the meeting, disclose the interest and shall not, unless the board otherwise directs, take part in any consideration or discussion of, or vote on, any question touching such matter.

---

[28] 1951 (1) SA 791 (A) at 828.

[29] [1967] 3 All ER 98 (CA) at 103.

[30] [1854] 1 Macq 461.

[31] See also *Transvaal Land Company v New Belgium (Transvaal) Land and Development Company* [1914] 2 Ch 488, and *North West Transport Company v Beatty* [1887] 12 App Cas 589 in which it was held that a contract which is voidable on account of a director's interest may be ratified by the company in a general meeting.

Subsection 6 of that section requires a disclosure of interest made under that section to be recorded in the minutes of the meeting at which it is made. Secondly, the fiduciary position in which a director stands in relation to a co-operative society entails that she cannot make a secret profit or divert opportunity from the co-operative society for herself.

Further, it should be noted that in addition to the common-law remedies available to erring directors, s 43(f) of the Co-operative Societies Act prescribes that a director shall cease to hold office if she 'is connected with, or participates in the profits of, any contract made between the co-operative society and any other co-operative society, company, organisation or individual in which that director has an interest; the fact of which that director knowingly failed to disclose to the board at or before the time the contract was made'

The repealed Companies Act, Chapter 388 of the Laws of Zambia, introduced some modifications to the common-law position. It also departs rather significantly from the provisions of the English Companies Act of 1985 on the issue of directors' interest in contracts involving their companies. Section 218(1) and (2) defines contracts in which directors would be deemed to be interested. Subsection (3) states that unless the articles of the company provide otherwise a director shall be entitled, subject to the Act, to enter into a contract with the company and such a contract shall not be voidable, nor shall the director be liable to account for any profit made thereby, by reason only of her being a director or of the fiduciary relationship thereby established. The section further obliges an interested director to any contract or proposed contract to declare the nature and extent of her interest at a meeting of directors or shareholders.

The newly introduced Companies Act 10 of 2017 replaces the section on contracts in which directors are interested by codifying the director's duties of good faith, avoiding conflict of interest and disclosing information about remuneration. The Act makes it clear that a director shall avoid a situation where that director has or is likely to have a direct or indirect interest such as deriving a material financial benefit that conflicts or is likely to conflict with the interests of the company. It would therefore follow that any contract the director enters into should not be in conflict with the interests of the company.

The extent to which s 218 of the repealed Companies Act and s 106 of the current Act should influence the operation of a board of a co-operative society is doubtful. A better approach, which is truly positivist, is to let the provisions of the Co-operative Society Act, without more, apply to a situation affecting a co-operative. There appears to be no direct legal provision either in the Co-operative Societies Act or in the Companies Act, save the ones already pointed out including ss 11, 13 and 82, which allows for the application of the provisions of the Companies Act to co-operative societies.

4.24 QUALIFICATIONS OF DIRECTORS OF CO-OPERATIVE SOCIETIES

The qualifications necessary for directors of a co-operative society are nowhere stated in the Co-operative Societies Act. Section 38 merely provides that the number of members of the board shall be prescribed in the by-laws and that such members of the board shall be elected by members of the co-operative from amongst its members. It follows, therefore, that one qualification for membership of the board of directors of a co-operative society is membership of the co-operative society itself.

A person will not be eligible for appointment to the board of a co-operative unless she is a member of the co-operative society. Since s 25 of the Act provides that any person who wishes to be a member of a co-operative society shall not exercise the rights of a member until that person has paid to the co-operative society the amount required for membership of that co-operative society, or such person has acquired such interest in the co-operative society, as may be prescribed in or under the Act or the by-laws, it seems to follow that a non-paid-up member or a member who has not fully paid her membership dues either in the form of payment for her shares or payment of her membership fees in full, if payment in full is what is required for membership, will not be eligible for election to board membership.

Failure to possess the share or other qualification for board membership was considered in a case concerning directorship of a company, but it is submitted that the holding by the court in the case of *Carbonic Gas Company Limited v Ziman*[32] applies with equal force to co-operative societies. Murray J stated as follows:

> [I]f the articles provide that the holding of a certain number of shares is qualification for election as a director, that shareholding must exist at the time of election, otherwise the appointment is defective and absolutely void; it cannot be rendered valid even by the subsequent acquisition of the prescribed qualification. If the articles, however merely provide that the specified shareholding is a qualification for holding office of director such a qualification may be obtained within 2 months (or such shorter period as the articles fix) but if at the end of such 2 months or shorter period the qualification has not

---

[32] 1938 TPD 102 (Transvaal Provincial Division).

been obtained, this is an automatic vacation of directorship with a relevant incapacity for reappointment until qualified as required . . .[33]

It is important to refer once again to s 19(1) of the Act which states that the by-laws of a co-operative society shall include provisions relating to matters set out in the Schedule. The Schedule then provides in Clause I that the by-laws of every co-operative society shall deal with '*(o)* the terms of office of the board of directors'. The by-laws will therefore spell out the other terms upon which directors serve.

4.25 VACATION OF OFFICE BY DIRECTOR OF A CO-OPERATIVE

In terms of s 43 of the Act the term of office of a director shall be prescribed in the by-laws. As the by-laws also prescribe the terms under which directors serve, vacation of office by a director will be very much a matter of prescription in the by-laws. However, the Act also indicates instances when a director may in any event vacate office. These include:

4.25.1 Death of a director

The death of a director is the most obvious and least contentious way of vacation of office by a director. When a director of a co-operative society dies, she ceases to be a director because she is dead. Her office is vacated in accordance with s 44(3)*(i)*.

4.25.2 Expiration of the period of office

A director shall vacate office at the expiry of the period for which she is appointed director. In the case of directors named in application for incorporation, the term of office expires at the end of the first annual general meeting of the co-operative.

Section 38(2) provides:

> The persons whose names appear in an application for the registration of a co-operative society shall upon registration, be deemed to have all the powers and duties of directors; and shall direct the affairs of the co-operative society until directors have been elected at the first general meeting of the co-operative society.

The by-laws will prescribe the tenure of office of directors and at the expiry of such period elections will be held by the members in a general meeting.

4.25.3 End of the sixth consecutive year

A board member who serves a co-operative society for six consecutive years will vacate office at the end of the sixth year but will be eligible for

---

[33] 1938 TPD 102 (Transvaal Provincial Division).

election as a director after a lapse of one year. This is provided for in s 43(2) which reads:

> Notwithstanding subsection (1), a director of a board shall not hold office for a period of more than six consecutive years from the time of the first election of that director but may be eligible for election as a director after a lapse of one year after the end of the initial period.

This provision seemingly imposes a disqualification for a director, rather than a reason for vacation of office.

4.25.4 Disqualification

A director shall cease to hold office if she is disqualified. She may be disqualified on any of the following grounds set out in s 44(3), that is to say, she is:

(a) declared bankrupt;

(b) declared to be of unsound mind;

(c) connected with, or participates in the profits of, any contract made between the co-operative society and any other co-operative society, company, organisation or individual in which that director has an interest; the fact of which that director knowingly failed to disclose to the board at or before the time the contract was made;

(d) sentenced to a term of imprisonment exceeding six months;

(e) lawfully detained for a period exceeding three months or the director's freedom of movement is restricted for a period exceeding three months under any written law;

(f) guilty of gross misconduct in terms of the by-laws; or

(g) ceases to be a member of the co-operative society.

4.25.5 Removal by resolution of the co-operative society

A member of the board may be removed before the expiry of her term of office by resolution of the co-operative society passed in a general meeting by at least two thirds of the members or delegates present. This is sanctioned by s 47(1) of the Act.

4.25.6 Holding remunerative office in the co-operative society

A director who holds any remunerative office or office of profit in the co-operative shall vacate office in accordance with s 44(3)*(c)* of the Act. It is probable that the by-laws would make the managing director or principal executive officer an exception.

4.25.7 Resignation

A director may resign her office by notice in writing to the co-operative society giving not less than one month before resignation. In reference to a company director, in *Glossop v Glossop*[34] Neville J observed:

> I have no doubt that a director is entitled to relinquish his office at any time he pleases by proper notice to the company and that his resignation depends upon his notice and is not dependent upon any acceptance by the company, because I do not think they are in a position to refuse acceptance . . . .

4.26 CANCELLATION OF A CO-OPERATIVE SOCIETY/ WINDING UP

Under s 81 of the Act, the Registrar may cancel a co-operative society for any of the reasons set out. Where a co-operative society is so cancelled the co-operative society shall cease to carry on any business and the assets and liabilities of the co-operative society shall vest in a liquidator appointed by the Registrar for the purpose. This effectively means that the directors of the co-operative stand dismissed.

KEY POINTS

- Co-operative societies (co-operatives) are a form of business association used by communities wanting to achieve common economic social and cultural goals while the members retain democratic control of the business entity.
- The directors of a co-operative society are responsible for the overall supervision and control of the co-operative society's affairs.
- A company registered under the Companies Act may convert into a co-operative society. The procedure for conversion of a registered company into a co-operative society is set out in s 11 of the Co-operative Societies Act.

---

[34] [1907] 2 Ch 370.

Chapter 5

REGISTERED COMPANIES

5.1 INTRODUCTION

The Companies Act 10 of 2017 regulates companies in Zambia. The purpose of the Companies Act as set out in the Preamble is a mouthful of aims—possibly a wish list. Unlike what has hitherto been the practice where a preamble to an Act captures in a few lines what the principal objectives of the Act are, the Preamble to the present Companies Act plentifully recites the objectives of the Act as follows:

> An Act to promote the development of the economy by encouraging entrepreneurship, enterprise efficiency, flexibility and simplicity in the formation and maintenance of companies; provide for the incorporation, categorisation, management and administration of different types of companies; provide the procedure for the approval of company names, change of name and conversion of companies; provide for shareholders' rights and obligations, the conduct of meetings and the passing of resolutions by shareholders; to encourage transparency and high standards of corporate governance by providing for the functions and obligations of company secretaries and directors; provide for issue of shares, share capital requirements, procedures for alteration and reduction of share capital and disclosure requirements of companies; provide for the public issue of shares, the issue and registration of charges and debentures; incorporate financial reporting provisions, maintenance of accounting records, and access to financial information of companies; provide for amalgamations; provide for the registration of foreign companies doing business in Zambia; provide for the deregistration of companies; repeal and replace the Companies Act, 1994; and provide for matters connected with or incidental to the foregoing.[1]

Although registered companies are primarily governed by the provisions of the Companies Act and by the rules and regulations laid down in the articles of the company and any shareholders' agreement, the nature of the company and/or the business it is intended to undertake normally determines what other legal requirements specified in other pieces of legislation will have to be complied with. Companies undertaking business as diverse as commodities trading, banking, mining, manufacturing and farming will use the legal framework set out by the Act for purposes of their set up before moving on to comply with other legal requirements under separate, specific Acts of Parliament or other regulations governing particular aspects of their business. For example, a company that wishes to undertake banking business

---

[1] As at the time of writing, the Act was not operational as the Minister had not yet set a date for the operation of the Act in terms of s 1 of the Act.

or financial services will inevitably have to also ensure compliance with the Banking and Financial Services Act 7 of 2017 and the regulations made under that Act. A company intending to undertake insurance will be required to comply with the provisions of the Insurance Act.[2]

A company set up to manufacture pharmaceutical products or to undertake mining activities will likewise have a whole host of laws and regulations to meet. A public company may have several rules and regulations to abide by as set out in the Securities Act 41 of 2016. It is also always important to bear in mind that there are various sector regulators which may also prescribe safety and licensing requirements which must be met before a business enterprise can commence or continue business.[3]

5.2 DEFINITION AND NATURE OF A COMPANY

There is no strict or technical meaning of the word 'company.' It may simply be defined as an association of persons with a common business purpose. Section 2 of the Companies Act defines the term 'company' as 'a company incorporated under this Act; or ... an existing company'. This definition is clearly not very useful because the term is not defined with reference to its features or its capacity. That great company lawyer, Buckley J, attempted the following definition of the term company in *Tennant v Stanley*:

> The word 'company' has no strict technical meaning; it involves two ideas—namely, first that the association is of persons so numerous as not to be aptly described as a firm; and, secondly, that the consent of all the other members is not required to the transfer of a member's interest.[4]

It is, however, easy to appreciate that this dictum does not apply to the modern phenomenon of the so called 'one-man' private company where transfer of shares by a member is ordinarily prohibited unless the other members agree. Marshall CJ's definition in the American case of *Dartmouth College v Woodward*[5] perhaps goes a little further in explaining the characteristics of a company. He defined a company as

> a person, artificial, invisible, intangible and existing only in the contemplation of the law being a mere creature of law. It possesses only those properties which the charter of its creation confers upon it, either expressly or incidental to its very existence.

---

[2] Chapter 382 of the Laws of Zambia.

[3] For example, the Bank of Zambia, the Competition and Consumer Protection Commission, the Securities Commission, the Energy Regulation Board, the National Council for Construction, the National Water and Sanitation Council, the Pharmaceuticals Regulation Authority, the Zambia Bureau of Standards, the Zambia Information and Technology Authority, the Weights and Measures Agency and the Environmental Council of Zambia.

[4] [1906] 1 Ch 131, 134.

[5] 4 Wheat (US) 518.

In Zambia, a registered company is one that is formed and registered under the Companies Act 10 of 2017. It also includes an existing company which was formed and registered under the former Companies Act. A company comes into existence when it is registered, ie when its name is entered into the register meant for this purpose under the Companies Act and a certificate of incorporation issued to it by the Registrar of Companies. The certificate issued by the Registrar is in a prescribed form and states that the company is on and from the date specified in the certificate, incorporated. It also specifies the type of company.

In terms of s 12(1) of the Companies Act, any two or more persons associated for a lawful purpose may form an incorporated company by subscribing their names to an application for incorporation that satisfies the requirements of the Act and lodging the application with the Registrar. Certain documents as set out in s 12 ought to accompany any such application. These are considered later in this chapter. Once an application which satisfies the requirements of the Act is received and considered by the Registrar, a company is incorporated by being entered in the Register of Companies and a certificate of incorporation is issued by the Registrar. From the moment a company is incorporated, it acquires certain attributes which in fact define its nature. This chapter now turns to these characteristics of an incorporated entity which define its nature.

5.3 CHARACTERISTICS OF A COMPANY

An incorporated company has several characteristics which define it and give it its identity and, in many instances, provide it with advantages over an unincorporated association such as a partnership. These attributes of a company explain the nature of a company and distinguish it from other forms of business association. These specified characteristics are:

5.3.1 Separate legal personality

A company is in law regarded as a legal entity separate and distinct from its members. As an artificial legal person, a company will be entitled to deal with other persons, natural or artificial, in its own name and in its own right. In terms of s 11 of the Companies Act, a company is deemed incorporated on and from the date of incorporation specified in the certificate of incorporation issued by the Registrar of Companies. By s 22 of the Act a company is invested, subject to the Act and to such limitations as are inherent in its corporate nature, the same capacity, rights, powers and privileges of a natural individual.

Because a company is distinct and separate from the persons making it up, it cannot be held liable for the acts of individuals in the company, nor can an individual claim a benefit due to the company, even if he holds a substantial interest in the company. The leading case that illustrates the concept of corporate status is that of *Salomon v Salomon and Co.*[6] Salomon, a trader, transferred his business as a leather merchant and wholesale boot manufacturer to a limited company formed by him for the purpose of taking over the business. The company had a nominal capital of 40,000 shares of £1 each. The shareholders of the company were Salomon himself, his wife, his daughter and four sons who each subscribed for one share. In consideration of the business, Salomon took 2,000 shares of £1 each, and debentures worth £10 000. This entailed that the company owed Salomon the company. Salomon was appointed managing director while his two sons were directors.

When a year later, due to trade difficulties, the company went into liquidation, it was found that the company's assets were worth only £6 000 while the liabilities amounted to £17 000. If the amount realised from the assets were to be, in the first place, applied in payment to Salomon under the debenture as a secured creditor, there would be no funds left for payment of the ordinary (unsecured) creditors. The liquidator and the other creditors alleged that the company was a mere alias or agent and that Salomon was liable to indemnify the company against the claims of the unsecured creditor and that no payment should be made on the debenture held by him until the ordinary creditors had been paid in full. The House of Lords held that 'Salomon and Co Ltd' was a real company fulfilling the requirements of the legislature, and it had a separate legal existence from its members and, therefore, that Salomon was entitled to be paid his dues first as a secured creditor. Lord Macnaughten put the matter thus:

> [W]hen the memorandum is duly signed and registered, though there be only seven shares taken, the subscribers are a body corporate 'capable forthwith' to use the words of the enactment 'of exercising the functions of an incorporated company'. Those are strong words. The company attains maturity on its birth. There is no period of minority—no interval of incapacity. I cannot understand how a body corporate thus made 'capable' by statute can lose its individuality by issuing the bulk of its capital to one person, whether he be a subscriber to the memorandum or not. The company is at law a different person altogether from the subscribers to the memorandum; and though it may be that after incorporation the business is precisely the same as it was before, and the same persons are managers, and the same hands receive the profits, the company is not in law the agent of the subscribers or trustee for them. Nor are the subscribers as

---

[6] [1897] AC 22.

members liable, in any shape or form, except to the extent and in the manner provided by the Act . . .

In *Macaura v North Assurance Company Ltd*[7] where the owner of a timber estate which he assigned to a company known as the Irish Canadian Saw Mills Ltd in which he was virtually the sole shareholder, insured the company's timber in his own name, the court held that the owner as mere shareholder in the company had no insurable interest in the timber belonging to the company. Lord Summer observed:

> [I]t is clear that the appellant had no insurable interest in the timber described. It was not his. It belonged to the Irish Canadian Saw Mills Ltd . . . He had no lien or security over it and though it lay on his land by his permission, he had no responsibility to its owner for its safety, nor was it there under any contract that enabled him to hold it for his debt. He owned almost all the shares in the company, and company owed him a good deal of money . . . The debt was not exposed to fire, nor were the shares, and the fact that he was virtually the company's only creditor, while the timber was its only assets, seems to me to make no difference . . .

Elsewhere in the Commonwealth, the courts have followed the same reasoning.[8] The Indian Supreme Court in the case of *Tata Engineering and Locomotive Company Ltd v State of Bihar*[9] summed up the concept of corporate status as follows:

> The corporation in law is equal to a natural person and has a legal entity separate from that of its shareholders; it bears its own name and has a seal of its own; its assets are separate and distinct from those of its members; it can sue and be sued exclusively for its own purpose; its creditors cannot obtain satisfaction from the assets of its members; the liability of the members or shareholders is limited to capital invested by them; similarly the creditors or the members have no right to the assets of the corporation. This position has been well established ever since the decision in the case of *Salomon v Salomon & Co.* which was pronounced in 1897 and indeed has been the well-recognised principle of common law.

The Supreme Court in Zambia cited with approval the case of *Salomon v Salomon* in *ZCCM and Ndola Lime Company Limited v Sikanyika and Others*[10] where it held that the change of ownership of shares in a company cannot result in the corporate entity becoming a new employer. The court

---

[7] [1925] AC 619.

[8] See for example in *Zimmerman v St Paul Fire Insurance Co.* [1967] 63 DLR (2d) 282 where an Australian Court followed *Macaura*. In *Lee v Lees Air Farming Ltd* [1961] AC 12, the appellant's husband founded Lee's Air Farming Ltd. He was the controlling shareholders as well as its director. He was employed as the company's chief pilot. He died while piloting an air craft in the course of the company's business. The New Zealand Court of Appeal had to determine whether he was a 'worker' for purposes of workman's compensation. It was held that he was not. The Privy Council held that the deceased and the company were distinct legal persons and had a contractual relationship.

[9] 1965 AIR 40.

[10] SCZ Judgment 24 of 2000.

recognised the distinction between the company as a body corporate and the shareholders in that company.

The case of *Miller v Miller*[11] lends support to the assertion that, as a separate legal persona, a company can engage in any lawful act and is entitled to the same rights as are available to any juristic person, such as submitting to arbitration.

5.3.2 Perpetual succession

Once incorporated, the company has perpetual succession. This simply means that a company has a continuous existence and it can outline its members. Shareholders in a company may come and go but the company remains. The continuity of the company does not depend on its membership. This, however, does not suggest that once a company is incorporated, it can never end. A company's life ends when it is wound up and struck off the register in accordance with the Companies Act.

Section 190(1) of the Companies Act provides:

> In the case of the death of a shareholder of a company the—
> (a) survivor or survivors where the deceased was a joint holder; and
> (b) personal representative of the deceased where the deceased was a sole holder or last survivor of joint holders;
> shall be the only persons recognised by the company as having title to the deceased's interest in the shares.

In the case of *ZCCM and Ndola Lime Company Limited v Sikanyika and Others*, the Zambia Supreme Court reiterated the concept of perpetual succession when it ruled that the company remains the same entity in spite of a total change in its membership. The death of shareholders will not affect the corporate existence of a company. Where a shareholder of a company dies, the legal representative of the deceased shareholder becomes entitled to shares by way of transmission.

5.3.3 Can own property in its own name

As a persona at law, a company can own property in its own name, enjoy such property and dispose of it. The property of the company will not be considered as the joint property of the shareholders of the company.

5.3.4 Has limited liability

An important attribute of a company is that the liability of its members is limited. This is arguably the principal advantage of a company as opposed to an unincorporated association such as a partnership.

---

[11] [1963] R & N 60. See also *Re H. R Harmer Ltd* [1958] 3 All ER 689.

5.3.5 Transferability of shares

The shares of a company are freely transferable and can therefore be sold and purchased in the share market. They are therefore transferable like moveable property. This is another advantage that companies have over partnerships.

The shares of a company are freely transferable and can therefore be sold and purchased in the share market. They are therefore transferable like moveable property. This is another advantage that companies have over partnerships. This characteristic of a company is recognised in s 188(1) of the Companies Act which provides:

> Subject to the articles, fully paid-up shares in a company may be transferred by entry of the name of the transferee on the share and beneficial ownership register and evidenced by registration with the Registrar.

It must however be noted that articles of a company may impose restrictions on the transferability of shares and transfer may only be done in accordance with the conditions laid down in the articles.

5.3.6 Capacity to sue and to be sued

Being a legal person with independent existence, a company can file suits against other persons in its own name. Likewise, it can also be sued in its own name. No action can be maintained in the company's name without authority of the company nor can a shareholder or director be a proper plaintiff in an action to redress wrongs committed to the company.[12]

5.4 TYPES OF COMPANIES

The provisions of the Companies Act and the rules and regulations laid down in the articles of the company govern registered companies. Section 13 of the Companies Act lists the types of companies that could be incorporated under the Act as

(a) public companies;
(b) private companies being:
    (i) private companies limited by shares;
    (ii) companies limited by guarantee; or
    (iii) unlimited companies.

Each type is now considered, though not necessarily in the order in which they are mentioned in the Act.

5.4.1 Public company

A public company is provided for and regulated by s 7 of the Companies Act. The Act provides that this company shall have share capital and have

---

[12] [1916] 2 AC 307.

articles of association that state the rights, privileges, restrictions and conditions attaching to each class of shares authority given to directors. A public company does not have a limit on how many shareholders may own shares in the company.

Section 7 lists a number of requirements that must be satisfied for a company to qualify as a public company. These are:

1   it must have a share capital;
2   its articles must state the rights, privileges, restrictions and conditions attaching to each class of shares, if there are two or more classes;
3   its articles must state the authority given to the directors to determine the number of shares in, the designation of and the rights, privileges, restrictions etc. attaching to each series in a class of shares, if the class of shares may be issued in series;
4   its shares must rank equally apart from differences due to their being in different classes or series;
5   its articles must not impose any restriction on the right to transfer;
6   it cannot transact any businesses, exercise borrowing powers or incur any indebtedness except for purposes incidental to its incorporation obtaining subscription etc. until it has applied to the Registrar in a prescribed form and the Registrar has issued it with a certificate; and
7   the nominal value of its allotted share capital must not be less than the authorised minimum (ie one million kwacha or such larger or smaller amount as may be prescribed instead).

It is curious that the Companies Act does not directly provide for the minimum number of members of a public company.

5.4.2 Private company

(i) *Private company limited by shares*
The vast majority of registered companies in Zambia are companies limited by shares. This type of company is accommodated in ss 8 and 9 of the Companies Act which provide that the company shall have articles of association that provide for the rights, privileges, restrictions and conditions attaching to each class of shares authority given to directors. Further, as is implied in the name, such companies must have a share capital. A company limited by shares is one in which the liability of its members (ie the shareholders) is limited to the amount, if any, unpaid on the shares they hold. Where the shares are paid for in full the liability of the members is nil. Where the shares are partly paid for, the liability of the members is limited to the extent of the amount remaining unpaid on shares in the company.

Lastly, the number of shareholders or members in all private companies is limited to 50.

(ii) *Private unlimited company*
An unlimited company is one having no limit on the liability of its members. The members of such a company are personally liable for the

company's debts and liabilities. Where, for instance, in the event of winding up of such a company it is established that the assets of the company are not sufficient to pay its debts, the members' private property can be attached for the purpose of settling the company's obligations. The Companies Act provides for such companies in s 11.

Following naturally from the concept of separate legal personality and the doctrine of privity of contract, creditors of such a company cannot commence proceedings directly against the members. Where an unlimited company is wound up, a member shall be liable to contribute without limitation of liability. It is obvious that members will only be obliged to contribute during the winding up process and that no such obligation attaches when the company is a going concern.

(iii) *Private company limited by guarantee*

Companies limited by guarantee are provided for in s 10 of the Companies Act. A company of limited members is limited to such amounts as the members undertake to contribute to the assets of the company in the event of the company being wound up. Section 10(1) of the Companies Act requires each subscriber to an application for incorporation of a company limited by guarantee to sign a declaration of guarantee specifying the amount that such subscriber undertakes to contribute to the assets of the company in the event of its being wound up. As in the case of companies limited by shares, the liability of members of companies limited by guarantee is therefore limited.

Two points must be emphasised: firstly, the guaranteed amounts may differ from member to member or they may be fixed by the articles. Secondly, the liability of the members can only be enforced during the winding up of the company. Members cannot be called upon to pay the guaranteed amounts during the normal existence of the company.

A private company limited by guarantee is the only type of company in the Act which is allowed to incorporate without share capital and not permitted to carry out business for the purposes of making a profit.

5.4.3 Foreign company

A foreign company relates to an entity that is incorporated outside Zambia but has a branch in Zambia. Every foreign company requires an established place of business in Zambia that can be an office, factory or mine or any other fixed place of business.

Section 303 of the Companies Act provides that a foreign company must appoint a local director who is resident in Zambia and empowered and authorised to conduct and manage the affairs, property, business and other operations of the company in Zambia.

5.5 PRIVATE AND PUBLIC COMPANIES

From a business point of view, the main difference between a private and a public company is that the former is suited to a small business or family trading enterprise where informality is desired and capital can easily be obtained privately, while the latter requires more formality and strict compliance with a great deal of legislation, can raise money by invitation to the public, and is thus suited to businesses having greater capital needs.

5.6 INCORPORATION

Section 12(1) of the Companies Act provides that two or more persons may apply to incorporate a company specified above for a lawful purpose. Section 18(8) of the Companies Act provides that an individual who is under 18 years of age, an undischarged bankrupt or of unsound mind and has been declared to be so by a court of competent jurisdiction cannot incorporate company. Notwithstanding this, s 14(2) states that the incorporation of a company shall not be invalid by reason only that an individual or individuals subscribed to the application for incorporation.

The documents required to incorporate a company under the Companies Act include the application for incorporation form, the articles of association, consent form signed by at least two directors and a company secretary to act in those roles, a statement of beneficial ownership in respect of each beneficial owner of the company and Statutory Declaration of Compliance which may require some professional input to formulate or complete. This may initially appear complicated for small enterprises that cannot afford professional fees. Such associations may, as an initial step, prefer registration under the Registration of Business Names Act, though this need not necessarily be so.

However, it is important to note that in terms of s 39 of the Companies Act, prior to incorporating a company, a person must apply for clearance and approval of their proposed name for the company from the Registrar of Companies. Only after this process is completed can the documents above be filed to complete the incorporation of a company.

5.6.1 Name clearance

The first formal contact with the office of the Registrar of Companies that any person wishing to form a company will have will be at the stage of name clearance. Section 39(1) provides that a person wishing to incorporate a company may apply to the Registrar for an opinion to give clearance and approval of a proposed name. This is in effect always one in practice and is called name clearance.

There is no doubt that certain names would be undesirable either because they are likely to cause confusion with the names of other existing companies, or they are suggestive of impropriety, or they are deceptive, or they are blasphemous etc.

A practical process, which is in fact the first step in the incorporation process, is name clearance. This involves writing a letter to the Registrar of Companies stating a number of possible names under which the company may be incorporated order of preference, coupled with a request for the Registrar to advise whether the name or names are available for registration. Where the name suggests that the company enjoys the patronage of the President the written consent of the Minister responsible for commerce must be sought. Upon receipt of the application for name clearance, the Office of the Registrar conducts a name search to ascertain whether, firstly, there is already an existing company using the same name or a name so similar as to cause confusion, and, secondly, if no existing company uses the proposed name, whether the name is in any other way undesirable, eg if the name is likely to cause offence, is suggestive of blasphemy or indecency etc. A search fee is payable in this regard.

The Registrar will only clear the name as being available for registration upon being satisfied with the result of the search or the name as aforesaid. Upon receipt of the Registrar's indication that the name is available for registration, the Registrar will reserve the name for a period of 90 days. The person must then incorporate the company within the period during which the name is reserved. Thereafter, within the 90-day period, there are some documents that need to be filed to incorporate the company. As mentioned above, once the issue of the name is resolved, persons wishing to incorporate a company would then have to complete and file the application for incorporation form and other incorporation documents.

Reservation of a name pending incorporation is rarely done in practice. Persons wishing to incorporate a company will most probably already have prepared all the necessary incorporation documents while awaiting name clearance and will therefore be ready to lodge the registration documents as soon as the name has been cleared. It is not certain what the legal position would be if two or more applications are made at the same time to reserve one name.[13]

---

[13] The case of *Builma (Cape) (Pty) Ltd v Registrar of Companies and Other* 1956 (3) SA 690 (SR) suggested that the Registrar has discretion in making a determination on the matter which could only

The Registrar may reject an application if the name registered is likely to cause confusion with an already registered company or a well-known name or trademark. The Act defines a well-known name or trademark as associated generally by the Zambian public with a registered company, products whether within or outside the Republic, and in respect of which confusion is likely to arise if the proposed name or trademark is registered by a company other than the company generally associated with that name. A court is empowered to grant an injunction against a company using a proposed name that created an impression that was similar to a well-known registered company.

The Registrar will also be permitted to reject the proposed name if it is undesirable to the public interest or calculated to deceive or mislead the public. This is in line with the case of the *Society of Motor Manufacturers and Traders Limited v Motor Manufacturers and Traders Mutual Insurance Company Limited*,[14] where the court held that the proposed name of the company was calculated to deceive as it created the impression that the company was associated with an already registered company.

Further, the Registrar may reject a name if the proposed name denotes the patronage of the state or of the President, government or administration of any foreign state, or of any department or institution of any foreign state, or, the registration would suggest or imply a connection with a political party.

5.6.2 Application for incorporation form

The application for incorporation form differs depending on the type of company. Section 12(4) of the Act outlines, for the first time, what the application for incorporation for shall include. These are the:

- name and address of the individual lodging the application;
- proposed name of the company;
- physical address of the office to be the registered office of the company;
- registered postal address, electronic mail address and phone number of the company where available;
- type of company to be formed;
- particulars of persons who shall be the first directors of the company;

---

be attacked on special grounds such as *mala fides*. That case was however interpreting a particular provision of the Zimbabwe Companies Act.

[14] [1925] 1 Ch 675.

- particulars of persons who shall be the first secretary or joint secretaries of the company; and
- nature of the company's proposed business or proposed activity.

Both the application for incorporation form and articles of association will include a clause outlining the objects of the company. The objects of the company according to s 6(1) of the Companies Act should be for a lawful purpose.

5.6.3 Consent form by at least two directors and a company secretary to act in those roles

Section 94 of the Companies Act provides that a person shall not be appointed as a director or secretary of a company unless that person has given consent to be appointed as such, in the prescribed form; and made a declaration that the person is not disqualified by the Act from holding the office.

5.6.4 Statutory declaration

Section 13 of the Companies Act provides that either a legal practitioner or person named as first director or secretary of the company shall sign a declaration made in the prescribed form stating that the requirements of the Act relating to incorporation have been complied with.

When the applicants for incorporation meet the requirements outlined above and do not submit any false information, in terms of the Companies Act, the Registrar shall register the company, issue a certificate of incorporation and a certificate of share capital within five days of the application being made. Once the certificate of incorporation has been issued, the company can commence business.

5.7 CERTIFICATE OF INCORPORATION

Once the company files all the requisite documentation for incorporation and meets all the requirements, s 14(1) provides that the Registrar shall within five days register the company and issue a certificate of incorporation. A certificate of incorporation is conclusive evidence that the company is incorporated from the date of registration and that the requirements of this Act regarding the incorporation of the company have been complied with.

A company can only commence business operations once the certificate of incorporation has been granted.

5.8 ARTICLES OF ASSOCIATION

The articles of association are defined in the Companies Act as the internal governing rules of a company. The Companies Act provides that every company must have articles of association. The articles provide details on important matters such as the object and purpose of the company, the appointment and powers of directors, meetings of the company, voting rights, dividends and matters relating to shares and share capital of the company.

Section 26(1) of the Companies Act provides that the articles of association of a company are a statutory contract that regulates the relationship between the company and its members and between the members themselves.

5.9 NAME OF THE COMPANY

It has already been stated that the name of the company should not be undesirable or identical with that of any existing company, or suggestive of enjoyment of the patronage of the President. The name should end with an appropriate word indicating the nature of the company—limited or unlimited or public. Where the name of the company so closely resembles the name of an existing company as to cause confusion, the Registrar may under s 43(1) of the Companies Act direct that the company changes its name. This, however, is assuming that the Registrar is of the opinion that the name would cause confusion with an existing name.

Where the Registrar is not of that opinion, he would not invoke his power under s 43(1) of the Act to direct that the name be changed. Even if the Registrar does not invoke the powers contained in s 43(1), any company whose name the name of a new company resembles, will be entitled to apply to court to restrain the new company with an identical name from using the name. As the name of a company is part of its business reputation or goodwill, the court will, on application, normally grant an injunction. In *Ewing v Buttercup Margarine*[15] the court granted an injunction against a company using a proposed name that was similar to that of a well-known registered company.

Where, however, the name does not create an impression that it is connected with an existing company, or where the business of the company is or will be different from that of an existing company, there may not necessarily be confusion and the court will not grant an injunction. Thus in *Society of Motor Manufacturers and Traders Limited v Motor Manufacturers and Traders Mutual Insurance Company Limited*,[16] the court declined to grant an injunction as it held that the proposed name of the

---

[15] [1917] 2 Ch 1.
[16] [1925] 1 Ch 675.

company was not calculated to deceive as it created the impression that the company was associated with an already registered company.

5.10 REGISTERED OFFICE

Section 28(1) of the Companies Act provides that a company shall have its registered office in Zambia to which all communications and notices may be addressed. In *Grand Eddy Knowles v Ohan Transport Limited*[17] the Supreme Court of Zambia reaffirmed the current s 28(2) of the Act which provides that the registered office of a company is to be used for service of writs and other legal processes.

The registered office of a company need not be the company's place of business. It is indeed not unusual for the registered office of a company to be the lawyer's or the accountant's office. In this regard, Geoffrey Morse explains the significance of a company's registered office in the following terms:

> The reason for requiring a company to have a registered office is that the company has a legal existence but does not have a physical existence, it is necessary to know where the company can be found, where documents can be served on it. A company need not, and very frequently does not carry on its business at its registered office. There is nothing, for example, to prevent a company with a registered office in England from carrying on its business abroad.[18]

Section 30 of the Act provides that a company shall keep its articles of association and a register of the company's members and beneficial owners, minutes of meetings and company records, financial statements and accounting records at the company's registered office.

5.11 COMPANY OFFICERS

As an entity, the company cannot act for itself. It necessarily must act through its human agents. The affairs of a company are thus usually entrusted to a small group of persons called directors who work closely with a management team. This position is well settled. It was recognised by the Kabwe High Court in *Jigry Auto Works Limited v M H Patel*[19] where the court was emphatic that a company, though a body corporate with a legal personality, can only do things through its officers as its organs. In *BP Zambia Plc v Interland Motors Limited*,[20] Ngulube CJ held as follows:

---

[17] [1978] ZR 8.
[18] G Morse et al *Charlesworth's Company Law* 13 ed (1987) 70.
[19] 1989/HB/129 [1993].
[20] SCZ Judgment 5 of 2001.

As a metaphysical entity or fiction of law which only has legal, but no physical existence, a company (though being a separate and distinct legal person from its members or shareholders) can only act through the humans charged with its management and the conduct of its affairs.

The affairs of a company are managed and governed by the directors of the company acting individually or collectively, or the shareholders acting collectively at a general meeting of the company. The directors manage all the affairs and operations of the company whilst the shareholders exercise powers reserved for them such as appointing directors and auditors and selling and leasing assets of the company.

Section 86(1) of the Companies Act provides that the business of a company shall be managed by, or under the direction or supervision of, a board of directors who may pay all expenses incurred in promoting and forming the company; and exercise all such powers of the company as are not, by this Act or the articles, required to be exercised by the members. Further, s 131 provides that the shareholders shall exercise the powers reserved for them but if the board of directors perform their duties, the shareholders may ratify their actions.

Although it is preferable, especially in relation to a public company, for a director to be a member of a professional body and to be a qualified professional, the position under the law is that a director need have no professional qualifications whatsoever. The Companies Act, however, does disqualify certain persons from holding office as a director of any company. A person is disqualified, in terms of s 92(3) of the Companies Act, from holding office as aforesaid if he:

(a)   is under eighteen years of age;
(b)   is an undischarged bankrupt;
(c)   has been declared by a court of competent jurisdictions to be of unsound mind; or
(d)   fails to satisfy any additional qualifications for directors provided in the articles.

Additionally, s 94 provides that a person shall not be appointed as director unless he has consented in writing. The articles of a company often set out more restrictions on eligibility for directorship in a company. The general purpose of provisions imposing such restrictions is to keep the management of the company out of the hands of unscrupulous or disreputable people.

5.12 COMPANY SECRETARY

Section 82 of the Companies Act provides that every company is obliged to appoint a company secretary. This officer is responsible for all the administrative duties of the company such as providing the directors, collectively and individually, with guidance as to their duties, responsibilities and powers and informing the board on reports relating to the operations of the company, ensuring statutory documents are filed and bringing to the attention of the board of directors any failure on the part of the company or a director to comply with the articles or the Companies Act.

The Companies Act in s 83 provides that a company secretary is responsible for providing the directors, collectively and individually, with guidance as to their duties, responsibilities and powers and informing the board on reports relating to the operations of the company, ensuring statutory documents are filed and bringing to the attention of the board any failure on the part of the company or a director to comply with the articles or the Companies Act.

5.13 COMPANY WINDING UP

The company's life as a separate legal entity and artificial entity can be ended by winding up and subsequent dissolution. Winding up or liquidation proceedings are associated with the ending of the company's existence. The winding-up process entails the appointment of a liquidator who is responsible for winding up the affairs of the company by assessing the state of the company, paying off the creditors and reserving any surplus to the shareholders of the company.

Where a company is wound up, every member at the time of the commencement of the winding up shall be liable to contribute to the assets of the company an amount sufficient for payment of its debts and liabilities and the costs, charges and expenses of the winding-up and for the adjustment of the rights of the shareholders among themselves.

The three types of winding up are voluntary winding up, creditors' winding up and winding up by the court. Voluntary winding up is a liquidation process that is initiated when the shareholders of a company adopt a special resolution for the voluntary winding up of a company following a declaration of solvency by the company's directors. Before the special resolution is passed to wind up the company, the directors of the company must make a statutory declaration of solvency asserting that the company meets the solvency test before issuing a notice for a meeting to wind up the company. Creditors' winding up is provided for in s 95 of the Insolvency Act and occurs when a winding up resolution has been proposed, but the directors have not made a declaration of solvency. When this occurs, the company is obliged to convene a meeting of the creditors who can then pass a resolution for a creditor's voluntary winding up.

Compulsory winding up by the court is provided for by s 57 of the Insolvency Act. The provision provides that the court may order the winding up of a company on the petition of a person other than the Officer Receiver if

(a) the company has by special resolution resolved that it be wound-up by the court;
(b) the company is unable to pay its debts;
(c) the period, if any, fixed for the duration of the company by the articles expires, or an event occurs in respect of which the articles provide that the company is to be dissolved;
(d) the number of members is reduced below two;
(e) the company was formed for an unlawful purpose;
(f) the incorporation of the company was obtained fraudulently; or
(g) in the opinion of the court, it is just and equitable.

KEY POINTS

- The documents required to incorporate a company under the Companies Act include the application for incorporation form, the articles of association, Consent form by at least two directors and a company secretary to act in those roles and Statutory Declaration of Compliance with these requirements.

- The articles of association are the internal governing rules of a company and a statutory contract that regulates the relationship between the company and its members and between the members themselves.

- The Registrar may reject an application if the name registered is likely to cause confusion with an already registered company or a well-known name or trademark.

- A company shall have its registered office in Zambia to which all communications and notices may be addressed.

- The affairs of a company are managed and governed by the directors of the company acting individually or collectively or the shareholders acting collectively at a general meeting of the company.

- The company secretary is responsible for exercising all the administrative functions of the company.

Chapter 6

PARASTATAL ORGANISATIONS

6.1 INTRODUCTION

One of the most notable, if not most troublesome, features in the law of business associations in Zambia is the existence of a breed of business organisations referred to as state-owned or controlled entities called parastatals. The concept of parastatal organisations is closely associated with the socialist ideology with its commandist economic values. It is, therefore, now largely a fading phenomenon. This is not in any way to suggest that there are not any state-owned business enterprises in Zambia, nor is it to imply that this kind of business activity is being phased out. The existing state-owned companies and other business entities have increasingly taken a different shape and form from that which they had in the one-party state under the first President of Zambia, Dr Kenneth Kaunda.

State-owned enterprises dominated Zambian business and commercial life for about two decades. It is estimated that the share of parastatals in industrial and commercial activity prior to 1991 was about 80 per cent with the private sector taking up the remaining 20 per cent. Parastatals dominated virtually all sectors of the economy including agriculture, communication and transport, construction, energy, manufacturing, mining, trading and tourism. They still occupy a prominent position in the economy of the country today. Their impact on the Zambian law of business associations and commercial life in general cannot, therefore, be ignored.

It must from the outset be mentioned, however, that the parastatal organisation as a form of business entity is not generally available to individuals as an optional vehicle for carrying on business. As the word 'parastatal' clearly suggests, these are state or semi-state enterprises that conduct business which private entities may also be involved in. It is not inconceivable though to have both the state and private entrepreneurs' own shares in the same business. It is their establishment in some cases, their ownership and the manner in which they are run that sets them apart from ordinary companies.

Because private companies are motivated by making profit and receiving high financial returns on their investments, several private entities are disinterested in the services these bodies provide as they do not provide high financial gain. For this reason, these bodies, especially the statutory corporations, were created to ensure social and economic growth and benefit for all citizens.

Parastatals have large or significant governmental control. It should however be noted that the level of state control varies, with the government having more control in statutory corporations due to their creation by statute. In parastatals, the level of shareholding by government can vary as these entities can have private shareholders. Notwithstanding being similar, as will be demonstrated in this chapter, the objects, share structure and financing of the two structures are different.

6.2 DEFINITION OF THE TERM 'PARASTATAL'

There is no one existing statutory definition of the term 'parastatal.' In the Zambian context the term parastatal or state-owned enterprise denotes a public enterprise (ie state-owned or controlled) which is quasi-autonomous and outside the regular civil service structure.

Parastatals comprise two categories of enterprises: those of a purely commercial nature set up under the Companies Act and statutory boards and organisations established under specific Acts of Parliament.

A statutory definition of the term 'parastatal' was first made as late as 1976 in the now repealed Parastatal Service Commission Act 18 of 1976. Section 2 of that Act defined a parastatal as

(a) any company, association, statutory board or corporation; or any institution of learning in which the state has a majority or controlling interest;

(b) any company, association, statutory board or corporation or institution of learning in which the state holds any interest and which the President may, by statutory order, declare to be a parastatal body.

What ought to be borne in mind, however, is that the Parastatal Service Commission Act was passed principally to establish the Parastatal Service Commission whose purpose was to deal with conditions of service for employees of state-owned or controlled businesses. The Commission was set up on 11 May 1977.[1] It was abolished with the repeal of the Parastatal Service Commission Act in 1977. Beyond that point, therefore, the statutory definition which it gave to the term parastatal is of limited significance. It, however, remains an important indication of the connotation of business attributed to the term.

There can be no doubt whatsoever that the definition contained in the repealed Act was broad. It covered not only entities which could be viewed as principally for business, but also institutions that had little to do with

---

[1] Statutory Instrument 89 of 1977.

business as it is known in the commercial world. Learning institutions such as universities and colleges neatly fell into the definition of parastatal as envisaged in the Parastatal Service Commission Act. This is probably why it is important to appreciate the nature of the available forms of parastatal.

To add to the difficulty of a statutory definition of the term 'parastatal', various statutes have definitions of either 'state-owned enterprise' or 'statutory corporation' or 'public company' in a manner which suggests state ownership or government interest in a business entity or indeed a utility firm. The Public Finance Act 15 of 2004, for example, has a definition in s 2 of the term 'statutory corporation' as 'any body corporate established by an Act of Parliament in which the Government has a majority or controlling interest, and includes a Government agency'. A government agency is defined in the same section of the Act as 'any unincorporated person or body of persons to which functions exercisable on behalf of the Republic, involving the use of public money or stores are delegated by or under any written law'.

The Public Audit Act[2] on the other hand contains definitions of both a public company and a statutory corporation. The former is defined in s 2 of the Act as 'any company limited by shares and incorporated under the Companies Act, in which the government is the sole shareholder.' The latter is defined in the same section as 'anybody corporate established by statute in which the state has a majority or controlling interest, and includes a statutory board.'

The Zambia Development Agency Act 11 of 2006 adds to the confusion around the identity of a parastatal body. It defines two terms which both tend to blur the definition of a parastatal body, namely, 'state institution' and 'state-owned enterprise'. A state institution is defined as including 'a ministry or department of Government, a public office or agency or institution, statutory body or company in which the Government has a controlling interest, a local government authority, a commission or body established under the Constitution'.

A state-owned enterprise, on the other hand, is defined as 'a corporation, board, company, parastatal or other body in which the Government has direct or indirect ownership, equity or interest and includes a partnership, joint venture or any other form of business arrangement or organisation in which the Government has direct or indirect interest, but does not include a Government ministry or department'.

---

[2] Chapter 378 of the Laws of Zambia.

6.3 THE POLITICAL BACKGROUND AND ITS IMPACT ON ZAMBIA'S ECONOMIC DIRECTION[3]

At the risk of digressing into the political arena, but in the interest of completeness and the need to establish a clear link between politics and the economy, it is imperative to examine the objective political conditions existing at that time which provided impetus to the government to undertake bold steps in addressing what it perceived as gross economic and social imbalances against the indigenous Zambians in favour of white settlers created by the colonial administration. There are striking parallels between what was happening in the political area and what the government wanted to do in the economic area.

After political independence in 1964, Zambia, like many other graduates of British colonial rule, embarked on an ambitious programme of nation-building and economic transformation. Although the Independence Constitution which created the First Republic provided for multi-partism, it had always been the objective of the then ruling party, UNIP, to introduce a one-party state through the ballot box. However, this avenue was closed by the mounting ethnic sectionalism within UNIP[4] and the awful possibility that UNIP might lose power to the combined forces of Nkumbula's African National Congress (ANC) and Kapwepwe's United Progressive Party (UPP), both of which were proscribed. Such political developments led to a decision that the single-party system would be instituted to promote national unity and development.

On 25 February 1972, President Kaunda issued a press statement in which he informed the nation that government had decided that Zambia would become a one-party participatory democracy and that practical steps were to be taken to implement that decision. The President said, among other things:

> Since independence there has been a constant demand for the establishment of a one-party state in Zambia. The demands have increasingly become more and more widespread in all corners of Zambia.

On 1 March 1972, the National Commission on the Establishment of One-Party Participatory Democracy in Zambia (the Chona Commission) was

---

[3] For a detailed narration of the political background that was later to give impetus to the movement for democratic reform, see M Malila 'The Legal Aspects to Zambia's Transition to Multi-Party Democracy' in J Oloka-Onyango, K Kivutha & MP Chris (eds) *Law and the Struggle for Democracy in East Africa* (1996).

[4] The Mulungushi Elections for UNIP's Central Committee in 1967 split the party into ethnic factions which spread to the provinces and which manifested themselves in the growth of provincial groups.

appointed with the mandate to consider and examine changes to be made to the Republican Constitution and in the practices and procedures of government which were necessary, and consequently to submit a new Constitution. This entailed the examination of the Republican as well as the UNIP Constitutions.

President Kaunda made it clear that a decision that Zambia should become a one party state was firm and that the study of the Commission was thus 'not to consider whether or not there shall be a one party democracy, but rather the form which it should take in the context of our philosophy and our belief in participatory democracy'.[5]

The Chona Commission considered both oral and written submission from members of the public. Some members of the public sought to give evidence as to why the introduction of one-party rule was not desired by the people. The Commission, however, refused to hear any submissions for or against the introduction of the one-party state as that was beyond their terms of reference. Not unexpectedly, Harry Nkumbula, the leader of the opposition ANC, appeared before the Commission and sought to give evidence expressing opposition to the introduction of the one-party state. The Commission declined to hear his evidence. Nkumbula then brought a petition under Article 28 of the Constitution, which stated:

> [I]f any person alleges that any of the provisions of Articles 13 to 27 (inclusive) has been, is being or is likely to be contravened in relation to him, then . . . that person may apply to the High Court for redress.

Nkumbula was seeking redress on the grounds of Article 13, which recognised and generally guaranteed everyone's rights to life, liberty, security, freedom of conscience, expression, assembly and association etc. Article 22, which specifically guaranteed freedom of expression, and Article 33, which protected freedom of assembly and association, were likely to be contravened with government's announcement of its intention to set up a one-party system in Zambia and the appointment of a commission to consider the form of such a system. The High Court held that the fact that Nkumbula could not put his views forward before a particular commission was not a restriction upon his freedom of expression and that Article 28 of the Constitution did not prohibit the advocacy of changes in the Constitution.[6]

---

[5] *Report of the National Commission on the Establishment of a One-Party Participatory Democracy in Zambia* (1972) 67.

[6] *Nkumbula v Attorney General* [1972] ZR 11. Article 28(5) of the Constitution provides that 'no application shall be brought under clause (1) on grounds that the provisions of Articles 13–27 (inclusive) are likely to be contravened by reason of proposals contained in any bill which, at the date of application has not become law'.

Nkumbula appealed to the then Court of Appeal for Zambia with the additional argument that the appointment of the Chona Commission under s 2 of the Inquiries Act 45 of 1967[7] was *ultra vires* and null and void because the matter to be inquired into could not be 'for the public welfare' within the meaning of those words. He argued that it could not be for 'public welfare' to prepare to derogate individual rights and freedoms. The appeal was dismissed.[8]

At the conclusion of its task, the Chona Commission made many recommendations, and key to those which were accepted and implemented was that UNIP be made the only political party allowed under the law.[9] Secondly, the UNIP Constitution was appended to the Republican Constitution. Thirdly, UNIP supremacy over all other institutions was asserted under the new Constitution. Members of Parliament had to be members of UNIP.[10] In this way Parliament was unwittingly made subject to UNIP control and its sovereignty thereby compromised. Fourthly, the Cabinet was subordinated to the control of UNIP's supreme executive body, the Central Committee. The Central Committee of the party became the supreme policy-making body of the party and members of the Central Committee enjoyed precedence over members of the Cabinet.[11] Zambia legally became a one-party state on 13 December 1972.

Alongside these developments went the increasing concentration of power under the President with all the dangerous consequences that this entailed. This was not surprising as it is typical of many one-party governments. As one scholar has noted:

> The entire government's activities under the one-party system revolved around the president. He is the real and ultimate authority upon which the entire executive, legislative and adjunctive functions of the state rest. He also controls the entire apparatus of the party. In a one-party state of the Zambian model, it can fairly be said that the president is in himself the government and the entirety of the state authority is consummated in him. He directed the operations of the army, the police, the parastatal bodies, institutions of learning, and the intelligence system. Indeed the list is discouragingly long to attempt to exhaust. There could therefore be no business of government without him.[12]

---

[7] Then Chapter 181 of the Laws of Zambia. This section empowers the President to set up a commission of inquiry on any matter of public interest.

[8] [1972] ZR 205.

[9] Article 8 of the Second Republican Constitution.

[10] Article 67 of the Second Republican Constitution.

[11] *Report of the National Commission on the Establishment of a One-Party Participatory Democracy in Zambia: Summary of Recommendations Accepted by the Government, First White Paper No.1 of 1972* (1972).

[12] L Shimba 'Role of the "Party" in Government under the One-Party Constitution of Zambia: Impact of Harry Nkumbula and Simon Kapwepwe cases' (1982) 5(1) *Lesotho Law Journal* 9.

6.4 THE ZAMBIAN ECONOMIC REFORMS

On the economic front, the picture was not that different. The zeal with which the one-party state directed and controlled the economy was phenomenal. The involvement of the government in running business enterprises was justified fairly easily. Like most post-colonial countries, Zambia at independence took over political power, but the economic sector remained largely in the hands of non-Zambians, particularly Asians and Europeans.

This unfortunate situation was a direct result of the colonial policy of denying economic opportunities to indigenous citizens of the territory. The net effect of the exclusion from economic activity and opportunity of Zambian entrepreneurship was that at independence, Zambia found itelf dependent upon foreign enterprises and established foreign trade partners, foreign banks and foreign production techniques. In other words, the industrial and trade sectors remained in foreign hands.

Further, banks continued to lend only to their established customers, mainly foreigners and settlers, while profits made by foreign-controlled enterprises were largely externalised. In addition, some of the foreign-owned business enterprises had resorted to practices that were intrinsically injurious to the national economy leading to gross under capitalisation and excessive local borrowing.[13] Externalisation of profits from local industry was commonplace.

The prolonged economic discrimination against Zambians in the colonial era left Zambians on the eve of independence with neither the capital nor the skill to participate meaningfully in economic activity except as consumers. 'In the circumstances, therefore,' said President Kaunda,

> it is only the Government of the people that can participate on their behalf and ensure that the nation has control of the vital resources in the country, and also provide avenues for the acquisition of skills pertaining to economic development and participation.[14]

Furthermore, it was considered ridiculous that after independence Zambia should continue to be represented in economic negotiations by non-nationals. There is always some suspicion when non-national officials or businessmen purport to act in the economic interests of the nation. In addition, Zambia at this time was going through a significant ideological crisis. The country was faced with that vitally important question of choosing its path to development in light of three possibilities, namely the two sharply contrasting systems of

---

[13] See the remarks made in 'Background to Economic Reforms in Zambia's Economic Revolution', Address by President Kaunda at Mulungushi on 1 April 1968.

[14] Ibid.

socialism in the first place, capitalism in the second and a possible mixture of aspects of both in the third place. This last option appeared to align itself with neutrality in ideological direction and provided greater promise of assisting the emergent local entrepreneurship assisted by the state.

The new nationalist government opted to have a mixed economy which accommodated both government and private participation. This option apparently favoured even well before independence, is reflected in the UNIP manifesto which stated that 'a conducive climate for private capital shall be created so that both public and private sectors shall support each other'[15]

Politically, the government, of course, considered it enormously satisfying that Zambians should be 'masters' in their own home—both politically and economically. It was considered a matter of political necessity and honour that a Zambian front was manifested in all key economic spheres. Above all the philosophy of humanism which Kenneth Kaunda propounded so affectionately had now been institutionalised as a national philosophy.[16] The President put the point beyond doubt when he declared:

> This shall be a land of equal opportunity for all. Since our emphasis is people and all activities are centered on serving the people, there is no better alternative under our present circumstances, in the light of bitter experience, and in view of the people's desire for economic self-determination, than to control the resources of the country and the means of production and distribution ... A newly independent country with a responsible government cannot stand by and let its resources be exploited for the benefit of foreigners alone. We object to having a nation of foreigners on one hand and capitalist masters on the other hand ...[17]

A combination of these reasons led to the economic reforms between 1968 and 1970.[18]

6.4.1 The Mulungushi economic reforms

The first of the economic reforms were the Mulungushi reforms, dubbed 'Zambia, Towards Economic Independence,' announced in an address by President Kaunda to the UNIP National Council on 19 April 1968.

---

[15] *UNIP Policy* (1964): The United Independence Party (UNIP) was then the sole political party in Zambia.

[16] See K Kaunda *Humanism in Zambia: A Guide to its Implementation, Part I* (1967).

[17] See 'The Watershed Speech: Towards Complete Independence' An Address by President Kaunda to the UNIP National Council, 19 April 1968 at 43.

[18] The reforms were: 'Zambia, Towards Economic Independence, An Address by President Kaunda to the UNIP National Council, 19 April 1968' also known as the Mulungushi Reforms; 'Zambia, Towards Complete Independence' Address by President Kenneth Kaunda to the UNIP National Council on 11 August 1969' also known as the Matero Reforms; and 'Zambia, This Now Completes Economic Reforms: Now Zambia is Ours', Address by President Kenneth Kaunda on 10 November 1970.

Punctuated as they were by nationalist undertones, the measures announced during the reforms were intended, in the estimation of the political leadership, to stabilise the economy, restrain unnecessary outflows of foreign exchange and ensure the development of the country.[19] The President made it clear that whether or not the companies earmarked for takeover accepted it or not the government was going ahead with the participation in the private sector companies:

> I hope the companies will agree to state participation in their undertakings. However, I wish to make it perfectly clear that in the event of failure of the negotiations Government will compulsorily acquire the shares in the companies. I anticipate that the partnership between the state and the private sector ... can be brought about by consent, but whether there is consent or not, I will ensure that this implementation of humanism is brought about.[20]

The measures announced by the President involved mainly the assumption of controlling interests in some enterprises mostly in manufacturing, transport distribution and construction. Twenty-six large companies and commercial firms carrying on various businesses were 'invited' to sell 51 per cent of their shares to the government.

It will be noted that at this time, these companies were private companies mainly limited by shares incorporated under existing companies legislation at the time. The newly acquired companies were brought under the umbrella of the Industrial Development Corporation (INDECO), a state holding company which had been set up in colonial times essentially as a device for stimulating industrial development. In the pre-1965 times the role of INDECO was confined to that of promoting and financing industrial ventures. The nationalisation that occurred in 1968 saw INDECO assume the nascent and expanded roles of holding company and shareholder as well as those of negotiating and acquiring majority shares of the designated new partners. The organisation was now to play a pivotal role in initiating industrial ventures as well as overseeing the operations of subsidiary

---

[19] The Mulungushi Reforms, Address by President Kaunda on 19 April 1968. At the time of the takeovers, some of the principal concerns of the Zambian Government were: (1) failure by the largely foreign investors to re-invest sufficiently in the economy, (2) excessive repatriation of profits at the expense of development in Zambia, (3) acute economic imbalances with the rural-urban gap accentuated by private investors' preference to concentrate activities in urban areas, (4) failure by private investors to develop local human resources with the result that virtually all aspects of the economy were under the control of foreigners or settlers of foreign origin, and (5) apparent impotence of the government of the day in directing the pace of economic development flowing from the above factors.

[20] 'Zambia, Towards Economic Independence' An Address by President Kaunda to the UNIP National Council, 19 April 1968, also known as the Mulungushi Reforms.

companies.[21] INDECO undertook the negotiations for the acquisition of shares in 25 out of the 26 designated companies. No agreement was reached in the case of one company, Solanki Brothers Limited, which resisted the takeover on the premise that it was a family business.

6.4.2 The Matero economic reforms

The second of the economic reform measures to be announced were the Matero Reforms in an address appropriately titled 'Zambia: Towards Complete Independence.' The address by President Kenneth Kaunda was made to the UNIP National Council on 11 August 1969. These had to do with the takeover of the mining companies. It need not be mentioned that the history of Zambia's economic politics, in as far as parastatal companies and organisations are concerned, cannot be complete if no mention, no matter how brief, is made of the giant copper mining industry. As someone observed, 'the fame and fortune of Northern Rhodesia have been bound up in the territory's copper mining industry'.[22] That observation was as true in 1962 as it is today.

While it is beyond the scope of this work to trace and give a historical account of the battle waged between the British South Africa Company on the one hand and the colonial government on the other over the control of the Zambian copper mines, it is significant to mention that mining operations were, before the majority share takeover in 1969, privately owned. The Roan Select Trust (RST) and the Anglo American Corporation (AAC) owned and controlled the mining companies.

The mining industry in Zambia has for many years formed the cornerstone of the country's economic structure. In the Mulungushi Reforms of 1968, the issue of state control of the mining companies was scarcely touched upon. President Kaunda is on record as having said, long before the Matero Reforms, that

> there is no question of nationalizing anything in Northern Rhodesia, but the circumstances under which the British South Africa Company acquired these royalties and the historical background to the question—places the whole question ... out of normal commercial or industrial activities in the world of today.[23]

The complexity of the entire venture, and the sadly incapacitating factor of a lack of a skilled workforce, inevitably compelled the government to postpone government takeover of the mines. Though these problems had

---

[21] INDECO was formed in 1960 and was intended to be a joint venture between government and private interest although the initial paid-up capital was paid entirely by government.
[22] K Bradley *Copper Venture* (1952) 16.
[23] President Kaunda in *African Mail* 3 April 1964.

arguably not been solved a year later, the government, in 1969 at Matero, finally announced a package deal regarding the control of the mining industry. Unlike the Mulungushi Reforms of 1968, the main purpose of the Matero Reforms of 1969 was to acquire control of the mining companies by the government. The Matero Reforms heralded the acquisition of 51 per cent equity holding in the mines owned and run then by AAC (Central Africa) and RST.

In his speech, the President expressed disappointment at the rate of development in the mining industry. He castigated the mines for not reinvesting their profit. Remission and payment of dividends to shareholders abroad was one obvious point of disagreement because the government was of the view that these should have been invested and put to further national developmental use. It was generally thought that having a controlling interest in the mines would enable the government to achieve economic independence.

The takeover of controlling interest in the copper mines was only done after protracted negotiations. The mining companies insisted that certain amendments be effected to the Companies Act before the transfer of the shares to the government. For prudential and tactical reasons, the mining companies sought to sell their shares to the government through a scheme of arrangement. This could not be done within the existing legal framework. The government was prompted to pass an amendment to the Companies Act 8 of 1970. The Act was amended in at least three respects. First it was amended so as to make provisions which empowered the High Court to order any dissentient member to abide by the desire of the majority of the members representing three quarters in value of shares or class of shares in scheme of arrangements. The Act was also amended to empower the High Court to make orders facilitating reconstruction and amalgamation of companies for purposes of transferring shares from one company to another in readiness for takeover.

Finally, the Act was amended to empower the High Court to dispense with detailed procedures for reduction of share capital provided the creditors were not prejudiced. These amendments were of practical significance to the shareholder in the mining companies who could easily have fallen foul of the law if they attempted to sell the shares to government before the amendments.

After protracted debate and discussion over the future of the mining industry in Zambia, a scheme of arrangement was effected and on 1 April 1982, Zambian copper mines started operating under one name; Zambia Consolidated Copper Mines Limited (ZCCM). The copper industry was a

perfect example of joint venture projects between private and state enterprises. When the takeover negotiations were concluded in 1970, the mines were re-organised into two groups:
(1)   Nchanga Consolidated Copper Mines (NCCM); and
(2)   Roan Consolidated Copper Mines (RCM).

Government created a new holding entity called Mining Development Corporation (MINDECO) which was to hold 51 per cent of the shares each in NCCM and RCM on behalf of the state.

6.4.3 The economic reforms of 1970

The final reforms in this series of economic reforms were announced in November 1970. The address 'Zambia, This Now Completes Economic Reforms: Now Zambia is Ours' was made by President Kaunda on 10 November 1970. These were aimed for the state assuming a participatory role in the financial sector of the economy made up of privately-owned commercial banks, insurance companies and building societies. With specific reference to the banks, the general feeling was that these had not contributed as they should to the creation of employment and the distribution of wealth principally because they were foreign-incorporated and had rather illiberal policies. The President stressed:

> We disapprove of many of the policies of the head offices of local banks and have not lacked courage to say so. I would merely say that they have been exceedingly conservative in their staff policies, in opening new branches in rural areas and in their credit policies.[24]

Of the five privately owned foreign banks in the country, namely Barclays Bank, Standard Bank, National and Grindlays Bank, Merchant Bank and Commercial Bank, Barclays Bank and Standard Bank were identified as the foremost banks and all the others were requested to merge with either Barclays Bank or Standard Bank and then the state would take 51 per cent in the merged banks. As with the industrial and commercial sector and the mining sector, the government attempted the route of negotiations for the acquisition of shares. Sadly, the negotiations to carry though the takeover proposals were unsuccessful and the government then issued a directive requiring all foreign banks to comply with two conditions, namely, they had to be incorporated locally and at least half of their directors had to be resident in Zambia. The directive was issued on

---

[24] See 'Zambia, This Now Completes Economic Reforms: Now Zambia is Ours' Address by President Kenneth Kaunda on 10 November 1970.

27 July 1971 and compliance with it had to be done from 1 January 1972.[25] If there was one thing that this directive was certain to achieve, it was that bank policies would henceforth be made locally.

While it appears as if the purpose of the reforms in all the other sectors was to enable the government to participate side by side with the private sector, this does not appear to have been the case with two areas of the financial sector. As far as insurance and building societies were concerned, the reforms were intended to give the government a monopoly in this area. Appropriate legislation was passed, requiring all privately owned insurance companies and building societies to cease operations by an appointed date.

In implementing the policy of state participation, the government sought to take control of the 'commanding heights' of the economy as it were and be able to dictate the pace and direction of economic development. It also sought to restore economic power to government and through government to the people of Zambia. In the absence of a fully developed local entrepreneurial class, government was to act as surrogate for the people. There was also the desire to check the excessive outflow of profits and ensure that more earnings were retained for reinvestment in the country. It was also hoped that income inequalities between rural and urban areas as well as between foreigners and locals would be addressed. In the process it was assumed that local human resources would also be developed.

6.4.4 Post 1970s reforms

Economically, it was evident that after 17 years of one-party rule the country's performance was far from satisfactory. By the mid-1980s, Zambia became one of the most indebted countries in the world, relative to its Gross Domestic Product (GDP). All economic indicators were negative. For example, the country's external debt by the end of 1984 was estimated at US $3.5 billion. Two years later it exceeded US $5.1 billion and reached US $6 billion. Considered on a per capita income basis it represented a debt in excess of US $700 for every Zambian, just about the worst in Africa. Comparable figures for other countries in the same period were for Gambia and Guinea Bissau US $341, Zaire US $228 and US $211 for Mozambique.[26]

---

[25] See *Enterprise Magazine* 2 of 1971.
[26] K Good 'Debt and the One-Party State in Zambia' (1989) 27(2) *The Journal of Modern African Studies* 5–32; and *The World Debt Tables, 1989-1990: External Debt of Developing Countries,* World Bank, Washington DC, as quoted by J Sangwa 'Zambian Human Rights after the Elections: The Need for Conceptualisation of the Concept of Human Rights' (unpublished seminar paper, 1993).

The International Monetary Fund (IMF) prescribed programmes intended to stabilise and restructure the economy and diminish the country's dependency on copper. Among the measures suggested were:

(1) removal of price controls;
(2) reduction of government expenditure;
(3) devaluation of the country's currency; and
(4) removal of subsidies on such things as food and farm inputs.

As could only be expected, removal of food subsidies resulted in huge increases in the prices of basic foodstuffs. The disquiet among the Zambian people was obvious. Riots broke out in some areas. The reaction of the government was to break ranks with the IMF in May 1987. The New Economic Recovery Programme was introduced in 1988. This did not improve the situation, however, and the government moved towards a new understanding with the IMF in 1989.

The poor state of the economy in Zambia was altogether attributable to one-party rule. As one commentator observed:

> Zambia's acute malaise is a consequence chiefly of internal factors derivative of the single-party state and Kenneth Kaunda's personal rule.[27]

While the UNIP government under President Kaunda was seeking a solution to the economic problems of the country in foreign aid, some analysts such as Good thought:

> As things stand debt concessions and additional foreign aid would rather worsen than improve this situation since it would strengthen and encourage an inefficient regime without bringing benefit to the majority of the people. Domestic reforms aimed at creating efficiency and democratization in the government, as well as the long term diversification of the economy, are the essentials for full development.[28]

The various parastatal companies in Zambia were run and managed by executives who were politically appointed, not necessarily based on qualifications and management skills. Inefficiency and loss making slowly became the norm rather than the exception. For example, in 1989, 18 out of 97 parastatals had incurred cumulative losses amounting to over K354 million.[29] As the parastatal companies became increasingly inefficient, the government lost more and more revenue in trying to subsidise them. The economic performance of the country was moving from bad to worse, and the country's financial obligations to international lenders became a matter of serious concern. In September 1987, Zambia was declared ineligible to

---

[27] Good (1989) at 297–8.
[28] Good (1989) at 297–8.
[29] See Annual Report of the Executive Board of the International Monetary Fund for the Financial Year ended 30 April 1987.

use the International Monetary Fund (IMF) facilities owing to the accumulation of overwhelming financial obligations to the IMF.[30] As a result of the suspension, Zambia had to endure economic hardships leading to dissatisfaction among the general populace.

The economic conditions prevailing in Zambia at the time, coupled with mounting pressure for democratic reform from virtually all quarters including the church,[31] put the UNIP government to its most severe test. As the economic conditions worsened, the government took structural adjust-ment measures such as the removal of reduction of subsidies on some commodities. The effect was that prices of goods including maize meal (the staple food) shot up. This proved to be both economically unpopular and political disastrous for the UNIP government. In May 1990 the National Council, UNIP's governing body, had made a decision to put the future of one-party rule in Zambia to the popular test in a national referendum scheduled for October of that year. Later the President announced that the referendum was postponed to August 1991. In June 1990, there were food riots in the capital, Lusaka, and other cities. At least 27 people died in the riots. The political climate was potentially explosive, and a coup was attempted on 30 June 1990. It was clear that procrastination in effecting democratic reforms was not going to help matters much.

In July 1990, a group of private persons made up of businessmen, trade-unionists, church leaders, disaffected UNIP politicians, university lectur-ers and students, among others, convened a national conference to discuss the issue of multi-party democracy in Zambia. A pressure group called the MMD was born at this conference and one of its purposes was to canvass the Zambian electorate to vote for the restoration of the multi-party system in the referendum.

The UNIP National Council at its meeting held in September 1990 decided to cancel the referendum and instead hold general elections under a multi-party constitution. The Council also decided that a commission to review the Zambian Constitution be appointed. A Constitution Review Commission was subsequently appointed in October 1990, headed by the then Solicitor-General, Professor Mvunga. In December 1990, the President assented to the Bill repealing Article 4 of the 1973 Constitution, thereby permitting new political parties to be registered under the law. The MMD registered as a political party in January 1991, and by the time inter-party talks were called to consider the proposals for constitutional

---

[30] IMF Press Release 95/62 of 6 December 1995, Washington.

[31] See the pastoral statement of the Catholic Bishops on 'Economics, Politics and Justice' (1990).

reform in July 1991, following the publication of the government white paper on the Mvunga Report in May 1991, at least 11 political parties had been officially registered.[32]

Besides the repeal of Article 4 of the Second Republican Constitution, perhaps the other significant turning point in the build-up to the Zambian democratic reforms was the institution of the Third Republic when a new Constitution was passed by Parliament in August 1991. Not long thereafter an announcement was made that general elections under the multi-party constitution were going to be held on 31 October 1991. Multi-party democracy was reintroduced. The die was cast when Parliament was dissolved in September 1991.

In 1991, with the end of the Cold War, Kaunda was forced to make a major policy *volte-face* and announced government's intention to partially privatise the parastatals. Furthermore, knowing that his authoritarian/ socialist regime was under pressure with Mikhail Gorbachev's announce-ment of a perestroika and glasnost, as well as severe economic decline, Kaunda called for multi-party elections and subsequently lost to the MMD. In November 1991, the MMD's Frederick Chiluba was inaugurated as the second President of Zambia.

With the advent of the winds of change that blew from the eastern bloc (the collapse of the Soviet Union and the fall of the Berlin Wall in 1989) the Zambian people clamoured for political change. In 1991 the MMD succeeded UNIP.

The government introduced new economic policies which sought to do away with the mixed economy which had as its main object the provision of social welfare. It undertook to introduce a fully-fledged Structural Adjust-ment Programme (SAP) in line with the International Monetary Fund (IMF) conditionalities.[33]

Before the MMD came into government, Zambia's economy had literally collapsed. Food queues and food riots were becoming the order of the day. The transport sector had virtually come to a standstill. It was obvious that about 80 per cent of industries, transport and energy companies that were under state control and energy companies that were under state control and management had failed to deliver. Government's direct involvement or intervention in economic activity had clearly stifled economic freedom, entrepreneurial activity, business efficiency, productive investment and economic growth.

---

[32] See C Lumbwe 'Carrying Irreconcilables: Democratization and institutional reform in Zambia, 1990-1992' (unpublished seminar paper).
[33] Available at http://www.globalcompetitionforum.org/regions/Africa/Zambia/competition (accessed 12 December 2018).

Government immediately embarked on an ambitious privatisation programme to liberalise the economy. Competition law in Zambia developed
as part of this process of liberalisation. A new competition law had
inevitably to be passed. The Ministry of Commerce, Trade and Industry in
introducing the Competition and Fair Trading Bill in the National Assembly
put the position succinctly as follows:

> The private sector was marginalised and pitted against heavily protected monopolistic
> state-owned enterprises. Because of such heavy protection, these state enterprises grew
> complacent, inefficient, and quality standards of their products fell to shameful levels. To
> finance these deficiencies and over employment overheads, enterprises resorted, more often
> than not, to hiking prices. They were protected monopolies . . . As the MMD Government
> continues in its irreversible march to building a free market economy through the
> privatization and free market program, there is need for safe guards against creating private
> monopolies from state monopolies. Monopolies, whether they are state or privately owned
> are enemies of the free market and breed anti-competitive trade practices.[34]

In 2010, the Competition and Consumer Protection Act 24 of 2010 was
enacted. This law repealed the Competition and Fair Trading Act 18 of
1994 and seeks to eliminate or curtail restrictive business practices which
hindered or had the potential to hinder or prevent business entities from
competing freely in the domestic market.

As is well known, the role of competition law is to give business entities
a chance to enter the market and make a profit while they are exposed to the
risk of failure. Although competition law in the form of anti-trust legislation
has existed for many years in developed countries,[35] for many developing
counties competition law is a new phenomenon. The reason for this state of
affairs is easy to appreciate. The rapidly changing political and economic
environment in the last 20 to 30 years has seen a shift in economic policies
of many developing counties and the institution of microeconomic reforms
involving greater reliance on markets and less emphasis on central planning.

The Zambian example has already been cited. Among the more
important changes have been a lowering of tariff barriers, the removal of
most quantitative import restrictions, the reduction of subsidies to domestic
producers, the liberalisation of the economy mainly through the privatisation of government business enterprises, the easing of foreign exchange
controls and the encouraging of foreign direct investment. A discussion of
competition law is both interesting and tempting. This however, should be a
subject for a different occasion.

---

[34] Hon Dipak Patel, the then Minister of Commerce, Trade and Industry. See Parliamentary Debates
of the Third Session of the seventh National Assembly of Zambia No 97 of 21 January to 17 March
1994 at 1523.
[35] In the case of Canada since 1889, the United States, 1890, and Germany, 1923.

6.5 CONSOLIDATION OF THE PARASTATAL SECTOR IN ZAMBIA

In what was initially conceived as a state participatory idea intended to complement private initiatives, the parastatal sector took off at a vigorous pace after 1969. Over the years, the government acquired more shares in more companies and virtually controlled and directed their operations. Parastatal companies over the succeeding years dominated and monopolised all major sectors of economic activity in Zambia. In the transport sector for instance, there was Zambia Railways Limited, a statutory corporation established under an Act of Parliament[36] and owned by the state which owned and ran all railway transport operations except those governed by another parastatal—the Tanzania Zambia Railway Authority, which is also a creature of statute.[37]

There was then the Zambia Airways Corporation which was also created under an Act of Parliament[38] and provided domestic air transportation exclusively with Roan Air, a subsidiary of another state-owned enterprise, namely Zambia Consolidated Copper Mines Limited. The National Airports Corporation, created to undertake ground handling services at airports throughout the country,[39] the United Bus Company of Zambia Limited and Contract Haulage Limited, both government-owned companies, 'competed', albeit very unfairly, with private transporters in road passenger and goods transport services respectively. Even in the wholesale and retail trading sector, parastatals such as the National Wholesale and Marketing Corporation Limited and the Zambia Consumer Buying Corporation Limited 'competed' side by side with individuals and private firms in commodity trading, although they, of course, enjoyed all preferences and support from the government in the acquisition and marketing of their products. The manufacture and distribution of the most popular brands of beer was left to the exclusive domain of two parastatals—Zambia Breweries Limited and National Breweries Limited— while the manufacturing and distribution of cement and other building materials were done by the parastatals Chilanga Cement Limited and the Zambia Steel and Building Company Limited. Insurance business was the

---

[36] Zambia Railways Act, Chapter 676 of the old edition of the Laws of Zambia. It was repealed by the Railways Act Chapter 453 of the Laws of Zambia.
[37] Chapter 454 of the Laws of Zambia.
[38] Chapter 444 of the Laws of Zambia.
[39] National Airports Corporation Limited (NACL) is a parastatal company which is 100 per cent owned by the government of the Republic of Zambia. It was established in 1989 through the amendment of the Aviation Act.

exclusive domain of the parastatal called the Zambia State Insurance Corporation. Major textile industries were the domain of parastatals Kafue Textiles Limited and Mulungushi Textiles Limited. Broadcasting was left exclusively to the Zambia National Broadcasting Corporation Limited, while the Zambia Electricity Supply Corporation Limited monopolised electric power supply. Some parastatals were even jointly owned between the government of Zambia and other governments. Tanzania Zambia Mafuta (TAZAMA) Pipelines Limited is one such parastatal company jointly owned by the Zambian and Tanzanian governments.[40]

Writing on the situation that presented itself following the growth of the parastatal sector in Zambia, a commentator observed:

> As the pace of nationalisation and direct state involvement in the economy picked up, it soon became clear that the inherited organisational structure of INDECO as a holding company would not suffice. On 31 March 1970, the Zambia Industrial and Mining Corporation (ZIMCO) was incorporated to provide a single holding company for government's numerous investments previously held under INDECO. The role of ZIMCO in its simple format then was essentially that of an agent of government—to hold its investments. It is important to note that at this time ZIMCO, the apex organ, was no more than a mere paper holding company with no executive management. The actual supervisory control over the boards and company managements was vested in respective line ministries. From its humble origins in the late sixties, the parastatal sector in Zambia grew to a position of such dominance that by 1972 it was estimated that the public/parastatal sector accounted for 53 per cent of total manufacturing GDP and its share in employment was 42 per cent. By 1980, the shares of parastatals in total GDP and formal employment were put at 56 per cent and 54 per cent respectively. Prior to the most recent organisation-restructuring of the ZIMCO Group in April 1993 (about which we comment later), the growth of this major category of SOEs was such that SOEs were the backbone of the economy.[41]

This brief background explains the establishment and position of parastatals as extraordinary companies which did not normally operate under the provisions of the Companies Act. There has never however been any such thing as the Parastatals Act in Zambia, or indeed any single legal instrument governing these enterprises save the Parastatal Bodies Service Commission Act which was repealed.

State-owned or controlled companies were either established under an Act of Parliament or were incorporated as companies in the usual manner under the Companies Act as it existed then, though they were not regulated under that Act as if they were ordinary companies. The Minister of Finance ordinarily

---

[40] It was established in 1966 under the Tazama Charter (Convention) to transport finished petroleum products from Dar-es Salaam to Ndola. Construction of the pipeline took about two years and it was officially opened in 1968. TAZAMA pumps crude oil and is running the Ndola Fuel Terminal on behalf of the Zambian government.

[41] EC Kaunga *Privatisation: The Zambian Experience* (undated).

owns shares in these companies for and on behalf of the government of Zambia. Appointment of directors was always a political act. The concept of corporate governance had very little relevance in such a setting.

6.6 TYPES OF PARASTATAL ORGANISATIONS

Two forms of parastatal organisations are identifiable in Zambia: those which are created by specific Acts of Parliament, also known as statutory corporations or boards, and those established by registration under the Companies Act.[42] These statutory organisations are controlled from respective line Ministries through their boards of directors. These include such entities as the State Lotteries Board,[43] the Dairy Produce Board (DPB),[44] the Development Bank of Zambia (DBZ),[45] the National Savings and Credit Bank,[46] the Zambia National Tourist Board,[47] the Bank of Zambia,[48] and the Zambia National Building Society.[49]

Statutory corporations are used chiefly as entities through which specific public services are undertaken or provided while realising a profit. Perhaps the best distinction between these two kinds of parastatals is to be found in the categorisation given in the Mwanakatwe Commission Report on Parastatals. The Commission used two different terms to identify parastatals, namely, statutory corporations and state-controlled companies. It defined a statutory corporation as

> [t]he body corporate established by statute with defined powers and duties in some specified area of action and subject to the control of a particular Minister who may give directions as to the conduct of its affairs. The nature of the organization can only be changed if its governing statute is amended or repealed and replaced.

The same report explains what a state-controlled company is in the following terms:

> The company limited by shares and incorporated under the provisions of the Companies Act, chap 686 of the laws of Zambia. It is the sole or majority interest by the state which distinguishes this type of parastatal from any other limited company and in legal terms, its structure is exactly the same as that of its purely private counterpart. Its operations are governed by its Memorandum and Articles of Association, by the provisions of the

---

[42] Chapter 388 of the Laws of Zambia.
[43] Chapter 328 of the Laws of Zambia.
[44] Chapter 230 of the Laws of Zambia. The Dairy Industry Development Act 22 of 2010 repealed and replaced this Act.
[45] Chapter 363 of the Laws of Zambia.
[46] Chapter 423 of the Laws of Zambia.
[47] Established under the Tourism Act, Chapter 155 of the Laws of Zambia.
[48] Chapter 360 of the Laws of Zambia.
[49] Established under the Building Societies Act, Chapter 412 of the Laws of Zambia.

Companies Act and by the decisions of its board. The direct shareholding of the Government varies but is 100 per cent in the case of the main controlling groups.

The establishment of parastatal organisations in Zambia is an interesting example of how the political, social and economic climate in any country can dictate either the content or the interpretation of the law. A meaningful explanation of the law relating to parastatal companies in Zambia as commercial entities calls for the examination, no matter how undesirable this may be, of the economic politics of the country following independence in 1964. One is justified to state that the political climate had a lot to do with the economic direction which the country took, characterised by the serious involvement of the state in the running of business through parastatal organisations.

6.7 DIFFERENCES BETWEEN THE TWO TYPES OF PARASTATAL ORGANISATIONS

Notwithstanding the similarities, there are several differences between the two kinds of parastatal companies.

6.7.1 Formation

Parastatals are incorporated under the Companies Act and therefore follow the procedures that any other company follows as prescribed by the Companies Act. Therefore, the documents required to incorporate a parastatal under the Companies Act include the application for incorporation form, the articles of association, consent form signed by at least two directors and a company secretary to act in those roles and Statutory Declaration of Compliance. All such statutory corporations are created by Acts of Parliament. Unlike parastatal companies, a statutory corporation is formed by and subject to the specific legislation that creates it.

The main objective of a statutory corporation is not to maximise profit, but to provide affordable services to the general public as stated in the main objective of why the parastatal body was formed. Statutory corporations deal in services that are critical to the nation's development, such as electricity generation and supply, telecommunications, railway transport and postal services. Statutory corporations have a duty to promote economic and social development.

6.7.2 Name

The name of the parastatal is provided for in the same manner as a normal company. On the other hand, the name of the statutory company will be explicitly provided for in the Act of Parliament.

6.7.3 Objects and management

The objects and purposes of a parastatal organisation are provided for in the parastatal's articles of sssociation. Just like any other company, the Company is bound to act in line with its articles.

Whereas a parastatal is akin to a company formed in terms of the Companies Act and therefore mandated to operate in a manner conducive to maximising profit, in the Companies Act, only companies limited by guarantee are permitted to carry on business without the purpose of maximising profit. A parastatal cannot be incorporated as a company limited by guarantee as the parastatal has shareholders like other companies and therefore the organisation is mandated to carry on business for the purpose of making a profit.

Parastatals are companies whose control, management and organisation are provided for in the articles of association. The appointment of directors is governed by the provisions of the Companies Act, articles of association or shareholder's agreement, in the same way as it is done for a private limited company or a public limited company.

The organisational structure of statutory corporations is prescribed by the statutes that create them. The statutes do not only identify the Minister under whose portfolio a corporation falls but also give her immense powers over the running of the corporation, including the appointment of the governing board and its chairperson.

Statutory corporations fall under specific ministries and the Minister under which the statutory corporation falls exercises power to appoint and dissolve the board and acts as the board in the absence of the board. Most statutes of such organisations state that in the absence of a board, the Minister can act as a board alone until such a time when the board is appointed. The statute also provides for what positions shall exist in the higher echelons of management.

6.7.4 Share structure

The share and capital structure of parastatals is in the form of authorised and issued nominal share capital. The types and classes of shares are specified in the articles of the parastatal and reflected on the Certificate of Share Capital.

Therefore, even where government has 100 per cent ownership of a parastatal, this should be in the form of shares and registered with the Registrar of Companies. In some parastatals where the state does not own a majority of the shares, the state will retain a special type of share called a golden share, which gives the state the power to outvote other shareholders.

Just like any other company incorporated in terms of the Companies Act, the Board of Directors may determine dividends for shareholders out of the profits of a company in terms of s 159 of the Companies Act.

Statutory corporations do not have a capital structure comprising various classes of equity, debentures or any other component that represents interest holdings in the business entity. They are wholly owned by government, but ownership is not in the form of shares.

Dividends in statutory companies are not usually paid out because parastatal companies are not formed for the purpose of making profit but to provide critical services to the nation. In cases where a profit is made, it is usually referred to as a surplus that is planted back into the company or redirected to another statutory body.

6.7.5 Financing the operations of the organisation

Parastatals raise their capital funds by allotting shares, by borrowing from private or public lenders, by issuing debentures or by investing retained earnings. They do not get free money such as appropriations by Parliament as in the case of statutory corporations, though it is true to state that when it is in the public interest, directly or indirectly, government does subsidise parastatals.

The main source of operational funds for statutory corporations is government revenue which is determined each year by Parliament. The finance granted to the statutory corporations considers money paid for services rendered, and money paid as grants or donations, though money sourced outside the Republic would be approved by the Minister on behalf of government.

Further, where a statutory corporation obtains external finance through a loan or another form of commercial credit, the government guarantees such debt. This was confirmed in *Tamlin v Hannaford*[50] where Denning LJ held that there are no shareholders to subscribe to capital in a statutory corporation and they can only raise additional finance by borrowing. The state guarantees such loans.

As a result of their finances being allocated by Parliament, the financial performance and affairs of statutory corporations are supervised and monitored by Parliament. The Auditor-General of Zambia is responsible for auditing their financial statements and accounts of parastatal companies. Further, the Public Accounts Committee of Parliament and the Parastatal Bodies Service Commission were established to ensure that funds on which

---

[50] [1950] 1 KB 18.

they depended were spent according to the purposes for which they were allocated.

6.7.6 Termination

Because the statutory corporation is created by statute, the entity comes to life by statute. It follows therefore that in the same way Parliament can also legislate for its death.

Again, in *Tamlin v Hannaford*[51] Denning LJ held that if a company is unable to pay its debts, the property of a statutory corporation is liable to execution and not wound up in the same way a company or parastatal would be. Further, it is submitted that when a statutory corporation is going through financial difficulties, it is the taxpayers who rescue the company as the government would usually use their resources.

This is in contrast with parastatal companies which can only conclude through a procedure outlined in the Companies Act, that is to say by liquidation, whether voluntary or compulsory.

6.8 THE LEGAL FRAMEWORK IN WHICH PARASTATALS OPERATED

As already pointed out, the companies in which the government acquired a majority interest were mainly private companies limited by shares and incorporated as such under the Companies Act then in force.[52] Before too long, it became obvious that the legal framework under which parastatals operated was ill-suited for the large conglomerates which the government was using as instruments of control of the economy. As the Mwanakatwe Commission on Parastatals observed:

> The problem of Government control over the parastatal companies stems from the legal nature of these companies. The parastatal companies are registered under the Companies Act, which means that they are cast in the mould intended for private enterprise and consequently they are to be governed in a manner befitting private enterprises, unless it is otherwise provided.[53]

Indeed, the legal framework with which parastatals operated was originally meant to govern private companies. Since parastatals are public enterprises in the sense of being financed or purchased using public resources a framework of their operations or relationship based on private law is, of course, not exhaustive.

---

[51] [1950] 1 KB 18.
[52] Chapter 388 of the Laws of Zambia.
[53] *Mwanakatwe Commission Report* (1975) 134.

6.8.1 Defiance of the law

One of the established company law principles which became an early casualty of the state ownership and control of what were essentially business enterprises was the concept of separate corporate personality of individual parastatals.

6.8.2 The concept of separate legal personality and parastatal organisations

A company is in law regarded as a legal entity separate and distinct from the members who make it up. As an artificial legal person, a company will be entitled to deal with other persons, natural or artificial, in its own name and in its own right. In terms of s 15*(b)* of the Companies Act a company is deemed incorporated on and from the date of incorporation specified in the Certificate of Incorporation issued by the Registrar of Companies.

In the post privatisation era, the Zambian Supreme Court has had occasion to consider the concept of corporate personality on numerous occasions. The court was, not unexpectedly, called upon in many cases before it to consider the question whether the change in the ownership of the shares in various previously state-owned companies amounted to a change in the companies themselves. In *Kankomba and Others v Chilanga Cement Plc,*[54] for instance, the appellants were employed by Chilanga Cement Ltd which was a wholly Government of Zambia owned company under ZIMCO (Zambia Industrial & Mining Company). In 1994 Chilanga Cement Limited was taken over by the Commonwealth Development Corporation (CDC). To be precise, the shares of Chilanga Cement Limited were bought by CDC and the company became a public company hence its title changed to Chilanga Cement Plc (Public Limited Company). This means that Chilanga Cement Company Limited was no longer a private company, but a public company. The line of business remains the same and the employees who included the appellants were the same. In due course, the new owners of the company changed management. In April 1995, the new management introduced new conditions of service which the appellants, in some cases, alleged were inferior to the previous conditions. They were particularly concerned that some allowances which were previously paid separately and in conformity with Statutory Instrument 99 were then fused into their salaries. Such allowances included lunch and funeral grants. Also, under the new conditions, the early retirement service period was

---

[54] SCZ Judgment 30 of 2002.

increased from 10 years of service to 20 years of service, contrary to what the statutory instrument provided (10 years). The appellants felt that, in view of these changes, their conditions of service were changed to their detriment and that they should have been given an option to retire as from 31 March 1995, on old ZIMCO conditions, and re-engaged under the new conditions for those who wanted to continue working for the company, and when they retired under the new conditions of service, be paid gratuity under the new terms.

The defence contended that there was no change of employer as what was involved was a mere change of shareholding and the company continued operating as a going concern. The employees were informed of the changes. The employees were free to resign and, in this spirit, the General Manager resigned. It was denied that the new conditions of service were discriminatory or inferior. On the contrary it was argued that they were superior. The funeral grant was increased from K30 000.00 to K50 000.00. In addition, coffin, transport, firewood, and money incidental to the funeral were to be given under the revised conditions. Further, under the new conditions of service, under redundancy the employee is to be given six months' notice as against one month under Statutory Instrument 99 of 1994, and three and a half months' pay as against three months' basic pay under the Statutory Instrument.

On the evidence and the long submissions before him, the learned trial judge found that most of what was pleaded was not supported by any evidence. He found as a fact that there was no change of employer so as to call upon the appellants and others to exercise their option of continuing to serve with the new employees; he found that the new conditions of service were not discriminatory nor disadvantageous to the appellants; instead they were superior conditions of service. He found that there was no need to request the appellant to exercise the option of whether to retire or continue serving under the new shareholders and management and that s 35 of the Employment Act did not apply to the appellants. He therefore dismissed the appellants' claims with costs. The Supreme Court agreed that a change in the shareholders did not mean a change of the company.

On identical facts the court came to the same conclusion in *ZCCM and Ndola Lime Company Limited v Sikanyika and Others*[55] where it cited with approval the case of *Salomon v Salomon*. It held once again that the change of ownership of shares in a company does not result in the corporate entity

---

[55] SCZ Judgment 24 of 2002.

becoming a new employer. The court recognised the distinction between the company as a body corporate and the shareholders in that company.

The concept of separate corporate personality, clear as it may seem in law, was largely overlooked when the parastatal sector was at its peak. The web of companies that was created through the holding and subsidiary structures under INDECO, ZIMCO, MINDECO and FINDECO made the whole corporate separateness of these entities unreal in practice. ZIMCO was the main holding company to all the other parastatals. It thus occupied a central place in directing and supervising the operations of the other parastatal companies as and when it deemed this necessary. In many instances the operations of ZIMCO's subsidiaries were supervised by what were referred to as 'portfolio Ministries'. ZIMCO holding companies were answerable to these Ministries. The ZIMCO Board of Directors comprised senior cabinet Ministers.

The practical effect of the rule that a company is an entity separate and distinct from its members, who are liable only to the extent of their unpaid amounts on the shares they own in the company, is that the individual subsidiaries within a conglomerate will be treated as separate entities and the parent company cannot be made liable for the subsidiary companies' debts on insolvency. In the case of the conglomerates that were created in the wake of the government's takeover of formerly private companies in various sectors of the economy, the individual subsidiary companies remained separate and distinct in law from the holding company.

6.9 PARASTATALS AND DIRECTORS

Private companies ordinarily have a pyramid-type management structure with the shareholders at the apex, followed by the board, with the management at the bottom. The shareholders of the company appoint the board of directors who in turn appoint the officers or operatives of the company. The management of a company is usually entrusted to small group of persons called directors. All registered companies must have a board of directors numbering at least two, if they are a private company, and three if they are a public company (see s 85(2) of the Companies Act). The number of directors and the way they are to be appointed is left to be regulated by the articles.

As with the term promoter, the position of a director in law is complicated by reason of the wide differences in their functions in one company as against another, eg a resident director in a copper company will perform completely different functions.

In *Re Forest of Dean Coal Mining Co*,[56] Jessel MR said

> . . . it does not matter much what you call them so long as you understand what this true position is, which is that they are really commercial men managing a trading concern for the benefit of themselves and other shareholders in it.

The definition of 'director' in the Act provides that for purposes of the Act any person who is appointed by the members of the company to direct and administer the business of the company shall be deemed to be a director of the company, by whatever name designated, whether or not she is called a director.

There is a lot to be said, especially in relation to public companies for requiring directors to be members of a professional body, and to have been properly qualified before acting as director, but a director need have no professional qualifications whatsoever.

The Act however does disqualify certain persons from holding office as a director of any company. In terms of s 92, the following persons are disqualified:

(a)   a body corporate;

(b)   a minor or other person under legal disability;

(c)   any person prohibited or disqualified from so acting by any order of a court to be of unsound mind or because she committed an offence or breached the duties of director in the last five years; or

(d)   an undischarged bankrupt.

Further to this, s 94 of the Companies Act provides that a person shall not be appointed as director unless she has consented in writing. Section 92(3)*(e)* provides that the articles may provide more restrictions on who can be a director in the company. The object of these provisions is to keep the management of the company out of the hands of unscrupulous or disreputable people.

The directors' basic function is to manage the company for other people, and it is therefore not surprising to find a body of common law which prohibits them from feathering their own nests at the expense of the company and its members.

Section 86 of the Act sets out in general terms the powers of the directors of the company; s 105*(c)*(i) on the other hand give statutory effect to the directors' duties to have the interests of the company at heart in performing their functions.

In performing their functions as a body, the directors are under an equitable duty to act bona fide in the interest of the company. As

---

[56] [1878] 10 Ch 450.

individuals, directors are in a fiduciary position in relation to the company. This means they have a duty to act in good faith. In the words of Centlivers CJ in *Rex v Milne and Erleigh*:[57]

It is of course clear that the duty of all agents including directors of companies is to conduct the affairs of the business in the interest of the principals and not for their own benefit.

The fiduciary position of the directors with regard to the company entails certain consequences in equity. Any contract in which a director has interest averse to that of the company is voidable in the absence of disclosure or authorisation of the company's articles.

Secondly, the fiduciary position of a director entails that she cannot make a secret profit nor can she divert opportunity from the company to herself. Section 106(*d*) of the Companies Act codifies the common law and provides that a director must disclose information about her remuneration in the financial statement of the company.

The common-law position regarding contracts involving directors is very clear. A contract made by a company with one of its directors or with a company or firm in which she is interested is voidable at the instance of the company. Thus in *Aberdeen Rly Co v Blaikie Bros.*[58] where the respondent had agreed to manufacture iron chairs for the appellant railing company sued to enforce the contract, it was held and upheld on appeal by the House of Lords that the railway company was not bound by the contract because at the time when it was made, the chairman of the board of directors of the railway company was also managing partner of the respondents.

6.10 METAMORPHOSING THE PARASTATAL SECTOR IN ZAMBIA: THE INDUSTRIAL DEVELOPMENT CORPORATION

Following the privatisation of the parastatal sector in Zambia, many state-owned or controlled business entities in various sectors remained operational in one form or another under a direct reporting arrangement to line Ministries. Permanent secretaries of line Ministries continued to sit on the board of directors for purposes of monitoring and policy guidance. This was somewhat disconcerting particularly given the manner in which government detachment from business was envisioned in the dawn of multi-party politics. Granted the actual difficulties encountered during the

---

[57] 1951 (1) SA 791 (A) at 828.
[58] [1854] 1 Macq 461.

privatisation process, the continued existence or reincarnation of state ownership of business entities appeared an unlikely prospect.

The truth, however, is that even after the ambitious privatisation process itself, and the virtual demise of the conglomerate ZIMCO and other once dynamic state corporations, notably INDECO and FINDECO in the 1990s, Ministries remain ill-equipped to direct commercial enterprise. They do not have the commercial and investment know-how and resources to ensure positive performance of these business entities. Political interference continues to be the order of the day. One of the consequences is that these enterprises have been unable to give government a return on its investment and contribute to the Treasury by way of dividends and taxes.

The phased approach of the privatisation process under which the sale of equity in parastatal companies was done provided room for more deliberate reflection on the immediate and medium-term consequences of the privatisation programme. In fact, angst, disappointment and regret in many cases consumed sections of the public in the period following privatisation. Many jobs were lost when new buyers of formerly state-owned businesses restructured these companies, involving, in many instances, downsizing of the workforce or the realignment of business. Some new owners of formerly state-owned businesses dismantled equipment in established manufacturing factories and shipped it out of the country.

One of the policy initiatives of the Patriotic Front Government as enshrined in its 2011–2016 Manifesto was the creation of INDECO. This was to be used as a vehicle through which the government was to deepen and support the country's industrialisation so as to create jobs and reduce poverty. The intention was clearly that government would continue to participate as a co-investor alongside private enterprise.

On 20 September 2013, government announced its desire to restructure and improve the system for supervision and control of parastatals to ensure their enhanced contribution to economic development and the reduction of unemployment.[59] Later, Cabinet sanctioned the launch of the IDC and the transfer of government interest in all state-owned enterprises incorporated under the Companies Act from the Ministry of Finance to the IDC. The latter was henceforth to hold the shares on behalf of government in state-owned enterprises. Cabinet also approved the creation of a Sovereign Wealth Fund to safeguard the interest of posterity.[60]

---

[59] President Michael Sata made the announcement at the Official Opening of the 3rd Session of the 11th National Assembly.
[60] At its 32nd meeting held on 16 December 2013.

The IDC incorporated in early 2014 an investment company wholly owned by the Zambian government through the Minister of Finance who, under the Minister of Finance (Incorporation) Act Chapter 349 of the Laws of Zambia, is a body corporate. Its mandate is to facilitate provision and raising of long-term finance for projects and to serve as an investment holding company for state-owned enterprises and new investments that would eventually generate earnings for the Sovereign Wealth Fund.

INDECO is now a shareholder and investor in sectors that include agriculture, forestry, manufacturing, financial services, mining, energy, telecommunications, logistics, healthcare, education, tourism, real estate and media.

Its portfolio of companies across sectors include Nanga Farms Limited, Zambia Forestry and Forest Industries Corporation, NIEC Business School, Afrox Zambia Limited, Indeni Petroleum Refinery Limited, Zambia Electricity Supply Corporation, Indo-Zambia Bank Limited, Zambia State Insurance Corporation, Zambia National Commercial Bank Plc, Times Printpak Zambia Limited, Zambia Daily Mail Limited, Zambia Education Publishing House Limited, Zambia Printing Company, Zamtel Limited, Engineering Services Corporation, Lusaka South Multi-Facility Economic Zone Limited, Mulungushi Textiles Limited, Mupepetwe Development Company, Nitrogen Chemicals of Zambia Limited, Zamcapitol Enterprises Limited, Lusaka Trust Hospital, Medical Stores Limited, Kagem Minerals Limited, Kariba Minerals Limited, ZCCM Investment Holdings Plc, Mulungushi Village Complex Limited, Mukuba Hotel Limited, Mulungushi International Conference Centre, Zambia International Trade Fair, Mpulungu Harbour Corporation Limited, Zambia Airways (2014) Limited, and Zambia Railways Limited.

A worrisome feature of the IDC concerns its corporate governance. The board of directors which provides overall guidance and direction in the management of the company's assets and investments is made up of three Cabinet Ministers, namely those responsible for finance, commerce, trade and industry, and agriculture. It also has two main civil servants: The Secretary to the Treasury and the Permanent Secretary for Commerce, Trade and Industry. There are then seven private sector members and three executive directors of the IDC acting as ex-officio members. The Republican President is the Chairman of the Board. The President appoints and dismisses Board members. In addition to the ordinary fiduciary duties to the company, the IDC board is also accountable to the President.

It is expected that IDC will publish its annual reports bearing its group financial accounts and portfolio performance. It will also declare dividends to its shareholders.

KEY POINTS

- Parastatals comprise two categories of enterprises: those of a purely commercial nature set up under the Companies Act, and statutory boards and organisations established under specific Acts of Parliament.
- A parastatal company can be defined as a business organisation which is not an integral part of the state but an institution or agency which is wholly or mainly financed or controlled by government.
- A statutory corporation is created by an Act of Parliament.
- The primary role and objective of INDECO is to stimulate economic development and growth, via industrialisation, and job and wealth creation in Zambia.

INDEX